THE QUEST FOR ANASTASIA

The Quest for Anastasia

Solving the Mystery of the Lost Romanovs

John Klier
and
Helen Mingay

A Citadel Press Book
Published by Carol Publishing Group

Carol Publishing Group Edition, 1999

A Citadel Press Book
Published by Carol Publishing Group
Citadel Press is a registered trademark of Carol Communications, Inc.

Editorial, sales and distribution, rights and permissions inquiries
should be addressed to Carol Publishing Group, 120 Enterprise Avenue,
Secaucus, N.J. 07094

Carol Publishing Group books may be purchased in bulk at special
discounts for sales promotions, fund-raising, or educational purposes.
Special editions can be created to specifications. For details, contact
Special Sales Department, Carol Publishing Group, 120 Enterprise Avenue,
Secaucus, N.J. 07094

Manufactured in the United States of America
10 9 8 7 6 5 4 3 2 1

Library of Congress Cataloging-in-Publication Data

   The quest for Anastasia : solving the mystery of the lost Romanovs
/ John Klier and Helen Mingay.
        p.   cm.
Originally published : The search for Anastasia. London : Smith
Gryphon, 1995.
Includes bibliographical references and index.
ISBN 0-8065-2064-7
1. Anastasia Nikolaevna, Grand Duchess, daughter of Nicholas II,
Emperor of Russia., 1901-1918. 2. Anderson, Anna. 3. Princesses-
-Russia—Biography. I. Mingay, Helen. II. Klier, John. Search
for Anastasia. III. Title.
Dk254.A7K58   1997
947.08'092—dc21
[B]   97-30242
                                                    CIP

CONTENTS

Acknowledgements

Our account of the present state of 'the Romanov business' has been made possible because of the assistance that we received from a number of institutions and individuals. These include, in Great Britain, the Luton Hoo Foundation, the Public Record Office, the Forensic Science Service and the British Library. In the United States, Richard Schweitzer, Penny Jenkins of the Martha Jefferson Hospital, in Charlottesville, Virginia, and the Charlottesville Courthouse helped us navigate the controversy involving Anna Anderson's last remains. In Russia, we acknowledge the assistance of the Recovery Foundation in Ekaterinburg, of Dr Sergei Mironenko of the State Archive of the Russian Federation and of the Russian State Library in Moscow.

We very much appreciate the willingness of numerous people involved to talk to us, directly or indirectly, in the search for the truth about the fate of the Romanovs and of Anastasia. This is especially the case because a number of them approach these matters from very different perspectives. In Russia, our interlocutors included Aleksandr Avdonin, Vadim Viner and Vladimir Soloviev. In Great Britain we were able to tap the expertise of Ian Lilburn, Michael Thornton, Julian Nott, Philip Remy and Dr Peter Gill. In the United States we were aided by Richard and Marina Schweitzer, Sydney Mandelbaum, Terry Melton, Dr William Maples and Dr Lowell Levine.

The maps for this book were prepared by Tim Aspden and Catherine Pyke of the Drawing Office of the Department of Geography of University College London. The genealogical table was completed with the assistance of Ian Chapman. The photographs were in part supplied by the Luton Hoo Foundation, the Public Record Office, Anatoly Grakhov, Ian Lilburn, Fen Montaigne, the Press Office of the Bonn Opera House (for photographs of the production of *Dornröschen*, choreographed by Youri Vàmos, with sets and costumes by Michael Scott) and the James Lovell Estate. Medical diagrams are reprinted from *International Medical Reviews* in St Petersburg. Practical assistance has been provided by Kathleen Franzen and Bruce Cohen in the USA, Leah Chapman, Claire Pickard and Armorer Wason in London, Iuny Gorbunov in Ekaterinburg, and Dr Aleksandr Lokshin in Moscow. Professor Robert Service of the School of Slavonic and East European Studies of the University of London and Dr Viktor Kelner of the Russian National Library (St Petersburg) rendered valuable bibliographical assistance. We especially appreciate the expeditious services of our copy editor, Helen Armitage.

The two generations in our life, our children Sebastian and Sophia, and Helen's parents George and Jean Mingay, have been especially patient and supportive during the flurry of foreign trips and late-night labours that produced this book. We would like to dedicate it to them.

Transliterations from Russian are based on a modified version of the Library of Congress system. All dates are translated into the modern calendar, since before the October Revolution Russia used a calendar that was 13 days behind that of the West. By this reckoning, the February Revolution took place in March, while the October Revolution ended in November.

GENEALOGY OF
NICHOLAS AND ALEXANDRA

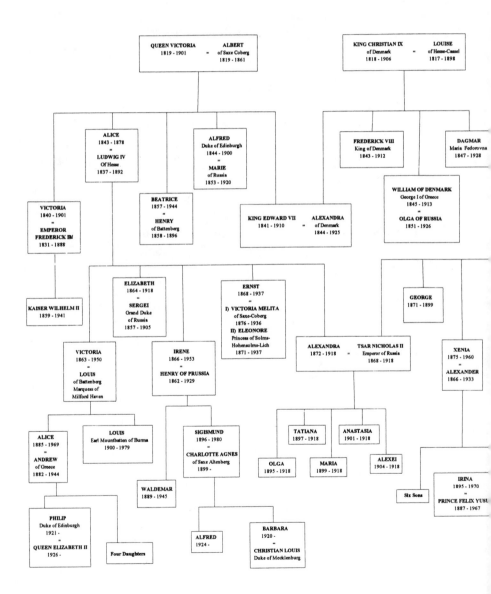

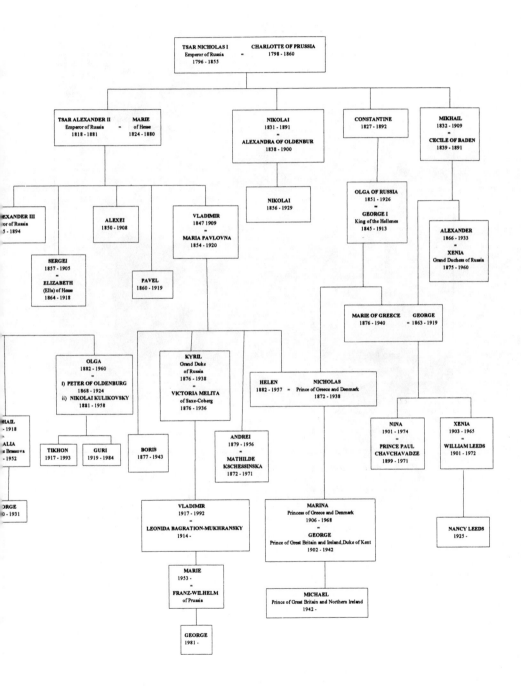

TSAR NICHOLAS I
Emperor of Russia
1796 - 1855
= **CHARLOTTE OF PRUSSIA**
1798 - 1860

TSAR ALEXANDER II
Emperor of Russia
1818 - 1881
= **MARIE**
of Hesse
1824 - 1880

NIKOLAI
1831 - 1891
=
ALEXANDRA OF OLDENBUR
1838 - 1900

CONSTANTINE
1827 - 1892

MIKHAIL
1832 - 1909
=
CECILE OF BADEN
1839 - 1891

EXANDER III
or of Russia
5 - 1894

ALEXEI
1850 - 1908

VLADIMIR
1847 1909
=
MARIA PAVLOVNA
1854 - 1920

NIKOLAI
1856 - 1929

OLGA OF RUSSIA
1851 - 1926
=
GEORGE I
King of the Hellenes
1845 - 1913

ALEXANDER
1866 - 1933
=
XENIA
Grand Duchess of Russia
1875 - 1960

SERGEI
1857 - 1905
=
ELIZABETH
(Ella) of Hesse
1864 - 1918

PAVEL
1860 - 1919

MARIE OF GREECE
1876 - 1940
GEORGE
= 1863 - 1919

OLGA
1882 - 1960
=
I) **PETER OF OLDENBURG**
1868 - 1924
ii) **NIKOLAI KULIKOVSKY**
1881 - 1958

KYRIL
Grand Duke
of Russia
1876 - 1938
=
VICTORIA MELITA
of Saxe-Coberg
1876 - 1936

HELEN
1882 - 1957
= **NICHOLAS**
Prince of Greece and Denmark
1872 - 1938

NINA
1901 - 1974
=
**PRINCE PAUL
CHAVCHAVADZE**
1899 - 1971

XENIA
1903 - 1965
=
WILLIAM LEEDS
1901 - 1972

HAIL
- 1918
=
ALIA
s Brassova
- 1952

TIKHON
1917 - 1993

GURI
1919 - 1984

BORIS
1877 - 1943

ANDREI
1879 - 1956
=
**MATHILDE
KSCHESSINSKA**
1872 - 1971

ORGE
0 - 1931

VLADIMIR
1917 - 1992
=
LEONIDA BAGRATION-MUKHRANSKY
1914 -

MARINA
Princess of Greece and Denmark
1906 - 1968
=
GEORGE
Prince of Great Britain and Ireland, Duke of Kent
1902 - 1942

NANCY LEEDS
1925 -

MARIE
1953 -
=
FRANZ-WILHELM
of Prussia

MICHAEL
Prince of Great Britain and Northern Ireland
1942 -

GEORGE
1981 -

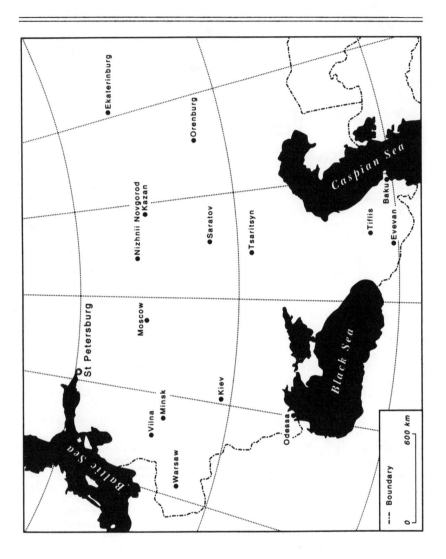

THE RUSSIAN EMPIRE IN 1917

Dick's Party

FROM THE PERSPECTIVE of a British journalist, no event of world-shaking importance ever occurs after 6:oo pm, the filing deadline for the next morning's editions of the serious broadsheets. The group of journalists gathered in the London headquarters' building of Channel 4 were thus understandably miffed. It was already 3:15 pm, and rather than the scheduled news conference, they were being put off with coffee and promises. The discomfiture of the journalists was fully shared by the event's organizers, who were engaged in frantic behind-the-scenes telephone calls to Britain's Forensic Science Service Laboratory in Birmingham, ensuring that their star witness, Dr Peter Gill, was authorized to share his official secret. The last chapter was about to be written in a mystery story that was born in the blood and violence of the Russian Revolution, played out in royal apartments and squalid bedsits and finally ended in Charlottesville, Virginia, in a pleasant suburban home overrun with cats. It has spawned an award-winning Hollywood film, television documentaries and docu-dramas, a popular song and enough publications to fill an entire wall in any well-stocked book shop. Peter Gill was about to step to the microphone and announce to the world the identity of a woman who for over 60 years had laid claim to the title of Her Imperial Highness the Grand Duchess Anastasia Nikolaevna, last surviving daughter of Nicholas II, the last Tsar of Russia.

Or, rather, Gill would announce who the mysterious woman was not. The scientific technique that he had pioneered, based on the testing of genetic matter, or DNA, was effective for establishing the connections of related Romanov family members. Gill then surprised the press by taking it one step further and suggesting a very different family background for the woman who first appeared as Anastasia in Berlin in 1920. His research on Anastasia was possible only because of the dramatic discovery of a mass grave, made some 15 years previously in a pine forest in Siberia, said to contain the remains of the last Russian Imperial Family.

Aside from the grumbling reporters, waiting for what might be sensational, front-page news, some of those in Gill's audience had not come to hear what he had to say. They already knew the answer. Dick Schweitzer had financed Dr Gill's research and had been given the results several weeks previously. Julian Nott, the producer of the Channel 4 extravaganza, had the cameras rolling when Dr Gill's call had come through to Virginia for Schweitzer and his wife, Marina, granddaughter of Dr Evgeny Botkin, the Tsar's personal physician, who had died along with the Romanovs. Firm in their own beliefs, they received the news with consternation and then quickly agreed that 'something went wrong.'

The audience included royals and royal watchers. Prince Rostislav Romanov was a scion of the Russian Royal Family in exile, which had fought the claims of the Charlottesville Anastasia almost from the first moment she had proclaimed herself in the early years of post-war Berlin. Historian and Romanov expert Ian Lilburn, who is also a genealogist, could boast of having sat through one of the longest cases ever to drag through the German courts, in a vain effort to establish Anastasia's identity. Writer and journalist Michael Thornton had chronicled the growth and flowering of the case for the readers of magazines and newspapers. The popular historian Robert Massie was as responsible as anyone for keeping the fate of the Romanovs in the public eye through the sympathetic portrait he drew of them in his bestseller, *Nicholas and Alexandra*. There were absent friends: the two rival biographers of Anastasia, the late James Lovell and the indisposed Peter Kurth.

This was, ultimately, Dick Schweitzer's party, and he had been very generous with the guest list. Also in the room was the German television producer Philip Remy, who had fought a legal action against Schweitzer for control of the tissue sample that formed the basis for Gill's work. He helped provide spoiler stories, which appeared in several Sunday supplements on the eve of the Gill announcement, presenting rival claims based on competing scientific expertise. He offered a very different identity for the Lost Princess. Yet Schweitzer bore no grudges. He had received the 'Romanov business' as a sort of marriage dowry through his wife, Marina Botkin, the granddaughter of Dr Evgeny Botkin. Everyone was welcome, if they would only work towards Dick's objective: 'All I want is the truth.'

This is the true story of Grand Duchess Anastasia, both in life and in death. It can be fully told because of the sea-changes that have occurred at the end of the twentieth century. These include not only the scientific discoveries pioneered by men like Dr Peter Gill but also the crisis and collapse of Communism in the former Soviet Union. 'The Romanov business', placed under an interdict by Stalin in 1928, and off-limits even for Russian specialists since that time, was suddenly reclassified as 'permitted' in the first heady days of Soviet glasnost. Investigators found a treasure-trove of information in the now open archives: secret, forged letters, which served as a pretext for the execution of the Royal Family; the last diaries and letters of the Tsar and Tsarina and their children; eye-witness accounts by the murderers themselves; and photographs of their secret burial. The changing climate also made possible an announcement that had been suppressed for a decade: the royal remains had been discovered in a hidden grave outside the Soviet city of Sverdlovsk, which has now reverted to its original name of Ekaterinburg. The story is not a simple or straightforward one – for history never is. There are rival claimants for the 'honour' of killing the Tsar and his family, of burying them and of digging them up again. Many of the accounts are contradictory.

Our narrative is based on a thorough examination of all the available written evidence relating to the fate of the family of the last ruling Russian emperor and his family. We have also travelled to Russia and the United States to speak personally to those involved in the discovery of the remains, and to leading genetic and forensic scientists who helped to identify them. The disappearance of the Royal Family in 1918 was a subject of controversy from the first moment they dropped from sight. We have had to navigate amid the conflicting claims and contradictions, and to present a picture that seems to us, on the basis of our research, to be the most accurate and plausible. Where it is impossible to make a decisive choice between rival versions, they are both noted. Nothing is invented or conjectured: every detail comes from written accounts, personal interviews or published scientific findings. We have chosen to relate our narrative without the distraction of scholarly footnotes. However, we include a select bibliography, which will indicate the scope of our work in published sources.

No author who has explored the lush literature produced by the 'Romanov business' could ever believe that they were writing the last word on the subject. Our account has the simple goal of offering the reader an accurate account of the contemporary scientific and historical consensus that has emerged concerning the events which took place in Ekaterinburg on the night of 16–17 July 1918 – and thereafter.

CHAPTER ONE

The Romanovs' Last Journey

'THIS IS THE first time in my life I have no idea how to act. Until now God has shown me the way. Right now tho' I cannot hear his instructions.' The former Empress of Russia, Alexandra Fedorovna, was facing an uncharacteristic moment of doubt in the late winter of 1918. God had always been a reliable interlocutor in days past, often speaking to her in the guise of holy men, most notably 'Our Friend', the peasant mystic and faith healer Grigory Rasputin. Her confidence in divine guidance had shielded her through all the vicissitudes of a troubled life: the deadly haemophilia of her only son Alexei; the tottering of the throne itself in the revolutionary year of 1905; the start of the World War in 1914, which threatened the very existence of the empire, and finally the revolution of February–March 1917, which swept away the 300-year-old Romanov dynasty. Now, as she sat in Siberian exile, the old certainties seemed far away.

Princess Alix of Hesse, as Alexandra was known before her marriage, was the youngest child of Grand Duke Ludwig IV of Hesse, a small German principality. Her mother was the British Princess Alice, who died when Alix was only six. Thereafter, she fell to the benevolent care of her grandmother, Queen Victoria. The young Anglo-German princess, nicknamed 'Sunny' by her mother, was a typical product of the cosmopolitan courts of

Europe, enjoying a gilded life while her elders went about the business of dynastic match-making. Her life rapidly changed when she was betrothed to the heir-apparent to the Russian throne, the Tsarevich Nikolai (Nicholas) Aleksandrovich, in 1894.

Alix was a conventionally pious Protestant. She found the required change of religion, a spiritual rebirth into the Russian Orthodox faith as Alexandra Fedorovna, to be extremely traumatic. She emerged from the process with all the enthusiasms of the recent convert. She became, in Prime Minister Alexander Kerensky's phrase, 'a wild Muscovite Tsaritsa'. Her particular brand of Orthodox religiosity contained a large dose of popular superstition and belief. Wonder-working icons, magic talismans, 'Holy Fools' and assorted mystics constituted a staple of her world-view. In particular she assimilated the religious imagery that underpinned Orthodox Russian rulers: the Tsar was an all-powerful ruler, whose strength came directly from God. He was the 'Little Father' of the Russian people, to whom he was bound by bonds of faith as the Lord's anointed, not the artificial constructions of democratic politics.

Since the Tsar's autocratic power was a divine gift, it had to be preserved and handed on from father to son, a belief that Alexandra held with special ferocity after the birth of her only son in 1904. Ironically, this new heir to the autocracy was born at the very moment when his father was being forced, in an effort to quell a rising revolutionary tide in 1904–5, to grant a constitution and a representative assembly, the Duma, to his people.

Alexandra's fate was linked to a ruler whom she knew lacked the ruthlessness that an autocracy required – although in fact the time had long passed when either the demonic energy of a Peter the Great or the fortress mentality of a Nicholas I could hope to control or prevent change in Russia. No past Russian ruler, not Peter, nor Catherine, nor Alexander I, could have hoped to deal effectively with the disorienting social, economic and political changes that bestirred the Russian Empire as it hurtled into the twentieth century. Yet Nicholas lacked even the firm hand of his immediate Romanov predecessors. He was a mild-mannered man, whose wavering nature caused him both to act impulsively and to dig in his heels at the most inopportune times. It was not true, as is often alleged, that Nicholas merely shared the opinion of the last person with whom he had spoken. Rather, his advisers were driven to distraction by their inability to decide which factors helped the Emperor to make up his mind. Sometimes he attributed his decisions to an 'inner voice', but there were strong suspicions that the Empress played a role or – even worse – Rasputin himself.

Much is revealed by Nicholas's relationship with two of his prime ministers, Sergei Witte and Peter Stolypin. These two men were evidence that late imperial Russia was quite capable of producing leaders of sophistication and skill, who recognized their country's manifold problems and devised policies to deal with them. Nicholas was forced to rely heavily on them, and he resented the sense of weakness and inadequacy that this instilled in him. He dismissed Witte in 1906, at a time of maximum political instability, and he regarded the assassination of Stolypin – which he witnessed in the Kiev Opera House – with something approaching equanimity.

Witte's sin was to have persuaded a reluctant emperor in 1905 to sign the October Manifesto, which limited the imperial, autocratic power and created a representative body, the Duma. Nicholas agreed only when he was assured that, lacking this gesture, it would be impossible to suppress the revolutionary movement without terrible bloodshed. While some liberal opinion accepted the new arrangements, more radical revolutionaries rejected 'the police whip wrapped in the parchment of a constitution'.

Disorders continued, while Nicholas observed sarcastically that 'it is strange that such a clever man [as Witte] should be wrong in his forecast of an easy pacification.' Before the first Duma even met, Nicholas despaired of Witte – '[I] have never seen such a chameleon of a man. That, naturally, is the reason why none believes in him anymore' – and demanded his resignation.

Stolypin combined a ruthlessness that Witte lacked – not for nothing did revolutionaries nickname the hangman's noose a Stolypin necktie – with an imaginative programme of controlled internal reform, particularly the modernization of Russia's archaic agricultural sector. He was also a minister who insisted on having his own way. On more than one occasion Nicholas, faced with a Stolypin threat to resign, had to concur in policies with which he had little confidence. Stolypin was well aware of the Tsar's displeasure with this state of affairs and was in daily anticipation of dismissal.

An assassin's bullet saved Nicholas the unpleasantness of dismissing him. Nicholas briefly mourned his dying minister and then went off to a military review. The Empress, jealous of Stolypin's power over her husband, saw the hand of providence in all this. She exhorted V. N. Kokovtsov, Stolypin's successor, to put aside mourning. 'Believe me, one must not feel sorry for those who are no more. I am sure that everybody does only one's duty and fulfils one's destiny, and when one dies that means that his role is ended and that he was bound to go since his destiny was fulfilled . . . I am sure that Stolypin died to make room for you, and this is all for the good of Russia.'

The crisis of 1905 demonstrated Nicholas's malleable character, and his ability to accept recommendations with which he did not fully agree. Alexandra was initially reduced to a stunned silence, but then embarked on a life-long effort to strengthen her husband's resolve and maintain his belief in his God-given power. In the name of supporting her husband and safeguarding the prerogatives of her son, she became a consummate political animal, but one with absolutely no understanding of the political realities of contemporary Russia, which she viewed through a romantic-mystical haze. She sought advice – which she passed on to Nicholas – from a bevy of adventurers and charlatans, of whom Rasputin was merely the most visible and damaging.

In particular the Empress detested the politicians produced by the parliamentary regime, and she continually urged her husband to rule lest he be ruled. This was advice that Nicholas was eager to take, since he himself despaired of anything constructive coming from the 'windbags' of the Duma. In particular, Emperor and Empress were united in their hostility to the sweetest liberal dream, a 'ministry of public confidence', which would be drawn from the elected Duma deputies rather than from the ranks of the professional bureaucracy. Nicholas's appointed ministers gazed across a political gulf at the elected Duma members. The resultant political instability did little to promote the evolution of new institutions required by a modernizing empire. Indeed, the death of the capable Stolypin was followed by a resurgence of political terrorism and popular discontent.

The outbreak of the World War in 1914 temporarily obscured these fundamental problems. Faced with the spectre of Germanic domination, the country rallied to the colours and to the Tsar, as the living symbol of the nation. Nicholas found himself the centre of an unaccustomed wave of popularity, exemplified by the huge popular demonstrations that accompanied the declaration of war in St Petersburg – now defiantly renamed as the more Russian Petrograd – and Moscow. Labour unrest dramatically declined, and the often truculent Duma unanimously passed the war budget.

The Russian leadership, like that of every other combatant, entered the war with a number of illusions. The first was that the war could be quickly won, and 'the boys home by Christmas'. When this proved illusory, it was replaced by confidence that one more push, one more break through the barbed-wire emplacements of no man's land would bring the war to a rapid end. Millions of men paid with their lives for these dreams of victory. The second illusion was that society could and would sustain the human and economic losses of the war indefinitely. To the contrary, war-weariness and disillusionment spread from the trenches to the civilian population in every combatant state. French generals shot their own rebellious troops *pour encourager les autres*, civilians in the Hapsburg Empire shot government officials and a growing sense of unease spread from Flanders fields to the British home front. In Russia recurrent military reverses engendered rumours that 'dark forces' were undermining the war effort. Increasingly this centred on the Empress and her entourage.

Alexandra detested Kaiser Wilhelm II and declared, at the outbreak of the war, that she was 'ashamed to be a German'. She threw herself into a number of war-relief charities, even establishing a medical clinic in the palace at Tsarskoe Selo. She and her daughters helped to tend wounded soldiers in the wards there. Yet the Empress remained obstinately blind to the need to placate public opinion. She chose to consider the dubious adventurers who surrounded her as the authentic and loyal voice of the Russian people. Most significant was Grigory Rasputin, the faith-healing peasant whose saintly reputation within the royal household was neatly balanced by a reputation for debauchery, which he acquired in the fleshpots of the nearby capital.

Rasputin's links to the Imperial Family were harmful, but not critical until 1915. In that year, following a series of Russian defeats, Nicholas determined to replace his uncle, Grand Duke Nikolai Nikolaevich, as commander-in-chief of the Russian forces. The intention behind this decision – made, typically, without consultation and announced in perfunctory fashion – was entirely honourable. The Tsar wished to take the risks and share the dangers of his soldiers at the front. There was also some logic to combining civilian and military authority. Finally, it was largely a symbolic decision, since the real conduct of the war would remain in the hands of General M. V. Alekseev, the Chief of the General Staff.

Yet every plus of this decision was balanced by an equally strong minus. The Tsar himself was widely regarded as ill-omened and unlucky – not for nothing had he been born on the church feast day of Job the Long-Suffering. Recurrent military defeats could only serve to discredit the dynasty and breed instability. Most importantly, in Russia's highly centralized political system, who was to be in charge if the Tsar was off at the front? Alexandra had a ready answer to this question: she would become the Tsar's 'eyes and ears' at home, loyally reporting on whatever mischief the Duma might get up to, especially after the creation of a Progressive Bloc, which had as its chief objective the creation of a 'government of public confidence'.

Certainly the public began to lose faith in the ministers the Tsar appointed, especially when they began to change with bewildering regularity, largely at the behest, it was rumoured, of Rasputin, whose advice was conveyed through the Empress. There was a mad scramble as opportunists paid court to Rasputin in the hope of political preference. Many succeeded beyond their wildest dreams. As the new Minister of the Interior, Aleksandr Protopopov, squealed in delight: 'All my life it was my dream to be a vice-governor, and here I am a minister!' In the 16 months when the Tsar was at the front, Russia had four prime ministers, five ministers of interior, four ministers of agriculture and three ministers of war. Even the lay head of the Russian Orthodox Church, the Ober-Procurator, was changed. Small wonder that one wag branded the process 'ministerial leapfrog'. The resultant chaos was laid to the malevolent influence of Rasputin. Salacious caricatures, bawdy rhymes and smutty jokes linked Alexandra and Rasputin. All this brought the dynasty into greater disrepute.

The growing crisis of confidence was there for all to see, and it ranged across the political spectrum. In the November 1916 session of the Duma, the leader of the liberal Constitutional Democrats made a sensational speech, listing all the failures of official policy and actually mentioning the Empress by name. After each policy disaster, he intoned rhetorically, 'Is this stupidity or is this treason?' At the other end of the political spectrum the reactionary Duma deputy Vladimir Purishkevich rounded on Rasputin, urging the Tsar to take action 'so that an obscure peasant shall govern Russia no longer.'

Criticism was not restricted to democratically elected politicians. Other members of the Romanov family grew alarmed that the activities of the Empress would fatally discredit the monarchy and lead to the destruction of the dynasty. A number of family ambassadors were dispatched to Nicholas at the front, to alert him to the danger. The Grand Duke Nikolai Mikhailovich arrived at the Stavka, the command headquarters, on 2 November 1916, with a letter of warning from the family. In it they lamented that the Empress 'has been led astray thanks to the malicious and utter deception of the people who surround her . . . If you are not competent to remove this influence from her, then at least guard against those constant interferences and whisperings, through your beloved spouse.'

Nicholas could think of nothing better to do than send the letter to Alexandra, provoking the inevitable furious response. She tried to depict the criticisms as a family squabble, complaining that Nikolai Mikhailovich 'has always hated & spoken badly of me since 22 years . . . during war & at such a time to crawl behind yr Mama and Sisters & not stick up bravely . . . for his Emperor's wife – is loathsome & treachery.' At the very least, she advised, Nicholas should have interrupted him and threatened to send him to Siberia if he ever touched on her person again. The Grand Duke thus joined a far from short list of Duma deputies whom the Empress had over the years expressed a wish to exile to Siberia – if they could not all be hanged!

Those fearful for the fate of the Romanov dynasty saw no recourse but to take matters into their own hands. On the night of 16 December 1916 Rasputin was invited to the Petrograd mansion of Prince Felix Yusupov, who had married the Tsar's niece, Irina, for an evening supper and entertainment. Waiting for him were five conspirators, including Purishkevich and a first cousin of the Tsar, the Grand Duke Dmitri Pavlovich. In the course of the revels, Rasputin was poisoned, shot, bludgeoned and dumped under the ice of the frozen Neva, where he drowned. French historian Marc Ferro has accurately called him 'a force of nature and a man of formidable temperament'. He was also a prophet to the last.

During the final month of his life Rasputin wrote a testament, in which he warned Nicholas: 'Tsar of the land of Russia, if you hear the sound of the bell which will tell you that Grigory has been killed, you must know this: if it was your relations who have wrought my death then no one of your family, that is to say, none of your children or relations will remain alive for more than two years. They will be killed by the Russian people.'

The imperial tutor Pierre Gilliard recalled his first glimpse of the Empress after she had received word of Rasputin's murder: 'Her anxious face betrayed, in spite of herself, the force of her suffering. Her grief was boundless. Her faith was shattered, they had killed the one who alone could save her son. Without him there loomed the possibility of any misfortune, any catastrophe. And there began the expectation, that agonizing expectation of the inescapable misfortune!'

The murder of Rasputin did nothing to restore Russia's failing military fortunes, nor did it endear Nicholas to his relatives. Grand Duke Dmitry Pavlovich and Felix Yusupov were exiled from the capital, and Nicholas dispatched a collective letter to the other members of the family: 'No one has the right to engage in murder, and I know that many have uneasy consciences, since Dmitry Pavlovich was not the only one mixed up in this.' Nonetheless, the Romanov family made one last effort to alert the rulers of the danger to the throne. They now decided to approach Alexandra directly and to persuade her to see reason. The Grand Duke Aleksandr Mikhailovich wrote to her with a request to see her alone, face to face.

On 10 February Aleksandr Mikhailovich arrived for his appointment with Alexandra, only to find that Nicholas was present. It was discomforting, he admitted, to reproach the Empress for leading the Tsar into the abyss when Nicholas himself was there. However, the Grand Duke did not mince words. When the Empress objected that his reproaches were exaggerated and that the people loved the Tsar, the Grand Duke demurred.

'The nation is loyal to the Tsar, but the nation is discontented because of the influence which Rasputin exercised,' he said. 'Nobody knows better than me how much you love Niki, but I still must recognize that your meddling in affairs of state is harming the prestige of Niki and popular ideas about the Autocrat. I have been a true friend to you for 24 years, Alix. I am still your true friend, but on that basis I want to make you understand that every class of the Russian population is hostile to our politics. You have a wonderful family. Why don't you concentrate your energies on the things that give your soul peace and harmony? Leave affairs of state to your husband!'

During the exchange of bitter words that followed between the Empress and the Grand Duke, the Tsar sat apart, silently smoking a cigarette. Alexandra's parting words to Aleksandr Mikhailovich were, 'You will see that I was right.' Before the end of the month, Russia would be in revolution.

After unpleasant scenes of this nature, Nicholas was always glad to return to the front, where there was no squabbling over who was the real enemy. As he reported from there on the day of his arrival, 'no ministers, no problems'. Still ringing loudly in his ears were the Empress's last words of advice: 'Dear One, be firm, show a strong hand, which is what Russians need. Let them feel your fist. They beg for it themselves – so many people have said to me not long ago – we need the whip. This is strange, but that is the slavic nature.'

Once again the Empress had misread the patience of the Russian people. Sitting in the comfort of Tsarskoe Selo, it was difficult to appreciate life on the streets of Petrograd in late February. This was the worst part of the Russian winter – not the beautiful fury of the first snowfall, but the piles of dirty, melting snow, with rotten ice underfoot. The meagre stores of food put up by householders were nearly exhausted, even without the added rigours of wartime shortages. Weary workers had to queue for hours in the cold and dark for their daily bread.

In the middle of February the district commander of Petrograd ordered bread rationing in order to protect the city's dwindling stores of flour. Bakeries began to sell out early, and this provoked disorder among those who had queued unsuccessfully for bread. On 23 February (8 March on the Western calendar) the socialist festival of International Women's Day was held, and a small demonstration by women was swollen by groups of striking workers. The protests continued on the following day, and then the next.

In general the demonstrations were good-natured, with little violence and much fraternization between soldiers and the crowd. On 10 March, however, the commander of the capital's military district, General S. S. Khabalov, received a no-nonsense telegram from the Tsar: 'I command you to suppress from tomorrow all disorders on the streets of the capital, which are impermissible at a time when the fatherland is carrying on a difficult war with Germany.'

The obedient Khabalov ordered the troops to employ force to dispel demonstrators. On the following day they opened fire, and civilian casualties began to mount. The most serious incident occurred when the Volinsky Regiment aimed machine guns into a crowd and killed 40 people. The soldiers were deeply disturbed by what they had done and spent the night in excited debate and resolved to disobey any instruction to fire at civilians. Challenged by their commanding officer the next morning, they murdered him before deserting their barracks and exhorting other regiments to follow them. Many did. The moment of true revolution had arrived: the tsarist regime could no longer depend on its armed might to maintain internal order in a national crisis.

The leaders of the Duma, meeting in the capital, were at a loss over what to do. Many deputies wished an end to Nicholas's leadership, but they were not eager to unleash a popular rebellion. As the situation in the streets worsened, the president of the Duma, M. V. Rodzianko, sent a series of panicked telegrams to the Tsar at military headquarters, urging him to make political concessions before the situation got completely out of hand. Nicholas dismissed this note of alarm, complaining to an aide that 'this fat Rodzianko has written me some nonsense, to which I will not even reply.'

Subsequent messages narrowed the Tsar's options. They announced that the city was entirely at the mercy of rebellious soldiers and workers, that troops sent to disperse them had deserted and that an emergency civilian government was being formed. Nicholas's first thought was to return to the capital, not only to quell the disorder but also because his family were trapped at suburban Tsarskoe Selo, just outside Petrograd. The imperial train was diverted by striking railway workers and left stranded at the provincial town of Pskov. If the revolution were to be suppressed, Nicholas would have to depend upon the loyalty of the army at the front. The chief of staff, General Alekseev, canvassed all the front-line commanders by telegraph. The answers trickled in throughout the afternoon of 15 March. A clear consensus emerged: the loyalty of the troops could not be counted on. To save the dynasty and the nation, Nicholas should abdicate.

Stunned by this desertion of his beloved army, Nicholas immediately drafted a telegram to Alekseev: 'In the name of the welfare, tranquillity and salvation of my warmly beloved Russia, I am ready to abdicate from the throne in favour of my son. I request all to serve him truly and faithfully.' Before the message could be sent, however, word arrived from Petrograd that the Duma was sending a delegation to call upon the Tsar. The telegram was recalled, and Nicholas sat down to await the Duma messengers who, themselves delayed by striking rail workers, arrived at ten in the evening. They were Aleksandr Guchkov, a leading Duma moderate, and the prominent conservative deputy, V. V. Shulgin.

They presented Nicholas with a bleak picture: revolution was growing, and only abdication could restore national unity and the prestige of the dynasty. Nicholas had already accepted the necessity of abdication, but since the morning's telegram he had pondered the implications of abdicating in favour of Alexei. The family would be broken up, the under-age Tsarevich placed in the hands of a regency, and his health problems would become general knowledge. Nicholas withdrew to consult with the court physician,

Dr Fedorov, who assured him that Alexei's condition was incurable. The Tsar returned to the Duma representatives to announce that he would indeed abdicate – but in favour of his brother, the Grand Duke Mikhail Aleksandrovich, rather than Alexei.

The first Romanov Tsar of Russia, proclaimed in 1613, was a Mikhail, and so was the last. On the morning of 16 March a delegation of Duma deputies called on the heir-apparent with grim news. So unpopular had the monarch become, that they could not guarantee his physical safety should he take the throne. Mikhail preferred discretion to valour and abjured the throne until it might be offered to him by a constitutional convention. This was never to come. Instead, the Tsar for a day would be murdered by a revolutionary gang in the wilds of Siberia, within days of the assassination of Nicholas himself.

A few miles away from where Mikhail was rejecting the Romanov heritage sat the one person in Russia who could be counted upon to demand that Nicholas should not relinquish his throne so easily, the Empress Alexandra. But the Empress found herself powerless: all her children had been struck down by a serious case of measles, and as she rushed about their darkened sickroom, she learnt that communications with Nicholas had been cut. The Tsar's 'eyes and ears' were blind and deaf. She could not give him the exhortation and advice that would be necessary to strengthen his will. Recalling the crisis of 1905, and Nicholas's fateful decision to sign a constitution, she drafted a frantic message to him and had it sewn into the uniforms of two Cossack messengers. 'Clearly they don't want to let you see me so above all you must not sign any paper, constitution or other such horror – but you are alone, without your army, caught like a mouse in a trap, what can you do?'

The Duma delegates who negotiated Nicholas's abdication had assured him that they spoke for the whole nation. Upon their return to the capital, they found many in the street who were ready to challenge their mandate. 'Who elected you?' was the shout of angry workers. Indeed, the elective Duma, created by Witte in 1905, had become increasingly undemocratic in the years before the war, as the government tampered with the electoral laws in order to secure a workable majority. The Duma was thus dominated by wealthy landowners, millionaire industrialists, liberal professionals and a smattering of peasants, but with enough representatives from the political extremes to keep the pot boiling. This body, based on a limited franchise, could hardly pretend to speak for all Russia. As revolutionary sentiment grew increasingly extreme, the more progressive members of the Duma could do no more than proclaim themselves to be a temporary, Provisional Government, which would hold power only until an elective constitutional assembly was convoked to map out Russia's political future.

Many in the crowd were unprepared to wait so long, as they knew they had a model close at hand. In 1905 the leaders of the revolutionary movement had succeeded in calling a general strike that paralysed the nation and brought about political concessions. A strike committee or Soviet had been founded, known as the St Petersburg Soviet of Workers' Deputies. It was dominated by revolutionary activists. Similar Soviets had sprung up all over Russia, to provide leadership for local strikes. These bodies were as democratic as could be: workers sent their representatives daily to the Soviet itself, which made its decisions by majority vote. While the 'gentlemen' of the Duma were meeting in the Tauride Palace in Petrograd to devise their Provisional Government, workers' groups were reinventing the Soviet, now rechristened the Petrograd Soviet of Workers' and Soldiers' Deputies.

In theory the Petrograd Soviet admitted one deputy for every 2000 workers or soldiers. In fact it grew into a huge, amorphous body, swelling to over 3000 deputies. Every day brought another deputy from some corner of the front or the empire, clutching his mandate in his hand. The practical work of the Soviet, as opposed to its noisy debates, passed into the hands of an executive committee, drawn from socialist activists. Since the old tsarist administration in the country, like the monarch itself, was discredited, similar Soviets sprang up throughout the country, laying claim to the reins of local government. All shades of opinion, from moderate to socialist and anarchist, were represented in the Soviets. As the months passed, however, the consensual view tended to become more radical.

The Petrograd Soviet did not actually seize power, but constituted itself as a revolutionary watchdog to ensure that the 'bourgeois' Provisional Government did nothing to infringe the newly won liberties of the common people. There emerged a system of Dual Power – on the one hand the Provisional Government, in power but without authority, and on the other the Soviet, with authority but with no elective power. Under pressure from the Soviet, the Provisional Government was pushed continually to the left. As assorted liberal politicians were swept away, the central figure in the Provisional Government was a representative from the Soviet, the moderate socialist Aleksandr Kerensky. Kerensky dominated the government from his post as Minister for Justice and became Prime Minister on 21 July 1917.

From the first moments of the revolution, Kerensky had been intimately involved in the fate of the Romanovs. His arguments had been decisive in convincing the Grand Duke Mikhail to reject the throne. When the Provisional Government decided to place the Royal Family under house arrest – ostensibly to protect them from the popular wrath – Kerensky, as Minister of Justice, was charged with supervising their internment.

A true revolutionary romantic, Kerensky always argued that the Russian Revolution must avoid the bloody excesses of past popular uprisings. Faced with a mob baying for the summary trial and execution of the Emperor and Empress, he boldly faced down the crowd with the declaration that he was not prepared to play the role of the Russian Marat, invoking the name of the French revolutionary leader who had used the guillotine to deal with political opposition. Kerensky developed a relationship with the Imperial Family that was based on a grudging mutual respect. There was an irony here, since in the turmoil that preceded the revolution in the capital, Alexandra had expressed the firm wish that Kerensky be hanged for an especially fire-breathing speech in the Duma.

Kerensky's government faced a daunting array of problems. The military situation continued to deteriorate, especially when attempts made to 'democratize' the army, forced on the Provisional Government by the Petrograd Soviet, effectively destroyed military discipline. A Russian offensive, begun on 1 July with some success, prompted a German counter-attack, which threatened the total collapse of the eastern front. Desertion was an increasingly desirable option for many peasant soldiers. Not only might they escape becoming cannon fodder but they might also arrive home in time to secure their share of the land that peasant communities were seizing from private estates, under the revolutionary slogan that 'the land belongs to those who till it.' The Provisional Government committed itself in principle to land reform, but hoped to conduct it in a controlled and orderly way. It thus received no credit when the peasants seized land on their own authority, while official criticism of such acts served only to alienate peasants from the state.

The characterization of the Tsarist Empire as the 'prison-house of nations' had always been an exaggeration, but dissatisfaction with Russian rule had grown alongside emergent national consciousness among many of the empire's national and ethnic minorities. In the chaos of wartime, Poles, Ukrainians, Finns and Armenians began to demand autonomy or even independence. The Russian nationalists who dominated the Provisional Government in its first months were never able to accommodate these demands. Instead they dreamt of a 'greater Russia' stretching all the way to Istanbul. Such dreams were clearly an impediment to the attainment of a 'fair and democratic peace', which became the slogan of most socialists, and expansionist hawks were forced from the cabinet.

Although Kerensky's cabinets added more and more socialists, they failed to satisfy the strident demands of radicals, especially the Bolshevik wing of the Marxist Russian Social Democratic Party (the SDs), led by Vladimir Ilych Ulianov (Lenin). Initially Lenin confined himself to the slogan 'all power to the Soviets', arguing that government should pass from the bourgeois Provisionals into the hands of the more democratic – and more radical – local Soviets. In mid-July a series of street disorders supported by the Bolsheviks, the July Days, almost toppled the Provisional Government. These protests ultimately failed, and the Bolshevik leadership fled into hiding, only to appear again with more deadly effect in October.

With these problems to consider, Kerensky clearly did not require the additional complication of the Imperial Family, living under opulent house arrest, the few miles away in Tsarskoe Selo, and stranded by the refusal of the British government to grant them asylum. There were recurrent rumours of an escape attempt by the right, and fears that a revolutionary mob from the left might take revolutionary justice into its own hands. Kerensky resolved to send the Romanovs far away, out of sight and out of mind. He decided on the remote Siberian town of Tobolsk, over six days' journey from Petrograd by rail and steamboat. The choice did not lack its ironic elements. Western Siberia had been a popular place of exile for political criminals convicted by tsarist courts. At the same time, it was very close to the settlement of Pokrovskoe, the home village of Grigory Rasputin.

Kerensky ensured that the move was carried out without a hitch. Strict secrecy was maintained, even from the Romanovs themselves. Nicholas hoped to be sent to family holdings on the balmy shores of the Black Sea, but was forewarned by Kerensky's advice to 'bring warm clothes'.

A special train, disguised as a Red Cross mission, was organized for the first stage of the journey. A huge entourage was permitted to accompany the Imperial Family, and 2700 poods of luggage was dispatched along with them. Most important of all, Kerensky recruited a picked detachment of elite troops to provide security for the family. Under the command of a military professional, Colonel Evgeny Kobylinsky, the troops conscientiously fulfilled their assignment, even amid rapidly changing political circumstances.

Early on the morning of 1 August the special train pulled out of Tsarskoe Selo. Nicholas carefully noted the station names and quickly realized that the family was bound for Siberia. After an uneventful trip, the Romanovs were ensconced on 13 August in the former governor's mansion in Tobolsk, renamed Freedom House after the revolution. In this spacious and comfortable dwelling, the family settled down to its languid existence, far removed from the political excitement of the capital.

Not that the Romanovs were totally isolated. Visitors and information continued to arrive from Petrograd, and Nicholas was even permitted to subscribe to foreign and domestic periodicals, although he frequently complained about the deficiencies of the post. An opportunistic officer, Boris Soloviev, arrived from Petrograd and wormed his way into the imperial confidence by marrying Rasputin's daughter Maria. Soloviev promised the family their imminent rescue. In fact he confined himself to embezzling funds provided for a rescue by loyal monarchists and denouncing rival projects to the authorities.

Much more important than local affairs was the dispiriting news that arrived from the capital during the period of Tobolsk exile. The military situation deteriorated. In September the Provisional Government was forced to suppress a coup headed by the army commander-in-chief, Lars Kornilov. In October 1917, Kerensky was overthrown by an armed insurrection led by Lenin's Bolsheviks. In December the long-promised and democratically elected Constituent Assembly, which was supposed to sort out Russia's system of government, was forcibly dispersed by the Bolsheviks, who did not intend to surrender any of their power.

The immediate repercussion of the Bolshevik revolution was the curtailment of state aid for the upkeep of the tsarist household. At the end of February, Nicholas had to arrange for the dismissal of some of his servitors in Tobolsk because of the absence of money to pay them. Members of the immediate entourage had to appeal to local monarchists for help. The royal household was unwilling to part with the substantial quantities of jewels that they had brought with them to raise funds – they were now the only family legacy. Moreover, they were no longer readily available. Under the supervision of the children's French tutor, Pierre Gilliard, and with the connivance of Colonel Kobylinsky, large numbers of jewels were smuggled out of Freedom House and into the care of nuns at the local convent. Later Alexandra and the girls were to sew many of the imperial jewels and pearls into special corsets and undergarments.

From the perspective of Nicholas and Alexandra, the worst possible news was the announcement of a cease-fire with Germany and subsequent peace talks at the Polish city of Brest-Litovsk. The resultant treaty, signed on 3 March 1918, was peace at any price for the Bolsheviks, who were confident that the coming world revolution would sweep away the German generals and diplomats with whom they were negotiating. In the meantime, the treaty provided for the virtual dismemberment of the Russian Empire. A truncated Russia lost her Polish, Ukrainian, Estonian, Latvian and Finnish territories, which amounted to 1,300,000 square miles and 62 million of the empire's inhabitants.

When Nicholas heard of the armistice, he lamented in his

diary 'Shame and horror!' and a few days later he noted that 'the Bolsheviks must agree to the degrading conditions of the German government, in view of the fact that enemy forces are moving forward, and there is nothing to stop them! A nightmare!'

On the anniversary of his abdication he recalled that it had been motivated by his desire to save the military situation. Instead, Russia was now being torn to pieces by internal and external enemies. 'It sometimes seems that there isn't strength to bear it, and you just don't know what to hope for, what to wish for.' When rumours reaching Tobolsk erroneously reported that provisions of the treaty provided for the transfer of the Royal Family into German hands, Nicholas complained that it was clearly a measure designed to discredit him. Alexandra exclaimed that she would rather 'die in Russia than be rescued by Germans'. When the final, dreadful reports of the Treaty of Brest-Litovsk were known, Nicholas could only gasp in disbelief, 'And they called *me* a traitor.'

Bolshevik influence soon became apparent even in sleepy Tobolsk. The soldiers of the guard set up a soldiers' Soviet, which began to challenge the authority of Colonel Kobylinsky, who was obliged to remove all indications of rank from his uniform. Nonetheless, a core of non-Bolshevik soldiers maintained strict discipline and ensured the safety of the family. Their military professionalism was required because of changing political circumstances outside Tobolsk.

Every region of Russia reacted to the Bolshevik coup in its own way. This was reflected in the composition of the local Soviets, which had been created after the February revolution. There were a few isolated pockets of support for political moderates such as the pre-war liberal party, the Constitutional Democrats (Kadets). More typically, the political consensus was on the left, where there was much more diversity.

Besides the Bolsheviks, there was the more moderate Menshevik wing of the Social Democrats, which stood in opposition to the Bolshevik seizure of power. In peasant-dominated Russia it was unsurprising that the largest political movement was the rural socialism of the Social Revolutionary Party. The majority, the so-called Right SRs, joined the Mensheviks in opposing Bolshevik power. The minority Left SRs not only joined Lenin's government but also, if anything, were even more extreme than the Bolsheviks themselves. The Left SRs were to pose a real problem to the Bolsheviks now that the latter were faced with the practical problems of running a government, instead of firing critical ideological broadsides at the policies of others. In many Siberian towns the local Soviet was dominated by an anti-Bolshevik coalition of Mensheviks and Right SRs.

Provincial Tobolsk was spared much of this infighting. However, nearby regional centres such as Omsk and Ekaterinburg, with large working-class populations, boasted pro-Bolshevik Soviets. Bolshevik activists cast envious glances at the royal captives of Tobolsk. Why should the Tsar luxuriate in comfort when the workers suffered the privations of Russia's economic collapse? Why should 'Nicholas the Bloody' escape retribution, when his generals, freed by the Treaty of Brest-Litovsk of the need to hold the front, began to organize armed resistance to the new workers' state? But to punish the Tsar, revolutionaries had first to get their hands on him and to wrest him from Colonel Kobylinksy's well-armed professionals. Both the Omsk and the Ekaterinburg Soviets sent armed detachments of Red Guards to Tobolsk. Kobylinsky denied them any entry into Freedom House, and so they fell to fighting with each other.

The political centre in Moscow was aware of the combustible situation in Tobolsk between the rival Bolsheviks. The ruling Central Executive Committee of the All-Russian Soviet received reports of the various conspiracies, real and imagined, to free the Romanovs. On 1 April 1918, the Praesidium of the Central Executive Committee resolved to move the Royal Family. The preferred solution was to bring them to Moscow, where a revolutionary tribunal, directed by Lev Trotsky himself, could be staged and would indict all the mistakes of Nicholas's reign.

The central problem concerned the local Bolsheviks, who were not eager to let Nicholas off so easily, especially since they suspected that the Moscow leadership was tempted to resolve the delicate problem of the Tsar by sending him abroad. Germany and Russia had just signed a peace treaty, and the Empress was a German. At the same time, it could not be anticipated how Kobylinsky's troops would respond to an order to hand over their prisoner. They had more than once manned the machine-gun emplacements around Freedom House when issued demands to surrender Nicholas. Great delicacy was required to extract the Romanovs from this volatile position.

In Moscow Lenin and Iakov Sverdlov, the powerful secretary of the Central Committee, decided to entrust the mission to one of their best, the veteran revolutionary Konstantin Miachin, better known under his revolutionary alias as Vasily Yakovlev. His revolutionary career was romantically dramatic, featuring 'forced requisitions' from banks and running gun battles with the police. He had played a crucial role in the Bolshevik revolution itself, serving with the armed band that seized the central telephone exchange. At the very moment that Moscow was deciding to act, Yakovlev arrived in the new capital on his way back to Siberia, having just fought his way across country to deliver 40 wagons of grain to Petrograd.

Yakovlev was called to Sverdlov's office, where he was given full power to take such action as the occasion might require. Three options were open to him: to bring the Tsar to Moscow via either Omsk or Ufa, or to transport him to Ekaterinburg. Moscow was the preferred destination, but Sverdlov was well aware that the Bolsheviks of Ekaterinburg considered Nicholas to be their prize. If the main options failed, the Tsar would be dispatched to the 'Red capital of the Urals'. The main concern was to keep in communication with Moscow, and Yakovlev was assigned a personal telegraphist and instructions to contact Moscow at every crucial juncture. In all communications the Royal Family were to be designated under the code-name of 'the baggage'. Time was of the essence because of the heated atmosphere in Tobolsk and because the imminent spring thaw was thought to be the moment in which monarchist rescuers would act.

Even as he made his way to Tobolsk with a picked detachment of troops, Yakovlev encountered reinforcements on the way to join the Ekaterinburg Bolsheviks. Soon after his arrival he had an unpleasant interview with the local representative of the Ekaterinburg Soviet, S. S. Zaslavsky. If Yakovlev had any illusions about the aims of the men from Ekaterinburg, Zaslavsky quickly dispelled them: 'We need to finish off this business,' he announced. Zaslavsky later suggested that the Romanovs could perish in an ambush laid by 'anarchists'. He warned Yakovlev darkly that he should not sit next to the Tsar in his carriage. After this exchange

Yakovlev needed no further warnings that he would need to watch his back.

For the moment Bolshevik enthusiasts could be cowed by Yakovlev's mandate, signed by Lenin and Sverdlov: it threatened the death sentence to anyone who did not instantly obey the commissar. Kobylinsky's troops proved less of a problem than Yakovlev feared, especially when he announced that he had brought their back wages, which had been forgotten in the months of revolution in the centre. In a special irony, Yakovlev had taken the precaution of bringing pre-revolutionary gold coins, 'Romanov money'. Any lingering hesitation vanished when Yakovlev invited the guards to send a few of their own along with him to ensure that the Royal Family was indeed conveyed to a secure refuge. The canny Yakovlev had taken the added precaution of spreading the rumour among the troops that the Tsar was being taken to the safety of Moscow.

These difficulties overcome, Yakovlev encountered unexpected resistance from the royal prisoners themselves. The ostensible objection was the sudden illness of the Tsarevich. Yakovlev was no doctor, but from Alexei's anguished groans he quickly convinced himself that the boy could not possibly be moved. There was an additional, deeper fear, which terrified the Empress. Why this sudden urgency to move Niki to Moscow? Of course, to sign the detestable, traitorous Treaty of Brest-Litovsk. Surely the Germans realized that the Russian people would never accept the treaty terms unless they were signed by the Tsar himself.

Nicholas responded to Alexandra's fears with the ringing declaration that 'he would rather cut off his hand than sign the treaty.' But later when they had Nicholas alone, 'caught like a mouse in a trap', anything was possible. In 1905 it had been a constitution; in 1917 it had been abdication. This last betrayal of Russia had to be prevented, and only Alexandra had the strength to steel her husband's resolve. Thus, even while her son lay upstairs crying in pain, Alexandra announced that if Nicholas must go, she would go with him.

Arrangements were quickly made: Nicholas, Alexandra, their daughter Maria, the Tsar's personal physician Dr Evgeny Botkin, the former chief Marshal of the Court Prince Aleksandr Dolgoruky, the valet Terenty Chemodurov, the nursery servant

Ivan Sednev and the chambermaid Anna Demidova travelled in the first echelon, to be joined by the rest of the family and their retainers when Alexei's health improved.

Early on the morning of 26 April, the family said their goodbyes. Nicholas betrayed his emotion through the jerky motions with which he made the sign of the cross over his remaining daughters. Alexandra was under greater control, determined that none of her children would show weakness before the 'Red enemies'. The entourage was bundled into peasant carts, and the journey began towards the railway junction at Tiumen.

It was not an easy passage, delayed by the spring mud and the breaking up of the ice on the rivers and streams that had to be crossed. Yakovlev kept a wary eye on the troops from Ekaterinburg who formed part of his escort. During a brief respite in the village of Pokrovskoe the little band of travellers stood for some time looking at the house of Grigory Rasputin, while 'Our Friend's' family stared back at them from an upstairs window. At nine o'clock on the evening of 27 April, by the light of a full moon, the weary travellers reached the Tiumen station and were moved immediately into a waiting train. As the Romanovs tried to clean off the mud from their clothes and boots, Yakovlev rushed off to the station's telegraph office.

Yakovlev's initial telegram summed up the situation:

ONLY JUST ARRIVED WITH PART OF THE BAGGAGE. I WANT TO CHANGE THE ROUTE BECAUSE OF THE FOLLOWING EXTRAOR-DINARILY IMPORTANT CIRCUMSTANCES. PEOPLE ARRIVED IN TOBOLSK FROM EKATERINBURG SPECIALLY DESIGNATED FOR JUST ONE PURPOSE, THE DESTRUCTION OF THE BAGGAGE. THEY WERE REBUFFED BY THE SPECIAL GUARD – BUT IT ALMOST CAME TO BLOODSHED.

Moscow must understand that, as matters now stood, to attempt to send the Romanovs to Ekaterinburg would guarantee their immediate execution and perhaps that of their special escort as well. Yakovlev suggested a change of plan. He would take 'the baggage' away from Ekaterinburg, in the direction of Omsk, and from there to a hiding place in the mountains, where the Tsar could be safeguarded from a rescue attempt by the right or the

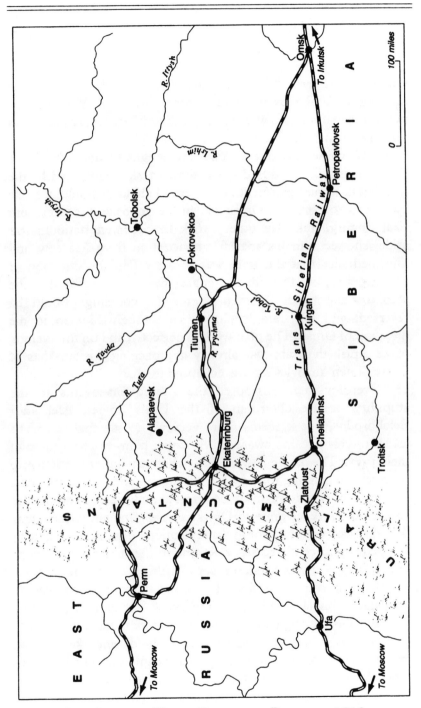

THE CENTRAL URALS REGION OF RUSSIA IN 1918

murderous attentions of the left. 'Give me an answer,' his message concluded. 'I'm standing in the station with the baggage.' A message direct from Moscow soon came through: 'Proceed to Omsk.' Did Sverdlov hope to snatch Nicholas from under the noses of the Urals Soviet and bring him to Moscow? Yakovlev was not to know until he could telegraph that the travelling party was safe in Omsk.

The chase was on, as Yakovlev sought to deny the Urals Soviet their most treasured possession, a task complicated by the fact that its armed representatives were all about. It would not take them long to catch on: Omsk was in the opposite direction from Ekaterinburg. Yakovlev quietly took the Tiumen stationmaster aside, showed him his special authorization from Moscow and informed him that the train was to set off in the direction of Ekaterinburg, but that another engine was to be prepared at the second station past Tiumen. Here, the couplings would be reversed, and the train would return through Tiumen in the direction of Omsk. The plan worked perfectly, and on the evening of 28 April, the train was already approaching the outskirts of Omsk. Then Yakovlev's plans collapsed in chaos.

Sverdlov later attributed the subsequent events to the stupidity of the chairman of the Urals Soviet, Aleksandr Beloborodov, but it seems more accurate to say that the Urals leader merely became aware of Moscow's plans to cheat them of their prey. The Urals Soviet dispatched an indignant letter to Moscow, demanding to know what was going on and announcing a general order that Yakovlev be arrested and the Tsar brought to Ekaterinburg. A telegram to Omsk, advising the authorities there that Yakovlev was 'a traitor to the revolution', demanded that he be stopped, by force if necessary. At one of the station stops before Omsk, Yakovlev was handed a copy of this message and realized that the game was almost lost. He stopped the train, uncoupled his passengers' carriage and went on to Omsk.

Even as the engine approached the station, he saw groups of Red Guards milling about the tracks. As he disembarked, he was surrounded by an armed mob. Yakovlev came very close to being lynched, but kept calm and demanded to see the chairman of the Omsk Soviet, an old Party comrade named Vladimir Kosarev. Fortunately, Kosarev was close to hand. 'Tell me what's going on, why are there cannons on the platform?' Yakovlev asked.

'They are all directed against you, you counter-revolutionary,' guffawed Kosarev. Yakovlev knew how close he had been to a violent end. Although a telegraph message from Moscow quickly confirmed that Yakovlev had been acting under the direct orders of the Central Committee, there was no escape now from Ekaterinburg for the Imperial Family. The Urals Soviet was forced to give a collective guarantee that the Tsar would arrive alive, then the royal train was turned around and headed back to the 'Red capital of the Urals'.

Nicholas immediately recognized the danger he was in. 'I would go anywhere at all but the Urals,' he confided to a member of the guard. 'Judging from the papers, the Urals are harshly against me.' But there was no turning back. As Yakovlev described the journey in his memoirs, it was 'the last trip of the Romanovs'. The baggage was approaching its final destination.

CHAPTER TWO

Delivering the Baggage

THE MOMENT YAKOVLEV turned the imperial train towards Ekaterinburg, the Royal Family was doomed. It was no longer even a question of who would die, but only where and when. Arguably the fatal moment had come even earlier, when Colonel Kobylinsky had handed over control of his prisoners to the commissar from Moscow. The Romanovs had then passed out of the hold of military professionals who had maintained discipline with codes of conduct that forbade the execution of civilian prisoners.

Now the family were in the hands of the hard men of the revolution, whose romantic ideal of a shining future had been coarsened by the realities of prison, exile, revolution and finally civil war. As Yakovlev had warned Moscow, the men of Ekaterinburg had only one goal, 'to destroy the baggage'.

The one who mattered most among the train-load of prisoners was 'Nicholas the Bloody'. This was the man whose troops had shot down unarmed workers and their families on Bloody Sunday in January 1905. It was he who had plunged Russia into a bourgeois war that had cost the lives of millions of peasants and workers. Now, the remnants of that army were trying to strangle the revolution. As for the rest of the family, they were at best the anachronistic Romanovs, unable to move without the help of flunkies and retainers, and at worst the remainder of 'the baggage', destined to share Nicholas's fate.

At no point did any of the revolutionaries give any thought to the possibility that individual members of the family might escape their common end. While the train headed for Omsk, there was still the possibility that some of the Romanovs might survive, even if the revolution took a bloody retribution from Nicholas in Moscow. But once the chance of a Moscow trial was gone, the centre ceased to worry about 'the baggage', except as to how to best dispose of it. The Politburo cared no more about the lives of the Romanovs than did 'the comrades' in the Red Urals. There had been a telling moment during Yakovlev's meeting with Sverdlov in the Kremlin, when the secretary of the Central Committee had given the Romanovs the code-name 'the baggage', and indicated how they should be moved. Almost as an after-thought Yakovlev had inquired: 'Should the baggage be delivered alive?' It was not a foregone conclusion.

If Nicholas had any doubts about the Urals being against him, they were dispelled upon his arrival at the main Ekaterinburg passenger station on 4 April 1918. The Tsar laconically recorded in his diary: 'Another wonderfully warm day. Arrived at Ekaterinburg at 8:40. We stayed at one station for three hours. There was a strong ferment between the locals and our commissars. Finally the former won out, and the train went off to the goods station.'

Yakovlev, who again found himself in the middle of a hornets' nest, left a more dramatic account. The station platforms were all filled with a boisterous crowd, and the local guards did little to keep them back. There were cries of 'Nicholas is finally in our hands!' and 'Hang them!' The station commandant himself, who was supposed to maintain order, hysterically shouted: 'Yakovlev! Get the Romanov out of the coach! I'll spit in his face!'

Yakovlev ordered the guards to bring out their machine guns to intimidate the crowd. To his astonishment, the crowd did not fall back. Instead, the station commandant cried triumphantly that 'we're not afraid of your machine guns! We've got cannons ready for you!' Yakovlev looked across the platform, and to his aston-ishment there were indeed several field pieces trained on him. In the nick of time a freight train passed between the Romanov train, standing at the platform furthest from the station entrance, and the crowd. Yakovlev used the opportunity to pull out and move the train to the Ekaterinburg freight terminal.

At the goods station, Yakovlev's – and the Tsar's – journey finally came to an end. A delegation arrived from the Urals Regional Soviet, led by its chairman, Aleksandr Beloborodov, along with Filipp Goloshchekin and Boris Didkovsky. Yakovlev handed over his prisoners and received a receipt – exactly as if he were delivering baggage. The royal travellers were placed in motor cars and driven towards the centre of Ekaterinburg. Already the culling began, however, as Marshal of the Court Prince Aleksandr Dolgoruky was taken off in a different direction, to the Ekaterinburg prison. He would never again be seen alive. His captors later claimed to have found money and incriminating documents on his person, which gave evidence of an escape plan. These allegations were used to buttress the claim that a large White Guard conspiracy was at work to save the Tsar.

The house of the retired military engineer and industrialist Nikolai Ipatiev must be one of the best-documented private homes in the history of Russia. Within a week of his arrival Nicholas had made a sketch of the floor-plan. His intention to send it to Tobolsk was stymied when it was confiscated – and used to justify the claim that the Romanovs were plotting their escape. Virtually every book devoted to the fate of the tsarist family includes a diagram of the house, with the south-central basement room marked with an ominous 'X'. Later investigators painstakingly explored and described every nook and cranny, and compiled a complete photographic record.

The house in question was a spacious, two-storey brick edifice, designed in the Russian Gothic style. It was located on a slight rise, virtually in the centre of the town. A small but pleasant garden was dominated by trees. Across the street was a large public square, fronted on the east by the imposing Ascension Cathedral. The house boasted unusual amenities for the Russian provinces: indoor toilets, hot running water and electric lights.

On 27 April 1918, Nikolai Ipatiev received a visit from a commissar of the Urals Soviet. He gave the family 48 hours to vacate the property, leaving their furniture behind. Since the penalty for disobedience was death, the house was quickly cleared. Two tall wooden fences were constructed around the dwelling and guard posts constructed. The Ipatiev House was thus transformed into the so-called House of Special Purpose. All was ready when the Romanovs arrived on 30 April.

It was immediately evident that the terms of their confinement had changed, and no attempt was made to spare their feelings. The Urals Soviet decreed a prohibition on the use of the old imperial titles, and Commissar Goloshchekin greeted the Tsar with the words 'Citizen Romanov, you may go in.' The family was subjected to frequent searches and arbitrary confiscations. This was all accompanied by constant pilfering of household possessions. Even the normally placid Nicholas lost his temper on one occasion, complaining to the vice-chairman of the Urals Soviet, Boris Didkovsky that 'heretofore I have dealt with honest and decent people.' Didkovsky asked the Tsar not to forget 'that you are under investigation and arrest'.

When the Tsar's children, Olga, Tatiana, Anastasia and Alexei arrived on 23 May, having come from Tobolsk by steamer and rail, the authorities were eager to demonstrate the change in their circumstances after the leniency of Freedom House. The princesses were forced to carry their own baggage as they disembarked on a rain-soaked, muddy platform. At the station another ominous reduction of the staff occurred. Of the royal entourage, only four were permitted to enter the House of Special Purpose. The children's French tutor, Pierre Gilliard, and their English tutor, Charles Sydney Gibbes, were freed, but most of the other travellers were packed off to prison.

Many of these followers, especially the more high born, were subsequently murdered. Even some of those who were admitted to the House, such as the servant Ivan Sednev and the Tsarevich's guard Klementy Nagorny, were removed on 27 May and subsequently shot at the end of June. An exception was made for the family's personal surgeon, Dr Vladimir Derevenko, who was allowed to take lodgings in the town and move about freely. 'They seemed to forget about me,' he said later, almost apologetically. His colleague, Dr Botkin, the Tsar's personal physician, who had travelled with Nicholas from Ekaterinburg, took up permanent residence in the Ipatiev House.

As first commandant of the House of Special Purpose, the Urals Soviet appointed Aleksandr Avdeev, a veteran Bolshevik who had been one of the Ekaterinburg stalwarts sent to Tobolsk to lay hands on the Tsar. A metalworker by profession, he became leader of the workers' council established to run the local Zlokazov factory. He was a fire-breathing activist, who proclaimed to the workers about the destruction of the rich bourgeoisie, with Nicholas at their head. He never spoke about the Tsar without using the epithets 'bloody' and 'bloodthirsty'. Thus, his appointment to guard Nicholas was a great honour, and Avdeev was not slow to boast about it at the factory. He was fond of announcing at workers' meetings: 'I'll take you all into the house, and show you the Tsar.'

Commander Avdeev required a cadre of professional guards to protect the house. In the first week of confinement Kobylinsky's soldiers who had escorted the royal party to Ekaterinburg were replaced by Magyars – Austro-Hungarian prisoners of war, who had gone over to the revolution. 'Professionals', in Avdeev's view, meant 'class-conscious workers', who were loyal to the Bolshevik cause. Recruitment took place in factories where the Bolsheviks had the strongest presence: 30 workers from the Sysertsk factory and 16 of Avdeev's pals from the Zlokazov works. The men made no secret of their reason for enlisting. It was not revolutionary consciousness, but the generous salary of 400 roubles a week for guard duty, in addition to payments that they continued to receive from their respective factories.

For all their fire-breathing rhetoric, Avdeev and his deputy, Aleksandr Moshkin, were seldom impolite to the Tsar, although they delighted in imposing petty regulations on the family and making arbitrary responses to requests. Avdeev was far too busy with other activities that derived from his new, privileged position, chiefly getting drunk at every opportunity. Nor did he drink alone. He invited workers from his old factory to come to the House of Special Purpose in order to assist him in his duties. In this way he was able to keep his promise to show the Tsar to the workers and also to secure fresh drinking partners.

Avdeev's drinking parties were frequently followed by raids on the storage rooms where Romanov goods were stored. The Tsar's monogrammed shirts became a fashion item around the town, while workers' girlfriends began to display perfume flasks with the legend BY SPECIAL APPOINTMENT TO THE ROYAL COURT.

When Avdeev was removed from his post on 4 July, the official reason given was the volume of theft under his administration. Professionals with skills other than drunkenness and petty theft were being moved into position.

Although he had a room on the same floor as the Romanovs, Avdeev spent his nights away from the Ipatiev House. A few days after the arrival of the Tsar and Tsarina, the lone sentry on the second floor was removed, leaving the family and their retainers in relative peace. As the number of guards from the factories increased, they could not be accommodated in the Ipatiev House, and an adjoining residence, the Popov House, was requisitioned for their use. Only the guards on duty remained on the ground-floor.

On her first day in the Ipatiev House, Alexandra, as was her wont, scratched the date and her lucky symbol, a swastika, on to a pane of glass in her bedroom window. The bored guards in the downstairs rooms also made alterations to the house. Much of it was the sort of graffiti that, in the words of one investigator, could be found on the walls of any public toilet. The identity of several of the guards can be established from their scrawls on the walls, and commandant Avdeev himself was not too proud to inscribe his name and title on the wall near the entrance. Pornographic sketches were a popular item as well, especially those illustrating the Empress and Rasputin. The frequent, obscene references to 'Grishka' (i.e. Rasputin) illustrated the hold that the wild Siberian still had on the popular imagination. The guards were forbidden to fraternize with the prisoners, and there was none of the fleeting banter between the Grand Duchesses and the troops that had characterized their confinement at Tsarskoe Selo or Tobolsk. The sole exception was when one of the princesses had to go to the toilet, when they were 'escorted' by guards who delighted in asking where they were going and what they were going to do.

Violence was always close to the surface. On 4 June, a guard accidentally fired through a window of the house. On 8 June, a bomb exploded, although without injuring anyone. When investigators later searched the house, they found strange cut marks on many door jambs in the house. They turned out to be casual cuts from bayonets. The bored guards were always practising.

● ● ●

Virtually all contemporary political events worked against the survival of the family. When the Soviet state signed the armistice with the Germans, the Russian military leadership was freed from the need to subordinate politics to the holding of the front. A number of them established anti-Bolshevik military forces, the so-called Volunteer Army, and the White movement was born.

Another military event occurred closer to Ekaterinburg, in Siberia. Large numbers of prisoners from the armies of Austria–Hungary had been captured by the Russians in the course of the war. The Allies, desperate for more cannon fodder to feed the war, had agreed with a suggestion, made by Czech nationalists, of organizing a volunteer force of Czechs and Slovaks, augmented by POWs, to fight against the Germans. As a reward, the Allies would support the creation of an independent Czech and Slovak state after the war.

The collapse of the Russian Empire left the status of these troops in limbo. Since both the Bolsheviks and the Allies wanted them out of Russia, an agreement was concluded whereby they were to be shipped to a suitable port for embarkation to the West. At the end of March 1918 it was agreed that the port would be Vladivostok in the Russian Far East, necessitating a lengthy train journey on the Trans-Siberian Railway. The Czechs and the Bolsheviks were mutually distrustful, and when, at the end of May 1918, local Bolsheviks attempted to disarm the Czechs en route, they rebelled. This uprising of the armed Czechs and Slovaks encouraged local anti-Bolsheviks, and the civil war came to Siberia. The initial successes of the Czech and White forces, which brought them into the Urals region, had a crucial bearing on the fate of the Romanovs.

The apparent weakening of Bolshevik strength encouraged resistance from those on the political left. In Moscow, the Left Social Revolutionaries plotted to sabotage the Brest-Litovsk Treaty, which they saw as a shameful surrender to German militarism. In Ekaterinburg itself, Anarchists organized demonstrations against the Bolshevik majority on the local Soviet. On 10 June one such demonstration by the Union of Veterans of the Front filled Cathedral Square and was only suppressed when armed Red Guards were brought into action. On 13 June several Anarchists were arrested in the Palais Royal Hotel, prompting an armed uprising of local Anarchists. So serious did the situation appear that Avdeev ordered the Royal Family to pack travelling bags and to be ready for evacuation to Moscow at a moment's notice. In the event, all the resistance was put down, and the ringleaders were executed.

A foremost role in the suppression of these disorders was played by a young commissar from the local Upper Iset factory, Petr Ermakov. He was a member of the local branch of the Extraordinary Commission for Struggle with Counterrevolution and Sabotage, the Cheka. This body, established shortly after the October Revolution by Felix Dzerzhinsky, one of Lenin's comrades-in-arms, was the chief agency of the Bolshevik regime for dealing with opposition from any quarter. Chekists like Ermakov were not fastidious in their choice of methods. When in doubt, they reached for their revolvers. Any matter touching state security involved the Cheka, and Ermakov was to play a crucial role in the events of mid-July.

As the political crisis deepened, the fate of the Romanovs became a recurrent issue among Bolsheviks in Moscow and Ekaterinburg. The attitudes of the latter were represented by Commissar Zaslavsky, who had told Yakovlev in Tobolsk that they must be 'finished off'. It is important to realize that throughout the period before the night of 16 July, local Chekists were 'finishing off' members of the royal entourage, even the most innocuous members. Thus, Nagorny, the Tsarevich's bodyguard, and Sednev, the nursery servant, were shot at the end of June. Marshal of the Court Dolgoruky and the Tsar's aide-de-camp, General Ilya Tatishchev, who had accompanied the children from Tobolsk, were disposed of on 1 July. But the best example of the homicidal malevolence of the Urals' Bolsheviks occurred not in Ekaterinburg, but in the Siberian town of Perm.

Nicholas's brother Mikhail, the erstwhile last Tsar of Russia, had chosen Perm as his place of exile. Here he led a placid existence in a suite that he rented at the ironically named Royal Rooms Hotel. On the night of 12 June a small squad of armed men, bearing an order from the local Cheka, took away Mikhail and his English secretary, Brian Johnson. The following morning the authorities announced that the Cheka documents had been forged, that the three men were 'unknown', and that Mikhail had

THE QUEST FOR ANASTASIA

escaped from custody. In fact, Mikhail and Johnson had been driven to the outskirts of Perm, where they were both shot dead. The 'unknown men' who carried out this summary execution were the head of the local Soviet, Gavriil Miasnikov, the chief of the Perm police, V. A. Ivanchenko, and several members of the Cheka. One of them, Andrei Markov, boasted in his memoirs that he had gone to Moscow to report on the deed to Lenin himself, who expressed his approval for this local initiative.

Exactly analogous was the fate that befell other members of the House of Romanov who were detained at the small town of Alapaevsk, not far from Ekaterinburg. On the night of 17 July, less than 24 hours after the execution of Nicholas, a group of Chekists executed the Grand Duchess Elizaveta Fedorovna (Alexandra's widowed sister), Grand Duke Sergei Mikhailovich, the three sons of the Grand Duke Konstantin – Ioann, Konstantin and Igor – and Prince Vladimir Pavlovich. The responsibility for their executions would have lain with the leadership of the Urals District Soviet – Beloborodov, Goloshchekin and Georgy Safarov – who, it will be remembered, were responsible for the captives of the Ipatiev House. A massive campaign of disinformation accompanied both of these summary executions, and one theme was foremost: the victims were presented as attempting to escape.

Thus the significance of a letter that was surreptitiously handed to Nicholas in the Ipatiev House by a member of the guard. It was written in French, and signed simply 'An Officer':

> *With the help of God and your sang-froid we hope to succeed without any risk. It is absolutely necessary that one of your windows be unblocked so that you can open it at the right moment. The fact that the little Tsarevich can't walk complicates things, but we have foreseen it, and I don't think that it will be too much of a problem. Write if you will require two people to carry him, or if one of you can do it. Would it be possible to sedate the little one for one or two hours in the event that you should know in advance the exact hour. This doctor [Botkin] should give his opinion but in the event of necessity we can supply something or other to deal with this. Don't worry: no attempt will be made without complete confidence in the outcome. Before God, before History and our consciences we give you our solemn promise.*

The excitement caused by this sudden ray of hope in the Romanov household can be imagined, but in all their dealings with this anonymous saviour, the family maintained an air of caution and realism. This was a proper response, because the letter, and those to the Romanovs that followed it, were forgeries. The real author was Petr Voikov. Voikov, nicknamed 'The Intellectual' in the revolutionary underground, had the necessary background to compose a note in credible French: he had spent years of exile in Switzerland. In 1917 he had returned to Russia through Germany together with Lenin in the famous 'sealed train', which the Germans had permitted to pass through their territory in order to spread revolutionary confusion in Russia.

At the beginning of 1918 he served on the Executive Committee of the Urals Regional Soviet as Commissar for Supplies. After composing the text of the 'Officer's' letter, he had a member of the Cheka, I. Rodzinsky, copy it out. The entire operation was thus a provocation that could be – and was – used as justification for the execution of the Tsar. But despite hints and encouragements, the Romanovs never wrote what was expected of them. The text that was finally published by the Soviet authorities, in *Izvestiia* on 3 April 1919, had to be heavily edited and distorted.

To begin with, the authorities pretended that Nicholas himself had responded to the original letter. In fact, the reply that the family passed on to 'an officer' was composed by one of his daughters:

The second window from the corner looking out on the square has been open day and night for two days. The seventh and eighth windows looking out over the square near the main door are always open. The room is occupied by the commandant and his assistants, who comprise the internal guard – somewhere around 13 men. At the least they are all armed with rifles, revolvers and bombs. None of the doors has keys except ours. The commandant or his assistant come in to us whenever they want. Whoever is on armed guard duty makes a circuit of the house twice every hour at night and we hear him talking to the permanent guard underneath our window. There is a machine gun on the balcony and another downstairs in case of a disturbance. We don't know whether there are others. Don't forget that we have the doctor and housemaid (two members of the domestic household [Dr Botkin and Anna Demidova]) with us and a little boy with us. It would not be proper on our side (although they don't wish to burden us) to leave them alone since they followed us into exile. The doctor has already been in bed for three days with a kidney complaint, but he is now better. We keep waiting for the return of two of our party who are young and strong, who were taken off to the town a month ago, and we don't know where or why. In their absence father will carry the little one through the rooms out into the garden. Our surgeon, who attends the little one almost every day at five o'clock lives in the city – don't forget that we never see him alone. The guards patrol of 50 men is situated in a small house opposite our window on the other side of the street. There are some unique things that we still have in cases in the storage shed. We are especially concerned for a little black box number 9 with the initials A.F., and the large box number 13 with the initials N.A. with old letters and diaries. Of course the rooms are full of boxes of bed linen and things at the mercy of the thieves who surround us. All the keys, and especially that for room No. 9, are kept by the commandant who conducts himself properly with regard to us. In any case, warn us in advance if you can and let us know if you can take our people. There is always an automobile outside the front door. There are signal bells connecting the commandant to all the guard posts, and there are connections linked to the guards' house and other places. If our people stay behind, can we be assured that nothing will happen to them??? Dr B[otkin] begs us not to think about him and the other people in order not to make the task still more difficult. Count on our women. God help us, and count on our sang-froid.

The 'Officer' promptly replied:

Don't worry about the 50 men living in the small house opposite your window – they won't be dangerous when it is necessary to act. Say something more precise regarding your commandant so to make it easier for us to start. We can't say now if we can take all of your people. We hope yes, but in any case they won't be with you after your departure from the house, with the exception of the doctor. We are taking all measures for Dr D[erevenko] and we hope well before Sunday to give you a detailed plan of operations. At this point they will take the following form: when you hear a signal, use the furniture to close and barricade the door that will separate you from the guards, who will be blockaded and terrorized inside the house. Special ropes will be used to hoist you through the window to where we will be waiting below, the rest won't be a problem, there is no shortage of means for getting away, and the escort will be the best there is. Give some thought to the important problem of how it will be possible to lower the little one. In any case, the father, mother and son should get out first, then the daughters and the doctor to follow them. Answer if this is possible in your opinion and if you can make the ropes since it will be difficult to get ropes to you in advance.

These warning letters were serious enough to cause the Romanovs to spend a troubled night on 13 July, lying in bed with their clothes on and awaiting the promised signal. The following day Nicholas noted in his diary that 'nothing happened, and anticipation and uncertainty was very agonizing.' In retrospect, the plan being hatched against the Romanovs seems all too apparent. They blockade themselves in their rooms, they force their way out of the window, and Nicholas, Alexandra and Alexei are first in the sights of the machine gun located below their window. Another set of Romanovs are 'shot trying to escape'.

The response of the Romanovs to the second letter reveals that their 'anticipation and uncertainty' were not caused only by their concern about the escape but also because they had already become very sceptical about the plans of the 'Officer', which had them swinging out of windows with a dangerously ill haemophiliac child. They might well have feared that their second letter would not reach their impetuous rescuers in time to warn them off. If Voikov and Goloshchekin intended the Romanovs to incriminate themselves, rather than attempt the reckless escape plan recommended to them, they were sorely disappointed. The Romanov response to the officer's second letter was short and to the point.

We do not want and we cannot flee, we are only able to be abducted by force such as that force which took us to Tobolsk. Don't count on any active help from our side. The commandant

41

has many helpers and change often and have become anxious. They are safeguarding our confinement and our lives honestly and our relations with them are very good. We do not want them to suffer because of us nor you to suffer for us and above all in the name of God avoid bloodshed. Confirm these things for yourself. Escape through the windows without steps is quite impossible. Even with helpers there is still great danger from the open window from the commandant's room and the machine gun from the lower floor, which commands the interior courtyard. Abandon any thought of abducting us, or removing us. If you are concerned for us, you can always come to our aid in the event of unavoidable or real danger. We simply don't know what goes on outside. We don't receive magazines or newspapers or letters. From the moment they permitted us to open our windows, our supervision has increased and we have even been forbidden to look out, at the risk of receiving a bullet in the face.

Although there was a further exchange of letters, the guards now recognized that their captives could not be tempted into anything rash. Out of frustration, they spitefully punished the family for their lack of cooperation. On 11 July, when the execution was less than a week off, the authorities installed iron railings on the open window, so that there was no possibility of using it as an escape route. Nicholas was critical of the new commandant in his diary: 'This type pleases us less and less.' They were virtually the last words he would ever write.

The military situation played the decisive role in bringing the Romanov problem to a head. In late June and early July the combined Czech–White forces made important gains in the Urals. At the beginning of July the Military Commissar of the Urals Regional Soviet, Filipp Goloshchekin, travelled to Moscow to evaluate the military situation and to warn that the city of Ekaterinburg, the target of an enemy advance, would almost certainly fall.

There is little doubt that he also discussed the fate of the Tsar. It is important to stress that Nicholas's destiny was never a matter of great concern to the Bolshevik leadership in Moscow.

Despite recurrent rumours to the effect, the future of the Royal Family was never discussed at Brest-Litovsk.

After the signing of a peace treaty, there is no evidence in the diplomatic correspondence of any German intervention on their behalf. As the final, decisive months of the Great War ensued, the Germans had many, more pressing concerns to raise with the Soviet authorities. German policy sought to do everything it could to normalize relations in the east, so that troops could be shifted to the Western Front. Of secondary importance was the enforcement of other provisions of the treaty, chiefly involving the evacuation of territory or the surrender of supplies. Moscow was well aware that the Romanovs were not a factor that needed to be considered at all in relation to the Germans.

Despite the rhetoric about Nicholas or Mikhail serving as a 'banner' or rallying-point for the counter-revolution, Lenin and the Bolsheviks never considered this a serious risk. Nobody who lived through the revolutions of 1917 could be in any doubt that the Romanov dynasty was completely discredited. The White leadership expounded on the need for a 'great and undivided Russia', but they were at pains to distance themselves from the House of Romanov, which had lost any popular resonance. If anyone tried to link Tsardom with the White forces, it was the Reds, who warned that their defeat would mean a return of the autocracy, its Tsar and its landowners.

Insofar as Moscow had an interest in Nicholas, it was as a focus for political propaganda. When the subject of the Tsar arose in meetings of the Commissariat of People's Deputies, such as the session of 4 June 1918, the consensus was that he should be brought to Moscow for a great show trial. Lev Trotsky dreamed of serving as public prosecutor and of heaping all the social, economic and political failures of the past upon Nicholas's head. But this was never more than a vague plan, which lacked real urgency or necessity.

On the other hand, Moscow was conscious of the murderous propensities of the Urals Bolsheviks. One of Lenin's cousins had been shot by them at the beginning of 1918 for leading a strike, and Lenin had to intervene personally in order to safeguard his uncle and the rest of the family. The Uraltsy were no respectors of rank or station. But then, these were just the sort of people Lenin wanted at the cutting edge of the Revolution – and at the front. Iakov Sverdlov's obscure negotiations on behalf of the Central Committee were motivated by the desire not to have Nicholas murdered by Ekaterinburg vigilantes somewhere south of Tobolsk. Ultimately a *modus vivendi* developed between Moscow and Ekaterinburg: Nicholas was to be kept safe in case he might prove useful in some way to the Revolution. Should the needs or risks of the moment necessitate it, however, he could be done away with. And if he were to be executed, the 'wild Siberian comrades' were to have the honour.

If this simple arrangement, which was respected by both sides, is kept in sight, it provides a clear answer to a question over which an ocean of ink has washed – did Moscow give the order for the execution of the Tsar? The answer, as will quickly be seen, was yes, but in response to the desires of the Urals Soviet. The family could easily have been evacuated – as were Bolshevik-held gold and valuables, including items worn by the late Royal Family – before the city was surrendered. It is therefore unsurprising that Moscow received the news of the Tsar's murder calmly and ratified it in a matter-of-fact manner.

This helps to explain the fate of the rest of the family. Nicholas posed the political problem, and his execution was the political solution. The Tsar's family and his suite were of secondary consideration and were left to the exigencies of the moment. Since the wholesale slaughter of all the Romanovs in the Urals, women and children included, proved to be too bloodthirsty for foreign consumption, efforts were made to deny or disguise their murders, or to attribute them to somebody else. But there is no doubt that they took place.

Even as Goloshchekin departed for Moscow at the beginning of July, plans were in motion for the liquidation of the inhabitants of the House of Special Purpose. On 4 July Avdeev and Moshkin were removed from their posts and replaced with a trusted member of the Urals Soviet, Yakov Mikhailovich Yurovsky. With the revised command came a new inner-guard, commonly called Latvians. The reference was to the regiment named the Latvian Rifles, whose enlisted men were an especially ardent group of Bolshevik supporters. Their services were employed whenever reliable troops were required, and their name was used casually for any specialist, non-Russian military group. The Latvians in question were actually prisoners of war from the Austrian Empire who had been recruited into special units by the Bolsheviks. Significantly, these foreign hand-picked troops were virtually unknown to the factory-worker Red Guards living in the Popov House. The Latvians were in the service of the Cheka and brought in especially for the executions. On the night, however, two of them declined this honour, since they refused to shoot women and children. The Ekaterinburg members of the Cheka showed no such scruples.

With the executioners in place, provision had to be made for the disposal of the bodies. Petr Ermakov of the Ekaterinburg Cheka was a local man, and so Yurovsky relied upon him to suggest an appropriate location. On 11 July the two travelled to a wooded area to the north of Ekaterinburg via a road that led to the small village of Koptiaki. The woods were dotted with lakes and abandoned open-pits, which had been dug to mine iron ore. There they encountered a mining engineer, Ivan Fesenko, who guided them to a part of the woods known as the Four Brothers, after a stand of tall trees growing there. Near the road was a clearing and an abandoned mine. While Yurovsky and Ermakov considered the site, Fesenko carved his name and the date on a nearby tree. The Four Brothers it is, thought Yurovsky as he walked away from the site.

The execution of the Tsar and his family has often been described as 'summary' and 'illegal'. This is true only to a point. By the dictates of the political morality of the day, in which terror played an increasing role, it was a well-considered act, which was approved up and down the chain of command. A formal trial was a luxury when the revolution came to deal with the 'class enemy'.

On 12 July a meeting of the Ekaterinburg Regional Soviet gathered to hear Goloshchekin's report from Moscow. He had much to tell them. During his stay in the capital a group of Left SRs, erstwhile coalition partners in the first Bolshevik cabinet, had sought to sabotage the Brest-Litovsk Treaty. On 6 July they had assassinated the new German Ambassador to Moscow, Count Wilhelm Mirbach, hoping to provoke a new war with Germany. A small force seized the Moscow post and telegraph office. This amateurish uprising was suppressed, and there was massive retaliation against the instigators.

At the first word of the outrage, Lenin rushed to the German embassy to offer condolences. The Bolsheviks had to squirm their way out of a German demand that a German battalion should be sent immediately to Moscow to protect embassy personnel. If the German government had shown any interest in the Romanovs, or if the Soviet government had seen any opportunity to use them as bargaining chips, this would have been the moment. In fact, not a word was said about the Imperial Family by either side. Indeed, Goloshchekin reported that the capital had no objection to the execution of Nicholas if the military circumstances warrented it, and a gloomy prognosis of the military situation was then delivered. The way was now clear, and the Soviet approved the following protocol:

'In view of the fact that the Czechoslovak bands threaten the Red capital of the Urals, Ekaterinburg, in view of the fact that the crowned hangman might flee the wrath of the people, the Praesidium of the Regional Soviet, fulfilling the will of the Revolution, resolves: the former Tsar Nicholas Romanov, guilty of countless crimes against the people, is to be shot.' At this juncture, it should be noted, the punishment was decreed only for Nicholas.

On Sunday, 14 July, the implementation of the verdict passed from the Soviet to the Cheka, which met in room three of the American Hotel in Ekaterinburg, where the Cheka had its headquarters. The meeting was chaired by the head of the Cheka's Executive Committee, Aleksandr Beloborodov, and attended by Yurovsky, Goloshchekin, Ermakov and others who would play their role in the execution. It resolved that the execution should be carried out no later than Thursday, 18 July. Full responsibility was assigned to Yurovsky, in his role as commandant of the House of Special Purpose. Apparently without any discussion, the Cheka resolution sentenced an additional ten people to death: 'It is resolved to liquidate the former Tsar Nicholas Romanov and his family and the servants living with them.' Goloshchekin also explained the rules of the game: Moscow was in agreement with their actions, but wanted to be consulted.

The following Monday was spent in preparations for the execution. A truck was ordered to carry away the bodies. Goloshchekin travelled to the woods to confirm the choice of the Four Brothers as the site at which to dispose of the victims. Yurovsky was especially busy. He instructed two novices from the

Novo–Tikhvinskii Convent, who had been supplying dairy products to the Tsarevich, to bring him 50 eggs. These would later serve as his breakfast while he supervised the burial of Alexei. Even more oddly, Yurovsky then found time for a friendly chat with his intended victim. Two women who came to wash the floors spotted him seated by Alexei's bed in animated conversation with the heir. Perhaps this motivated Yurovsky's one act of restraint throughout this period. The following day he ordered that the kitchen boy Leonid Sednev, who doubled as a playmate for Alexei, be removed to the Popov House, thus saving his life. A kitchen boy would live, while the pampered Tsarevich was to suffer another fate.

CHAPTER THREE

'Not Easy to Kill'

ALL THE MORE poignant because it was their last day alive, 16 July was an entirely uneventful day for the Romanovs. They took their usual walks and entertainments. Tatiana and Alexandra did their customary reading from the Bible, choosing the Prophetic Books of the Old Testament. Nicholas and Alexandra played bezique until 10:30 pm, when they retired. Dr Botkin was still working on his last letter when the executioner came to call.

All around the unsuspecting Romanovs there was hustle and bustle. During the day Yurovsky was again seen on the Koptiaki road. At six o'clock in the evening Goloshchekin took him aside and ordered the executions to proceed. While Goloshchekin went off to the telegraph office to send the final word to Moscow, Yurovsky summoned the head of the interior guard, Pavel Medvedev. He instructed him to collect the guards' revolvers, all standard issue Nagan, and verify that they were loaded and fully operational. 'Tonight, Medvedev,' Yurovsky warned him, 'we are going to shoot the whole family.'

At eight o'clock the guard assembled to plan the executions. It was at this point that two of the Latvians refused to participate. The rest of the detachment, over a couple of glasses of vodka, chose their victims. Yurovsky had ordered that each marksman should have a specific target, and that they should aim for the heart in order to make the death quick and prevent the flow of too much blood. Meanwhile Medvedev made the rounds of the external guards' posts, telling each man not to be alarmed if he heard gunfire from within the house after ten o'clock.

Yurovsky had ordered the Fiat truck to arrive at midnight. He hoped to use its noisy engine to cover the sound of shots. He complained of the delay in bringing the vehicle to the gate of the courtyard, but there was good reason. The telegraph lines to Moscow were unreliable that day, and the telegram notifying Lenin of the impending execution had to be sent via Petrograd, and the powerful Party chief of that city, Grigory Zinoviev, relayed it to Moscow. It was not until 21:22 that it arrived there:

TO SVERDLOV IN THE KREMLIN, COPY TO LENIN, FROM EKATERINBURG THE FOLLOWING MESSAGE IS TRANSMITTED: TELL MOSCOW THAT DUE TO URGENT MILITARY CIRCUM-STANCES IT IS IMPOSSIBLE TO WAIT FOR THE TRIAL ARRANGED WITH FILIPP [GOLOSHCHEKIN]. IF YOUR OPINION IS TO THE CONTRARY, LET US KNOW IMMEDIATELY. GOLOSHCHEKIN, SAFAROV. COMMUNICATE ON THIS MATTER WITH EKATER-INBURG YOURSELF. ZINOVIEV.

The affirmative telegram from Moscow came through to the American Hotel at shortly past one in the morning. The truck, sent from the nearby central garage, had been waiting for some time, its driver a member of the Urals Soviet, Sergei Liukhanov. Petr Ermakov and another Cheka man, Mikhail Medvedev-Kudrin, leapt into the cab of the truck as it raced off to the Ipatiev House. They did not want to be late for the great event. Yurovsky had almost lost patience when the truck arrived at half past one. He was eager to start.

As soon as the truck arrived, Yurovsky went into action. He interrupted Dr Botkin at his writing desk and asked him to rouse the family and servants. It took them about 30 minutes to wash and dress. Yurovsky then informed them that the military situation in the town was unsettled and asked them to retire to the basement, where they would be safer. The Romanovs were aware of the seriousness of the military situation. They had heard Red Guards marching past with a brass band on their way to the front. Distant artillery resounded almost every night. Thus there was nothing sinister in Yurovsky's invitation.

The Tsar picked up Alexei in his arms and carefully followed Yurovsky down to the cellar. Alexandra, whose legs constantly gave her pain, was helped down the stairs by Olga. Anastasia held her little dog, Jemmy. The maid Demidova carried two pillows for Alexei and Alexandra. As Yurovsky later gloated in his memoirs, proud of a job well done, they all came tranquilly and peacefully, not suspecting a thing.

The room had been selected by Yurovsky with care. It had plaster walls, to reduce the risk of ricocheting bullets. It faced on to the back garden, and was half below ground-level, which would reduce the sound of shots. It had been entirely cleared of furniture. Alexandra was the first to notice this and was imperious as ever. 'What! Can't we sit?' she exclaimed. One of the guards, Okulov, was sent out for a chair for the Tsarevich. 'He wants to die sitting down,' he muttered.

Meanwhile, the Ipatiev House had begun to fill up. In the room next to where the Romanovs partly stood and sat, the six Latvians waited, fiddling with the safety-catches of the Nagan revolvers. Yurovsky's deputy Prokopy Nikulin made his way into the room. Members of the Ekaterinburg Soviet arrived for the historic occasion. One of them was Goloshchekin, who spent the next half hour walking nervously around the house. Two members of the watch, Ivan Kleshchev and Nikita Deriabin, warned of the impending execution, stationed themselves so that they could witness the events through the open door. Yet another guard, Alexei Kabanov, was supposed to man the machine gun in the attic of the Ipatiev House. Instead, he came down to the basement and joined the firing squad.

Yurovsky began to arrange the group into rows, as though they were posing for a formal portrait. 'Please, would you stand there, you there, all in a row.' The Romanovs were in the front row, with Alexei and Alexandra seated in the two chairs that Okulov had brought. Behind them stood Dr Botkin, Anna Demidova, Ivan Kharitonov the cook, and Alexei Trupp the valet. The doors to the adjoining room opened, and the Chekists and the Latvians entered the room. With Yurovsky they numbered eleven men, one for each of their victims. The party still suspected nothing and sat calmly, looking at the line of men in front of them. The onlookers crowded outside the open door.

Yurovsky stepped up to the Tsar and pulled a small piece of paper out of his pocket. His other hand rested inside his jacket, where it clutched his Colt revolver. 'Nikolai Aleksandrovich,' he read, 'your relatives wanted to save you, but they did not succeed, and so we have to shoot you.' Nicholas appeared not to understand, perhaps because the engine of the truck outside had roared to full throttle. He turned to his family and then back to Yurovsky. 'What? What?' he asked. Yurovsky hastily read the declaration once more and ordered the firing squad to prepare themselves. Nicholas again turned to his family. Alexandra and Olga began to cross themselves, and the other girls started to scream. Then the firing commenced.

Nicholas was the first to fall, toppling over backwards. Yurovsky, Medvedev-Kudrin and Petr Ermakov all claimed to have shot Nicholas, and two of them donated their weapons to historical museums to celebrate their claims. All three may have been telling the truth. Faced with such a tempting target, most of the squad probably fired at Nicholas, eager to become 'the man who killed the Tsar'.

Yurvosky's plan to have his marksmen aim for the heart and end it all quickly completely broke down. Although the execution had been carefully planned, some of the squad were already drunk, and Nikulin was too nervous to aim properly. The air was filled with screams and the barking of dogs. Bullets ricocheted around the room. As the men fired wildly, they gave each other powder burns. One after another the victims began to drop, like targets in a shooting gallery. The air became thick with smoke, and it was almost impossible to see. The maid Demidova ran back and forth against the wall, trying to shield herself with the two pillows. There were groans coming up from the floor.

'Stop firing!' Yurovsky shouted. 'The shots will be heard on the street. Finish them off with bayonets.' The bayonet practice of the guards, which had left so many marks on the doorframes, appeared to have been wasted. The Grand Duchesses were mysteriously hard to pierce and had to be dispatched with blows from rifle butts. One such swipe killed the dog Jemmy. Demidova proved especially hard to kill, and when she finally lay still, there were 32 stab wounds on her body. Even after this, not all the victims were dead. Anastasia suddenly revived and began to scream, until silenced by more bayonet thrusts and blows from rifle butts.

There was one more unexpected survivor. Alexei, whose life had always seemed so ready to slip away, survived the initial assault and moaned softly from where he lay on the floor. Yurovsky's Colt was empty, so he pulled out a second weapon, a Mauser, and stepped over the little boy, with whom he had been amiably chatting two days earlier. He aimed and fired several shots point blank into his head. When the White authorities recovered the Tsarevich's diary from looters some time later, they found one of his last entries, written in Tobolsk: 'If we are going to be murdered, then let us not have to suffer long.'

The room was now awash with blood, and the electric light shone weakly through the smoky atmosphere. The whole execution, from start to finish, had taken no more than three minutes by Yurovsky's reckoning, but he still called it 'a long ordeal', perhaps because the bayoneting continued when one or another of the bodies showed signs of life. As Yurovsky was to recall in his later account of the night, 'It's not easy to kill people.'

For some of the spectators, the execution was not the exciting event they had anticipated. The guard Deriabin complained that it was just 'butchery'. The hardened Chekist Pavel Medvedev felt sick and had to go outside into the courtyard for a breath of air. He was relieved when Yurovsky ordered him to go and tell the guards not to be concerned if they had heard shots. Sure enough, Medvedev encountered Ivan Starkov and Konstantin Dobrynin running from the Popov House, bursting with questions.

There were already doubts about what had happened before the corpses were even cold. 'Did they shoot Nicholas II? Are you sure they didn't shoot somebody else in his place, because you'll have to answer for it!' Medvedev told them that there was no doubt. He had seen the dead bodies, covered with wounds. Blood was everywhere. In fact, his detail had to do something about the blood. He rousted other guards from the Popov House, including two men, Aleksandr Proskuriakov and Egor Stolov, who had been locked up in the bathhouse for coming in drunk for their shift.

Others viewed the murders with much more equilibrium. Alexei Kabanov calmly returned to his machine gun in the attic, while Yurovsky set about checking the bodies for pulses. Ermakov used sheets from the Romanovs' beds to fashion makeshift stretchers to transport the corpses to the truck. Twenty minutes after the firing had begun, the guards began to move the dead bodies to the truck that stood in the courtyard. All in all, it was a messy business. Blood dripped on the floors of the rooms through which the dead Romanovs were carried. At one point, Petr Ermakov used a cloth to wipe the gore from his hands and then tossed it into a corner, where investigators later discovered it.

Yurovsky appointed three reliable men to oversee the operation, during which the guards began to loot the personal effects of their victims. He announced that anyone caught with valuables would be summarily executed. After what had just transpired, this was a believable threat, and the guards grudgingly returned their booty, including gold watches and a diamond-encrusted cigar case.

The Urals Soviet had given Ermakov and his Red Guards the responsibility for disposing of the bodies. Yurovsky, however, had already noted that Ermakov was drunk and decided to accompany him to the Four Brothers disposal site. They threw a tarpaulin over the corpses, opened the gates and drove out into the street. It was three in the morning, but there were still people about, and a number of them later recalled seeing and hearing the truck. Further along the road a resident was feeling unwell after a night of drinking. At 1:30 he heard shots coming from the Ipatiev House. He met a neighbour who had been awakened by the noise. 'Did you hear it?' he asked. 'Heard it.' 'You know what it means?' 'I know . . .'

In 1825 the tsarist authorities executed five leaders of the Decembrist uprising, an effort by idealistic army officers to give Russia a constitutional regime. When the gallows trap was sprung, two of the hangman's ropes broke. The survivors, one with a broken leg, were hauled up to be hanged again. 'Poor Russia', lamented one of them, 'she can't even hang men properly.' After 100 years and a reversal of executioners' roles, Russian efficiency in state executions had still not improved. At least the tsars could still bury men properly. The Ekaterinburg Bolsheviks had yet to master this skill.

As Yurovsky and Ermakov drove away, the clean-up detail,

comprised of Latvians and some of the Russian guards, was set to work in the ground-floor of the Ipatiev House. Blood was lying in pools on the floor and splattered on the walls. There was so much of it that it began to seep through the floorboards. The cleaners tossed sand on the floor and then washed it with buckets of water. The work took several hours. When it was done, someone decided to write a epitaph to what they had seen. One of the German-speaking prisoners of war recalled a poem of Heinrich Heine, which he had memorized at school, and which seemed strikingly appropriate. It was based on the episode in the Book of Daniel, where the prophet foretells the death of the Babylonian king. He neatly wrote the slightly misquoted verses on one of the walls of the death chamber:

> Balsatzar ward in selbiger Nacht
> Von seinen Knachten umgebracht
>
> Balthazar was on the same night
> Murdered by his own slaves.

Not to be outdone, one of the Russians offered his own less poetical version of Nicholas's reign, with its bitter memories of Bloody Sunday: 'Nicholas said to the people, "F— you, here's your republic."'

Elsewhere in and around the Ipatiev House, people were busy with more serious work. Nikulin and some of the Latvians went through all the Romanov luggage to sort out the valuables. When Medvedev returned the next morning at around nine o'clock, he found a pile of gold and silver objects, many marked with the tsarist monogram, heaped up on a table in the commandant's office. While Nikulin was distracted by compiling an inventory of these priceless effects, Medvedev wandered around the upper rooms, where baggage was scattered about in complete chaos. He found three silver rings, engraved with some sort of prayer, and 60 roubles, which he discovered under a catechism that the Empress had been reading. He quietly slipped them into his own pockets.

Medvedev's caution was not really necessary, since a general distribution of Romanov loot was soon under way to the guards. When the Whites took Ekaterinburg a few days later, they found the attics of humble wooden houses crammed with unexpected items: fine porcelain and silver cutlery with the imperial crest, golden crosses, electric lamps, the latest Kodak camera, silk shirts and socks, military decorations studded with diamonds, the account book of the imperial court and even the personal diary of Tsarevich Alexei. The most exotic find of all, in the middle of provincial Russia, was a thoroughbred King Charles spaniel, which did not understand a word of command in Russian. It was Joy, the pet of Alexei. The guard Mikhail Letemin found it waiting patiently outside the royal rooms on the morning of 17 July. You'll be waiting a long time, he thought, before deciding to take the animal home.

As the truck carrying the dead Romanovs passed into the Koptiaki Woods, Yurovsky was pleased to see that the cordon of mounted troops was already on patrol, ready to keep away unwanted visitors from the burial site. Although he had scouted out the route on several occasions prior to this night, it was very dark, and he depended on Ermakov, the local man, to do the navigating. Ermakov, drunk and exhausted after his zealous efforts with revolver and bayonet earlier in the evening, was in no fit state to guide anyone. He failed to warn the driver Sergei Liukhanov of the marshy ground near the road, and just as it crossed a railway line by a signalman's box, the vehicle skidded and got stuck. When Liukhanov revved the motor, the engine overheated. He had to wake the signalman to provide water for the engine.

The marshy area was covered by planks and old railway ties that enabled the truck to move slowly on. Eventually they arrived at the encampment of Red Guards, mates of Ermakov from his factory, who had been recruited to help deal with the bodies. But Yurovsky was to receive an unpleasant surprise: apparently Ermakov had promised them more than just the chance to dispose of corpses. 'Why didn't you bring them to us alive?' they shouted.

With a bad spirit, the Red Guards began to shift the bodies to the light carts they had brought to transport them closer to the mine site. Suddenly their enthusiasm revived, as jewels began to drop out of the clothing. Yurovsky had at last discovered where the Romanovs had hidden the bulk of their jewels: they were sewn into the women's undergarments. Where

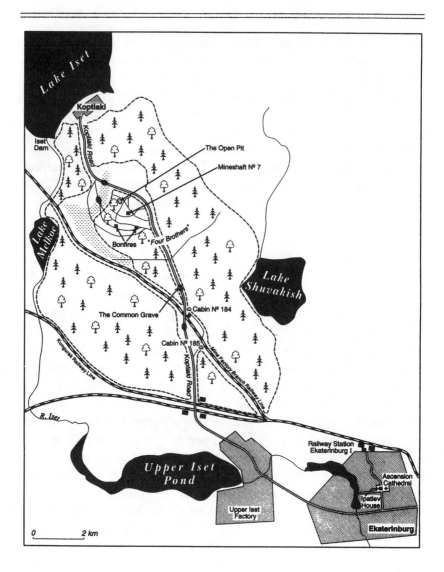

EKATERINBURG AND THE KOPTIAKA WOODS IN 1918

these garments had been torn by bullets, diamonds were visible. The Empress herself was wearing a sort of girdle, constructed of ropes of pearls looped together and sewn into a linen cover. The final count was more than 18 lb of gemstones. The difficulties attending the execution now became clear. Their bejewelled corsets afford the girls some partial protection from bullets and bayonet thrusts, ironically making their eventual deaths even more savage and brutal.

Dawn was breaking, but the guards were very slow to find the Four Brothers site. Yurovsky sent on his own scouts who returned to announce that nothing had been prepared. There were not even shovels with which to dig a grave. The disposal party set to work only after six in the morning – it had taken three hours to reach the Four Brothers from the centre of town. As there was no possibility of digging a grave, Yurovsky decided on the simplest expedient: the bodies would be stripped and searched, and disposed of down the mine shaft, and the bloodstained and bullet-torn clothing would be burned in a few makeshift bonfires.

Yurovsky immediately understood that he would not be able to prevent Ermakov's Red Guards from looting the Romanov treasure, and so he chose a few to work with him and his own men, and sent the rest away. As he had done earlier at the Ipatiev House, Yurovsky threatened summary execution for anyone who was caught looting. He realized at the same time that he would have to examine the corpses carefully before he disposed of them. Yurovsky's detail worked quickly, and precious gemstones and personal effects fell to the ground and were trampled into the mud. These included a military decoration and Dr Botkin's false teeth. In the haste, some jewels remained on the bodies, but one ring proved too tempting, and a finger was severed in order to retrieve it.

One group searched the bodies, while another started bonfires and burned the clothes. Finally, the corpses were dragged 50 metres to the mine shaft and tipped in over the edge. The water did not entirely cover the bodies, and some ash, dirt and tree branches were thrown in after them. As a macabre last offering the body of Anastasia's dog and the severed finger were tossed in as well. With the burial complete, Yurovsky and his men then tried to collapse the mine shaft with hand grenades. However, the shaft remained relentlessly intact. Yurovsky did no more than gather up the jewels and head back to Ekaterinburg.

Many members of the Urals Soviet had been present at the execution, but the leadership still had to be informed of the progress of the burial. Yurovsky reached the Soviet headquarters in Ekaterinburg after ten o'clock, finding Beloborodov, the chairman, and Safarov, his deputy, in attendance. The successful burial meant that Moscow could now be given formal notification of the execution, along with an appropriate cover story. The telegram reached Moscow sometime after midday:

> TO THE CHAIRMAN OF THE SOVIET OF PEOPLE'S COMMISSARS (SOVNARKOM) COMRADE LENIN. TO THE CHAIRMAN OF THE CENTRAL EXECUTIVE COMMITTEE (TsIK) COMRADE SVERDLOV.
>
> YOU ARE CONNECTED TO THE PRAESIDIUM OF THE REGIONAL SOVIET OF THE WORKERS' AND PEASANTS' GOVERNMENT. IN VIEW OF THE APPROACH OF THE FOE TO EKATERINBURG AND DUE TO THE DISCOVERY BY THE CHEKA OF A LARGE WHITE GUARD CONSPIRACY, WHICH HAD AS ITS OBJECTIVE THE SEIZURE OF THE FORMER TSAR AND HIS FAMILY (THE DOCUMENTS ARE IN OUR HANDS), BY DECISION OF THE PRAESIDIUM OF THE REGIONAL SOVIET, ON THE NIGHT OF 16 JULY NICHOLAS ROMANOV WAS SHOT. HIS FAMILY HAS BEEN EVACUATED TO A SAFE PLACE. ON THESE GROUNDS WE HAVE ISSUED THE FOLLOWING NOTICE:

> In view of the approach of counter-revolutionary bands to the Red capital of the Urals and the possibility that the crowned hangman might escape a people's tribunal (a White Guard plot aiming to free him has been discovered and com-promising documents found), the Praesidium of the Regional Soviet resolved to shoot the former Tsar N. Romanov, guilty before the people of innumerable acts of bloody violence. On the night of 16 July, the sentence was executed. The Romanov family, under guard along with him, has, in the interests of civil security, been evacuated from the city of Ekaterinburg. The Praesidium of the Regional Soviet.

THE DOCUMENTS CONCERNING THE CONSPIRACY ARE BEING
SENT WITHOUT DELAY BY SPECIAL COURIER TO THE
SOVNARKOM AND THE TsIK. WE URGENTLY ASK FOR A REPLY.
WE ARE WAITING AT THE TELEGRAPH APPARATUS.

A response came quickly from Sverdlov in Moscow. 'Today I
will report about your decision to the Praesidium of the VTsIK.
There is no doubt that it will be approved. Notice about the
execution must follow from the central authorities, refrain from
publication until its receipt.' Sverdlov was as good as his word. On
18 July a meeting of the government, the Council of People's
Commissars, was read the first Ekaterinburg telegram as a 'point
of information'. They unanimously approved it. Before moving on
to other business they ordered the telegram to be publicized in a
press release. This was to become the official version of events,
when it was published by the central government on 19 July, word
for word as received from Ekaterinburg. The Regional Soviet text
was also printed on posters and distributed about Ekaterinburg.

The disinformation programme that would surround the
execution of the Imperial Family was already in full swing, for
Moscow had been told of the true fate not only of Nicholas but
also of the rest of the family. Some time after nine in the evening
of 17 July, the Urals Soviet sent another telegram to Moscow in
code. It read simply: 'Moscow. To Secretary of the Sovnarkom
Gorbunov. Tell Sverdlov that all the family suffered the same fate
as the head, officially the family perished during evacuation.'

This should have tied up matters nicely, since it referred back
to the official version that an evacuation had taken place. The
slaughter of women and children, as well as innocent servants, was
attributed to the accidents of war. Their deaths could actually be
blamed on enemy action, not on the Ekaterinburg Bolsheviks. For
some reason the centre never utilized this cover story, leaving the
fate of the Imperial Family open-ended and unresolved.

By the time Yurovsky had completed his report to the Urals
Soviet, informers arrived with unsettling news. The central market
in Ekaterinburg was buzzing with stories of the execution of the
Tsar. There was nothing surprising in this, for almost all the
guards, onlookers and executioners themselves felt compelled to
share their secret with the world. The Soviet would later put up

posters to confirm the execution, as soon as approval was received from Moscow. What was more important was that people were also talking with complete accuracy about the location of the Romanov burial at the Four Brothers.

Ermakov's Red Guards were now having their revenge. They had been denied the satisfaction of murdering the Romanovs, or even of disposing of their jewel-laden corpses. But nothing could prevent them from telling what they had seen. They had ridden straight from the Koptiaki Woods to report what was going on. It was clear that Yurovsky's duties were not finished: he would have to plan a more secure burial. One of the members of the Soviet, S. Chutskaev, advised Yurovsky that the Koptiaki Woods also contained some very deep mines, which would be eminently suitable for hiding the bodies.

The early afternoon of 17 July found Yurovsky again in the woods, and once more in trouble. The car he had brought got stuck in the mud, and he was forced to search for the mines on foot. He eventually found three pits that appeared to be perfect, for they were extremely deep and filled with water. Yurovsky worked out a plan: he would again seal off the woods with guards and bring a carload of Chekists to patrol the forest paths and scare off any travellers. The bodies would be moved from the Four Brothers site, weighed down with stones and dumped into the deepest pit. In the midst of these ruminations, Yurovsky encountered a mounted traveller on the road and requisitioned his two horses. He returned to the mine for another look, but the horse stumbled, and Yurovsky was badly shaken up. He began to realize that moving the bodies might not be so simple a task and devised alternatives. Perhaps the corpses could be disposed of at the Four Brothers mine after all, but partially destroyed and disfigured to prevent positive identification.

Returning to Ekaterinburg, Yurovsky explained to his colleagues in the Urals Soviet that he would require additional supplies. He dispatched the Commissar for Supplies, Petr Voikov, to the local chemical depository to order a large quantity of sulphuric acid. The highly corrosive fluid was widely used for mining and for making jewellery: the intense heat it generates was commonly employed by goldsmiths to work platinum. When Robert Wilton, the London *Times*'s Russian correspondent, found himself in Ekaterinburg a year later, assisting the Sokolov investigation, he tried to order a platinum ring, a regional speciality. No platinum jewellery was available, however, because the stores of sulphuric acid had still not been replenished.

A large number of jerry cans containing petrol were secured by Voikov, and vehicles ordered from the central Soviet motor pool. Having made these arrangements, Yurovsky returned to the mine to keep watch and to arrange for the quarantine of the area. He had little time to rest or eat due to these constant comings and goings. Part of his nourishment consisted of the boiled eggs that he had ordered on 15 July for Tsarevich Alexei's last meal.

The day of 18 July dawned at 5:09 am and found Yurovsky and his assistants already at work. They aimed to dig shallow graves and bury the remains after disfiguring and burning them, though Yurovsky was already aware of a cardinal rule of forensic science: it is not easy to destroy a human corpse without leaving any trace. Before long, this plan too was abandoned, when it became obvious that the nature of the terrain made it almost impossible to disguise newly dug pits, and Yurovsky still hoped to prevent the discovery of any remains. He decided to reactivate his earlier plan of disposing of the corpses in the deep pits. This required transport, and he sent a request to the Cheka headquarters at the American Hotel for a fleet of cars and trucks to ferry the bodies, the petrol and the acid.

It was nine o'clock in the evening before the vehicles arrived. In the growing darkness a volunteer was lowered into the burial pit, where he stood in icy water sending up the naked bodies by ropes, one by one. One of the participants was later asked if the Grand Duchesses were pretty. 'Death is never pretty,' he replied. Although the cool conditions of the mine had preserved the corpses somewhat, they were mangled by the hand grenades and were beginning to decompose. As the bodies were naked and had open wounds, as well as the rents and tears caused by the grenade explosions, they were already crawling with maggots. It is easy to understand how the burial detachment might misidentify the corpses of the women, and especially the Grand Duchesses, who were relatively close in age.

A night operation had the advantage of shrouding Yurovsky's activities in darkness, but it also meant another elaborate negotiation of the treacherous roads in the Koptiaki Woods. Predictably, the truck carrying the bodies got stuck once again around 4:30 in the morning. The burial crew followed what was by now a familiar operation. They went to the signalbox located by a nearby railway crossing and found a pile of rotten ties, which they used to create a small bridge for the vehicle through the low-lying mire. While this was going on, Yurovsky had yet another change of plan. Why bother to go further, when they would only get stuck or break down again? Why not dispose of the bodies right here, on the roadway?

Many commentators have said of Yurovsky that he was a man of strong nerves, and he surely proved that now. He attempted first to burn the corpses. A pyre was built and doused with petrol and set alight. The logical thing was to ignite the smallest body first, and so the remains of Alexei were hauled over to the blaze. Yurovsky decided to set fire to what he thought was the corpse of Alexandra next, but the bodies were in such a state that it was hard to identify it. Later, Yurovsky decided they had burned the body of the maid Anna Demidova, while another participant argued that it had been the Grand Duchess Anastasia.

It became clear that cremation would not remove all traces of the bodies – bits of bone and teeth from Alexei lay near the pyre – so Yurovsky decided on his final change of plan. He ordered the squad to dig a shallow pit in the middle of the road. The grave was less than four feet deep, and about seven feet in diameter. Before dumping in the remaining bodies, the guards stove in their faces with rifle butts and poured acid over the corpses. This had the double effect of rendering them unrecognizable and preventing the decomposing flesh from making too much of a stench. The ceramic jars, which had held the acid, were thrown down into the pit, and it was then filled in. The ties that had been used to make a small bridge through the mire were replaced in the roadway, and the truck, by now hauled out of the mud, was driven back and forth across the burial site.

Yurovsky's task was finished at last. Nothing remained of the fires or of the corpses. It was just another spot in a muddy path. By eight o'clock Yurovsky could leave the Koptiaki Woods, where he had already spent three sleepless nights, for good. The truck, covered with mud and splattered with blood, was returned to the central garage. His helpers, including Ermakov, hastened to the bar of the workers' club to drink and celebrate their service to the revolution. Commissar Voikov, who had signed the order for the sulphuric acid was especially pleased with himself. 'The world will never know what we did with them!' he boasted.

CHAPTER FOUR

'Lies of the Capitalist Press'

THE KREMLIN TELEGRAPH line to Ekaterinburg was busy on 16 July. At 1:27 pm Lenin's office received a request from the editor of the Danish national newspaper *National Tidende*: 'There are rumours that the former Tsar has been killed. Please report the facts.' At 4 pm Lenin's office replied: 'The rumours are not true, the former Tsar is still alive. All the rumours are only the lies of the capitalist press. Lenin.' The telegram failed to reach Copenhagen only because the Moscow–Denmark line was down. By the time the wires were again open, the Kremlin could no longer pretend that any part of its reply was true, and the message was never sent. It does, however, illustrate that hours before bullets and bayonets cut down the Imperial Family, a massive campaign of disinformation was conducted by the Communist authorities. Lies and half-truths complicated and confused every subsequent investigation.

The cordon around the Ipatiev House was withdrawn on 20 July, and formal control of the premises returned to engineer Ipatiev on 22 July as the Soviet forces evacuated the city. The property was the worse for wear, with rooms defaced by graffiti and pornographic drawings, clutter in every room, half-burned objects spilling out of the stoves and, of course, bullet holes in the walls of one of the basement rooms. Ipatiev himself had left

Ekaterinburg, and the house stood empty until the evening of 25 July, when White military forces occupied the city. The house immediately became a magnet for curious citizens. They roamed the halls, explored every room, and took away 'souvenirs'. Everything conspired to obscure the scene of the crime.

Lines of authority in Ekaterinburg were no clearer. A moderately democratic administration, the Urals Regional Government, was formed under the leadership of P. V. Ivanov, the former chairman of the Ekaterinburg stock exchange. The Czechs formed a Czechoslovak National Committee, which worked closely with members of the right wing of the Social Revolutionary Party, including some who had been members of the Russian Constituent Assembly dissolved by the Bolsheviks. There was also a military authority, headed by the commander of the town garrison, which paid little attention to the civilian administration. In the fluid political and military situation, the fate of the Tsar, whose execution had by now been formally announced by the Moscow government, was of minor importance. There was no authority that might automatically conduct an investigation, nor any indication of where to begin. Moreover, any investigation would by its very nature carry political implications.

It was the military, where some faint loyalty to the Imperial Family still lingered, that was the first to act. On 27 July, one of the regional commanders of Ekaterinburg, Captain V. A. Girsh, received a visit from Lieutenant Aleksandr Sheremetevsky who had been hiding in disguise behind enemy lines. He had heard from local peasants of strange activities conducted by Red forces in the region of the Four Brothers. Military patrols had denied them access to the forest, the road from the village of Koptiaki to Ekaterinburg had been blocked, and explosions could be heard in the woods. The official explanation was that Red army units were conducting a military exercise. This did not explain, however, the curt warning that anyone entering the area would be shot. When the cordon was lifted, local peasants rushed to the spot to investigate, accompanied by Sheremetevsky. They found the remains of several bonfires near an open-pit mine. In the ashes were uniform buttons, corset stays, fragments of jewellery and a military decoration. One peasant was lowered into the mine shaft, but a cursory search revealed nothing.

On the basis of these ominous findings, Girsh appointed a team of military investigators. Wishing to maintain an air of legality, he sought to appoint a civilian court investigator. The logical candidate, Deputy Prosecutor of the District Court, A. T. Kutuzov, was nowhere to be found, and Girsh's choice fell on one A. Nametkin, the District Court Investigator for Very Important Cases. Nametkin tried to refuse the appointment, but early on the morning of 30 July a group of young army officers rousted him out of bed and demanded that he go with them to the Four Brothers site. When he continued to object, one of the garrison staff officers, Dmitry Malinovsky, told him bluntly that there were 12 armed soldiers who demanded his presence: 'He understood my hint, got ready and came.'

Accompanying the officers and Nametkin were two of the Tsar's former entourage. Dr Vladimir Derevenko, the family surgeon, had been living freely in the city and making daily visits to examine the Tsarevich, and Terenty Chemodurov, the royal valet who had been taken from the Ipatiev House on 24 May and dispatched to the local prison. Too insignificant to be shot, Chemodurov was still languishing there, forgotten, when the Whites took the town. No one was more knowledgeable than Terenty Chemodurov: he had helped to dress the Tsar for ten years and had personally packed the clothes that Nicholas had brought from Tobolsk. The 69-year-old servant recited the litany of the Tsar's wardrobe throughout the visit to the Four Brothers: 'one dozen nightshirts, one dozen day shirts, one dozen flesh-coloured silk shirts, 200 handkerchiefs.' With growing alarm he identified a number of Nicholas's personal effects at the mine and later at the Ipatiev House.

Having confirmed that tsarist artefacts were present at the Four Brothers, the Officers' Commission made a concerted effort to complete its investigation by finding the royal corpses, although General Mikhail Diterikhs, who later took over the inquiry, rightly complained that they worked like dilettantes, without a system or plan. Their obvious starting-place was the shaft of the open mine, around which lay the remains of bonfires. Initial attempts to pump the chest-high water from the mine were unsuccessful. While they awaited a better pump, they chased after every lead and rumour. Employing the labour of Austrian prisoners of war, they drained the municipal pond, dug up graves in the town cemetery and excavated the entire garden of the Ipatiev House, all the while dogged by abysmal weather.

On 15 August the water was finally cleared from the open pit. A few objects were found, but no trace of any bodies. There were over 60 abandoned pits in the Koptiaki Woods, and an effort was made to search them all, with the help of 50 boy scouts assigned to the task. For one exciting moment they thought they had succeeded, when five bodies were found in one mine, but they proved to be those of Austrian POWs. Nonetheless, this appeared to confirm that the Bolsheviks were in the habit of disposing of their victims in this way. No further finds were made, however, and the searches petered out.

In the meantime Deputy Prosecutor Kutuzov returned to the city. He made a cursory inspection of the Ipatiev House, but it was enough to convince him that there were grounds for conducting a criminal investigation. He formally appointed Nametkin as chief investigating officer. Nametkin was never happy with this appointment and conducted his inquiry in a desultory manner. He refused to go again to the Four Brothers site and worked his way extremely slowly through the rooms of the Ipatiev House. Kutuzov recognized the unsuitability of Nametkin for this work and on 7 August replaced him with a judge, Ivan Sergeev.

Sergeev's investigation has always been dogged by a bad reputation. He has been charged with inaction and complete incompetence. His chief critic, General Mikhail Diterikhs, claimed that he lacked any professional competence, was in any case opposed to the inquiry and carried out his duties without any commitment. Noting that Sergeev was executed by the Bolsheviks when they retook Ekaterinburg late in 1918, Diterikhs drily noted that 'if it is true, then he cannot have been shot for anything having to do with his participation in the investigation of the case of the Tsar.'

Diterikhs was hardly a neutral observer. He was an ardent monarchist and a political reactionary who saw all of Russia's sorrows flowing from a Jewish–Masonic conspiracy. He was a typical servitor of the reactionary government that was created when Admiral Aleksandr Kolchak seized political power in Siberia through a military coup on 18 November 1918. As Kolchak's government grew ever more reactionary, individuals with vague leftish sympathies like Sergeev fell completely out of favour.

Kolchak placed the overall direction of the investigation in the hands of Diterikhs, and the latter succeeded in replacing Sergeev with the more conservative Nikolai Sokolov, an investigator for the Omsk regional court, in February 1918. In the final analysis Sergeev's greatest sin was the failure of his investigation to confirm Diterikhs' heart-felt belief that the murder was a vast conspiracy of 'non-Russians' (i.e. Jews). Not surprisingly Diterikhs made a 'discovery' that explained the cover-up: Sergeev, he claimed, was the son of a converted Jew and consequently had no loyalty or sense of duty to Russia.

In fact Sergeev was an active inquisitor and compiled much of the evidence upon which later investigators like Sokolov based their findings. He did pay careful attention to the Four Brothers site, even if he was guilty, as Sokolov later claimed, of a fundamental research error: instead of walking to the site, he took the train from Ekaterinburg to the nearest station and then travelled by carriage. He extracted from the Impatiev House portions of the walls with bullets embedded in them and removed the most important graffiti on the wallpaper of several rooms.

Sergeev made the discovery that, more than any other, advanced the investigation. In the stove of one of the ground-floor rooms, he found masses of ash left from the destruction of documents relating to the administration of the House of Special Purpose. Two sheets of paper had been caught by the updraft of the fire and lodged in the chimney. Sergeev recovered them both. The first was a receipt, dated 20 July 1918, for money that Yurovsky had given to Pavel Medvedev, severance pay for the last guards. The second paper was an investigator's dream: a neatly typed list of all the men who had been recruited to guard the Ipatiev House.

This list precipitated a manhunt for the 'regicides'. Those who had been too incautious to flee were apprehended and interrogated. Medvedev's wife was located and provided testimony, which constituted a virtual death sentence for her husband: his description to her of his role in the murder of the Imperial Family. The changing fortunes of the civil war, which had been raging from May 1918, led to the apprehension of several of the Tsar's guards, including Pavel Medvedev. Any prisoner of war with an Ekaterinburg connection was liable to have his name checked against the fatal record, and those whose names appeared paid with their lives. Anyone connected with the Ipatiev Guard would have been seen as having Bolshevik sympathies at the least and to have been broadly implicated in the Tsar's death. Moscow may have approved, but local officials carried it out.

If Sergeev was not as poor an investigator as he had been depicted, Sokolov was nonetheless an inspired choice as his successor. He combined real investigative talent, professionalism and an obsessive commitment to the case. Chased out of Russia in 1920, he spent five years of exile in western Europe still pursuing leads and interviewing participants. The security agents of the Soviet state paid him the ultimate compliment of burgling his apartment in France, in order to get a look at his famous dossier. When he died of heart failure in France in 1924, his colleagues and associates, with Diterikhs at their head, honestly believed that he had sacrificed his life to the hunt for the truth. Sokolov was doubly valued by Diterikhs for his shared hatred of the Bolsheviks and penchant for conspiracy theories. Trapped at the outbreak of the civil war behind Bolshevik lines in Penza in central Russia, Sokolov disguised himself as a vagrant peasant and made his way on foot across hundreds of miles to safety in Siberia. He displayed the same dogged persistence in his inquiry into the fate of the Romanovs.

Besides the investigation of the Officers' Commission, the commander of the Ekaterinburg garrison, Major-General Vladimir Golitsyn, assigned investigative responsibilities to the army's counter-intelligence unit. Another military-intelligence operation was launched the following year in Perm. Typically, the two inquiries did not cooperate.

The recruitment of 'Spooks' to the task had its positive and negative consequences. They proved quite capable of ferreting out suspects who had gone to ground, especially when armed with Sergeev's list. Their greatest coup was the identification and arrest in Perm of Pavel Medvedev, the leader of the guards at the Ipatiev House and one of the participants in the execution of the family. On the other hand, they were quick to enter that 'wilderness of mirrors' that so often seduces spies and counter-spies.

The investigation by the Kontragenstvo or military security proved particularly susceptible to false leads and to conspiracy theories, which took aback even the near paranoid Diterikhs. He complained of how they were completely seduced by Soviet misinformation that suggested that Nicholas's family had been 'sent to a safe place'. They enthusiastically pursued rumours that Alexandra and the children had been dispatched to Perm as part of a German plot to smuggle the family to Germany. They credulously accepted the story that the Grand Duchess Anastasia (and in another version Tatiana) escaped while in Perm, only to be recaptured by the Cheka and savagely beaten. How could this Anastasia story possibly be true, Diterikhs inveighed, when the chief witness, Dr Pavel Utkin, was a Jew?

Diterikhs's obsession with a 'Judeo-Masonic conspiracy' led some investigators to devalue all of his conclusions. Thus, Anthony Summers and Tom Mangold cited Diterikhs's anti-Semitism in order to discredit his rejection of the Perm escape thesis, upon which they built their own best-seller, *The File on the Tsar*. They also accused Sokolov of a cover-up, since he rejected testimony that he had collected about the Perm thesis and did not include it in his published works. In fact, a reading of the evidence in question suggests that Sokolov ignored it because it was not particularly convincing. The Perm thesis lacked the substantiation by physical evidence and corroboration by other witnesses that was the hallmark of Sokolov's own approach.

Summers and Mangold have their own deficiencies as investigators, particularly their propensity to give equal weight to every piece of evidence, no matter how implausible. They also favour a particular form of argument characterized by the assumption 'if . . . then', whereby they make a generalization and then drive it to an exotic conclusion. Thus: 'If the family were guarded only by senior Bolshevik officials, this must have made the task of procuring first-hand evidence of their presence in Perm all the more difficult for the CID [military intelligence]', or 'If Moscow needed a reliable person to supervise or keep a watching brief on the arrangements for the surviving Romanovs, then Zinoviev's secretary made an eminently sensible choice.'

Summers and Mangold assume that if a statement is 'sworn testimony' it must be given special weight – as though no malefactor ever lied under oath to save his own skin! While they are able to cite numerous persons who claimed to have heard that the Romanov women were secreted in Perm, they have only one eye-witness, Natalia Mutnykh. They proceed to give two different versions of her testimony. Whatever their other faults, Diterikhs and Sokolov at least sought to differentiate between differing versions of the same story, recognizing that they could not be all equally valid.

Most of all, they recognized that revolutionary Russia was a rumour mill of almost unimaginable dimensions. Even Summers and Mangold's star witness, Natalia Mutnykh, admitted that 'there was every possible kind of rumour about their presence, and nobody knew what to believe.' Nonetheless, her description of a two-minute visit, without any conversation, with four women confined to a dark basement 'by the weak light of a tallow candle' serves as the cornerstone for their whole imaginative edifice.

While one can question the investigative techniques of Summers and Mangold, they did identify some critical short-comings in Sokolov's investigation, most particularly the absence of human remains. Moreover, their book, smuggled into the Soviet Union, helped to inspire other amateur sleuths like themselves, whose searches did finally close 'the file on the Tsar'.

When Diterikhs first met investigator Nikolai Sokolov he was unimpressed: 'Medium height, lean, even emaciated, round-shoul-dered, with nervously twitching fingers and a nervous habit of constantly chewing his moustache . . . he had a glass eye which gave the impression that he was always looking off to the side.' But Diterikhs was seeking someone who understood that 'the whole rest of his life would be dedicated exclusively to uncovering this nightmarish crime,' and Sokolov was that man. The general and the investigator quickly established a close working relationship. Even while their side was losing the civil war that swirled around them, Diterikhs was able to provide Sokolov with men, including 1000 soldiers, and resources such as no other investigator could approach. He was given a special railway carriage, in which to live and work in Ekaterinburg, and an armed guard. The general's influence also enabled him to overcome the tacit opposition of a number of people in the Omsk government: those on the political right who wished to believe that the Imperial Family had somehow escaped execution, and, before they were purged from Kolchak's government, those on the left who saw no reason to waste time with 'this tsarist business'.

Sergeev had already collected most of the physical evidence and interviewed the most important witnesses. Sokolov went over all the documentary material again. His greatest accomplishment here was his persistent investigation of texts that the retreating Bolsheviks had left behind in the central telegraph agency in Ekaterinburg. One of the telegrams was in an apparently unbreakable code. Sokolov took it with him when he left Russia and did not succeed in having it deciphered until 1920. It turned out to be the telegram from Beloborodov informing the Moscow government that, in fact, all the members of the Imperial Family had been killed.

Sokolov arrived in Ekaterinburg in mid-March of 1919 to begin the examination of witnesses and materials there. He searched the Ipatiev House again and located a few bullets in the walls that Sergeev's team had missed. He also discovered more graffiti on the plaster walls of the death chamber, including the 'runes' – allegedly a set of cabalistic letters – that were the basis for later claims that the execution had actually been a ritual murder by Jews. That Sergeev had overlooked this vital piece of information has been taken as yet another example of his incompetence. However, it seems not to have occurred to his critics that he did not describe the death-chamber graffiti in August 1918, because it was not yet there. From the time of the Bolshevik surrender of the house to the start of Sokolov's investigation, the property had not been secure, and it is impossible to state with precision when these marks might have been added to the wall. By linking the 'letters' to the night of the murders, anti-Semites attempted to find some exotic meaning in what were, it now seems quite apparent, insignificant scrawls.

We have seen how difficult it was for Yurovsky and his men to move in the Koptiaki Woods even in the 'drier' (since it did rain almost every day) conditions of a Siberian summer. There was no possibility of accomplishing anything in the snow, dirt and mud of the late winter and early spring, so it was not until May 1919 that

Sokolov began a serious exploration of the Four Brothers site. From youth Sokolov had been a keen hunter and outdoorsman, and he literally approached the woods in a different way from Sergeev, who had ridden there by train. Sokolov walked the entire route, seeing the path in much the same way as had Yurovsky and Ermakov. In fact, as he trudged along, Sokolov found that he could easily retrace their journey: here the truck broke down; there it was hauled out of the mud and here railway sleepers were laid over the marsh to facilitate the passage. Sokolov described the route in meticulous detail and also made a photographic record of every step of the murderers' progress, such as the tiny bridge they had made of sleepers on one of the forest paths.

There was no doubting the significance of the open mine and the grassy clearing near it. Even a superficial examination revealed more objects – broken jewels, corset stays – and Sokolov resolved to concentrate his efforts at the Four Brothers. His later discoveries were equally impressive as the work expanded, which involved the total excavation of the site. The most important and poignant new find, made on 25 July 1919, at the bottom of the open mine, was the body of a small dog, which witnesses identified as that of Jemmy, Anastasia's lapdog.

Taken all together, the circumstantial evidence of the Four Brothers' site was very nearly conclusive, especially when linked to forensic evidence and personal testimony that claimed the family had been shot in the Ipatiev House. Eyewitnesses established the presence of the chief executioner, Yurovsky, at the site before, during and after the night and morning of 16–17 July. Trucks had brought petrol and sulphuric acid into the woods. The remains of clothes, including buttons from uniforms, jewels known to belong to members of the Imperial Family, corset stays and the dentures and spectacles of Dr Botkin had all been found at the site. There was even the ghoulish evidence of a severed finger and patches of skin. Several witnesses had seen Anastasia walking down the stairs on the night of the murders with Jemmy in her arms.

There was just one persistent problem: it is very difficult to destroy completely just one human corpse, to say nothing of eleven. Robert Wilton, the London *Times*'s Russian correspondent who assisted Sokolov with his investigation, reported that every day one man came to the site of the excavations and sat morbidly looking on. This was Ivan Fesenko, the mining engineer who had guided Yurovsky to the Four Brothers site, and who had absent-mindedly carved his name and the date on to a nearby tree while Yurovsky examined the mine. As soon as the Whites occupied Ekaterinburg, Fesenko had discovered it was not a good idea to leave one's name and the date at the site of a capital crime. He was arrested and closely examined, and released only because the authorities thought that he might lead them to bigger game.

Instead he began his vigil at the main site of the investigation. Every day he muttered the vexatious question, 'Where are the cinders? Where are the cinders?' If, as Sokolov asserted in his report, the bodies had been stripped, dismembered and burned with the help of petrol and sulphuric acid, where were the ashes and charred bones? Diamonds, discoloured by heat, had been recovered. Where were eleven sets of human teeth, which are also especially resistant to fire?

Wilton gave the obvious answer that 'they must be hidden somewhere.' But he also rejected an important lead, dismissing as Bolshevik propaganda the persistent rumours that the bodies were buried in one place, then reburied in another. Despite his tremendous exertions, Sokolov was never able to find the ashes, which would have provided the decisive proof that he needed.

Historians jokingly reduce philosophies of history to two: the cock-up theory, which attributes all historical events to accidents and random acts; and the conspiracy theory, which explains all phenomena through the working of a mysterious, hidden hand. The irony of the Sokolov investigation is that it was a quintes-sential example of the cock-up theory in action, which caused it to give rise to innumerable conspiracy theories. If Yurovsky and Ermakov's burial detail had left the bodies in the open pit, they would have been found immediately. Had they burned the corpses and scattered the remains, or buried them in the clay pits at the Four Brothers site, Sokolov's investigation and excavations would certainly have located them. Had Yurovsky's truck not become stuck in the mud, and had he disposed of the bodies in the deep mines, they would have been discovered either by Sergeev's boy scouts or by the hundreds of soldiers that Sokolov had scouring the woods. Between them these two groups examined all 60 mines in the vicinity, some of them twice over. Every logical step that

Yurovsky took to hide the bodies was deciphered and pursued by Sokolov. Sokolov planned for everything except a random act – Yurovsky's despairing decision to 'bury them right here, in the road'.

Aleksandr Nikolaevich Avdonin, the man who discovered the grave in 1979, calls this burial 'a cynical deed'. Rather, it was an act of genius. Sokolov was looking in pits and ponds, while Yurovsky had left the quarry literally under his feet. The White investigator walked over the site numerous times, took photographs of it and described it in his reports and books. The one thing he did not do was to examine it closely. Once again in the historical annals chance triumphs over rational planning. Unable to find the corpses where all evidence suggested they should be, the investigators were thrown back on plots and conspiracies, the tendrils of which stretched far away to Berlin and Balmoral.

Sokolov tried to keep his investigation going as the White cause crumbled around him. Almost a year to the day after the murders, however, he was forced to evacuate Ekaterinburg, as the Red Army took it back for good. His subsequent ports of call are a litany of the failure of the anti-Bolshevik cause: Tiumen, Ishim, Omsk, Chita, Verkhine-Udinsk – towns that grew smaller and smaller in size, and further and further to the east. Sokolov continued to interrogate witnesses whom he encountered along the way, but in December 1919 General Diterikhs took control of the materials, as part of a plan to send all the remaining Romanov possessions to the Imperial Family abroad, in the person of the Tsar's sister in London, Grand Duchess Xenia Aleksandrovna. Diterikhs dispatched 50 cartons of personal effects, clothes, household objects and even parts of the wall that Sergeev had removed from the Ipatiev House. By the time they arrived at Vladivostok and were loaded on the cruiser HMS *Kent*, their number had been reduced to 29. When they were opened in England, most were found to contain rubbish. A few of Alexandra's jewels did arrive, because a sensible servant had hidden them in a pile of old clothes.

Britain had rejected the Romanov cause yet again when the British consul refused to transport boxes containing the scraps from the Imperial Family found at the Four Brothers. Instead, after the intervention of the tutor Pierre Gilliard, the French military attaché, General Janin, agree to dispatch the boxes to France. The box containing the relics has disappeared, which is unfortunate since they would have proved useful as sources of DNA for testing.

By March 1920 the remnants of the White cause were washed up in the Russian colonial outpost of Harbin in China. There Diterikhs stayed on, dying in China in 1937. Sokolov determined to take his investigation, and his documentation, to western Europe, where he died in 1924, still fighting for a resolution to his inquiries. Copies of Sokolov's original report circulated in Europe, and two were acquired by American libraries. As late as 1990 Sotheby's auction house offered some of Sokolov's documentation for sale, but they failed to reach the reserved price. Later, parts of the file, including Beloborodov's coded telegram, were sold privately to a collector.

The four men who played the greatest role in investigating the fate of the Imperial Family – Gilliard, Wilton, Sokolov and Diterikhs – all published books on the subject in the early 1920s. In a sense each man used his writings to exorcise his own personal demon, which had arisen in the course of the investigations and out of the events surrounding them.

Pierre Gilliard, who returned to his native Switzerland from the Russian Far East in 1920, wrote several books on his life at court in Russia, but the volume he published in Paris in 1921, *Le Tragique Destin de Nicholas II et de sa famille*, dealt specifically with the Romanov family's last months and the investigation of their murder, based on the Sokolov files. His book is an affectionate portrait of his young charges and a balanced depiction of their parents. It is his valedictory to a vanished world. Gilliard was not admitted to the Ipatiev House, so the bulk of his book deals with the confinement of the Romanovs in Tobolsk, where he lived alongside them in Freedom House. He was especially critical of the absence of any serious attempt to rescue the family, which could easily have been expedited with the cooperation of Colonel Kobylinsky. Gilliard was well placed to testify to the possibility of help from Kobylinsky, since the Colonel was a conduit for the well-organized smuggling of jewels out of the house. He must have worked with Gilliard in this regard, since the latter kept a list of all the items that were secretly syphoned off at that time in an attempt to safeguard the Romanov inheritance.

Even as Gilliard lamented the absence of 'a few energetic men, ready to act with method and resolution', he also recognized the obstacles that Nicholas himself placed in the way of rescue. When the topic was broached, the Tsar set two conditions: family members must not be separated from one another, and they must not be transported outside of Russia. This, of course, was the same intransigence the Tsar demonstrated when confronted with rescue offers from the fraudulent 'officer' in Ekaterinburg. The arrival of the Omsk Red Guards a few days later, as Gilliard immediately recognized, put paid to any chance of rescue.

While Gilliard conveyed the sense of shock and horror he felt when he was told that even the children had been shot, he was content to condemn the murderers as criminals, without the accompanying character assassination that accompanied some other accounts. He noted only that the assassins were 'a Jew, Russian convicts and Austro-Hungarians'. Their determination to hide their murderous deeds was easily explained: 'Yes, it is from the Russian people that they are hiding, these men who pretend to be their representatives. They are the ones who are afraid, who fear their vengeance.'

Gilliard's book recalled another incident that foreshadowed his future activities. While he was still in Siberia, Admiral Kolchak asked him to interview the first in a long line of pretenders, a young lad claiming to be the Tsarevich Alexei. There was a certain superficial resemblance, but when Gilliard began to question him in French, the boy stood mute. When Gilliard switched to Russian the youth explained that he had understood all of Gilliard's French conversation but, for reasons that he could not reveal, he was pledged only to speak Russian. Gilliard disgustedly rejected the boy's claim, just as he would do later when confronted with another pretender in the West, Anna Anderson.

Given the intense interest manifested by the London *Times*, their Russian correspondent Robert Wilton was sitting on a scoop of significant proportions with his own copy of the Sokolov report, which he had obtained from Diterikhs. He delayed publishing it, however, and was beaten at his own game by Kolchak's former justice minister, George Tellberg, who published the interrogations of several of the alleged assassins reproduced from its text. This omission eventually cost Wilton his job, 'flung out on the streets virtually penniless'. Before his departure, he published in 1920, with *The Times*'s enthusiastic approbation, a lengthy series on the murders, which was republished in book form that same year as *The Last Days of the Romanovs, from 15 March 1917*.

It is difficult to judge whom Wilton detested more, Jews or Germans. Probably the cream of his hate should go to the Germans, for the Jews were merely their servants: 'In 1917, the Germans had sent Lenin with a horde of Jewish revolutionaries to take possession of Russia. A Red government, composed of persons selected in Berlin, was now in power, but they were vassals.' The Germans and their agents were literally everywhere. Rasputin was their man, and 'the Germans had almost as much to do with the Rasputin scandal as they had to do with Lenin and the exploits of his hundred Jews. The Czech Legion, it transpired, were the soldiers of Wilhelm and his Austrian henchmen, who acted under the orders of the two Kaisers.' The fate of the Romanovs was under the total control of the Germans. They hoped to force Nicholas to ratify the Treaty of Brest-Litovsk and then 'seize the reins of power with the help of German bayonets, and to give his only son to be a lawful Tsar under German tutelage. This meant the intervention of Russia in the war again, but on the German side.' When Nicholas refused to cooperate, he was eliminated. Indeed, 'all the Romanovs who died violent deaths were, like the Tsar, inconvenient to German as well as to internationalist plans.'

Their subordinate status did not save the Jews from a full helping of Wilton's bile.

The Germans knew what they were doing when they sent Lenin's pack of Jews into Russia. They chose them as agents of destruction. Why? Because the Jews were not Russians and to them the destruction of Russia was all in the way of business, revolutionary or financial. The whole record of Bolshevism in Russia is indelibly impressed with the stamp of alien invasion. The murder of the Tsar, deliberately planned by the Jew Sverdlov (who came to Russia as a paid agent of Germany) and carried out by the Jews Goloshchekin, Syromolotov, Safarov, Voikov and Yurovsky, is the act not of the Russian people, but of this hostile invader. . . . Sovietdom has consecrated three heroes to whom monuments have been erected: to Karl Marx, to Judas Iscariot and to Leo Tolstoi, the three names that are associated with Revolution, Apostasy and Anarchism; two of them Jews.

It was Wilton who helped to spread the legend that the graffiti in the Ipatiev murder room directly linked the slaying to the Jews in some ritualistic way. 'The writer was quoting a Jew whose poem expatiates on the overthrow of a Gentile sovereign who has offended Israel.'

General Mikhail Diterikhs, brooding in his exile on Russia's Pacific coast, had dragons of his own to slay when he published his book based on Sokolov's report, *The Murder of the Tsarist Family and Members of the House of Romanov in the Urals*, in Vladivostok in 1922. To say that Diterikhs was an anti-Semite would seem an understatement to any reader of his book. He was a convinced devotee of *The Protocols of the Elders of Zion*'s description of a Jewish conspiracy to undermine Christian civilization and take over the world. He motivated his troops by providing them with a pamphlet entitled *The Jews Have Killed the Tsar*.

Before describing Diterikhs's basic obsession in full, it is worth noting that he had an additional foe: any politician anywhere to the left of the Union of the Russian People, the anti-Semitic, pogrom-mongering, ultra-monarchist and chauvinistic pre-war political movement.

The Jews were not alone in bearing guilt for the disaster that had befallen Russia. Democratic politicians had removed the steady hand of autocracy from the tiller of the ship of state; they had ruined the army with their stupid democratic reforms; they had indulged extremists like the Bolsheviks and then proved unable to keep them from power. Even now these alliance partners of 'a diseased political tendency' were sabotaging the White political movement, not least by undermining the investigation of the Tsar's murder. All this was to be expected – after all, the chief democratic villain, Aleksandr Kerensky, was a Jew: not Aleksandr, but 'Aaron'; not Kerensky, but 'Kipniss'. This was, of course, fanciful nonsense.

The Jews were 'sons of the Father of Lies', willing helpers in the effort to bring about the advent of the Antichrist. 'Jews created the revolution. Jews brought Russia to ruin. Jews shed the blood of our fathers, mothers, brothers, sisters and children of city and village, the hills and dales of Mother Russia. The Jews brutally destroyed the Royal Family. The Jews are to blame for every evil befalling Russia. *The Jewish people* should answer for this.'

The preeminent role of the Jews explained a number of the mysteries surrounding the Ekaterinburg murders, such as their extreme brutality. The Romanovs in Alapaevsk had been killed much more humanely by Russians than had the Tsar and his family by the butcher Yurovsky. Diterikhs forgot for the moment that the Alapaevsk victims had been bludgeoned, thrown down a mine shaft while still alive, bombarded by hand grenades and then left to die. Since the Jews were so bestial, they had no qualms about chopping up bodies, disfiguring them with acid and burning them. Their depravity explained another problem: if the bodies had been burned, where were the teeth, which can survive fire? The answer was obvious: Yurovsky had decapitated the bodies, placed the heads in alcohol and sent them off to Moscow as trophies.

The Jews had to destroy what remained from this butchery because the Tsar was the living symbol of the faith and the nation, and only by extirpating all traces of him could the Jews destroy the faith of the people. They had left plentiful evidence of the nature of the killings. The poem on the wall was in Yiddish, Diterikhs claimed. It was, in fact, standard German in non-Gothic script. 'Balthazar was on the same night murdered by his own slaves' read the inscription, written on the wall of the room of the shooting and shedding light on the spiritual dimension of the historical tragedy that took place there on the night of 16–17 July. This had been a ritual murder celebrating the victory of Jewish socialism over Orthodox Christianity. Diterikhs never tired of reiterating the theme and purpose of his book: to show the world that it was not the Russian people who killed their Tsar, but Jews.

Nikolai Sokolov, whose files provided the raw material for the works of Gilliard, Wilton and Diterikhs, was the last to publish his book, in part because he continued his investigations in exile. He was a proponent of conspiracy theories as well. He was more than ready to accept the role of the Jews in the murder of the Tsar. His faith even earned him a trip to Dearborn, Michigan, to consult with the automotive magnate Henry Ford, who was seeking confirmation of his own beliefs, again exemplified by the *Protocols*, that the Jews were trying to take over the world.

In the turgid world of exile politics, however, Sokolov's paranoid fancies had even more room to grow. A curious aspect of his investigation was the extent to which he explored the prehistory of the regicide. He studied events that, while interesting in their own right, bore little relation to what happened in the Ipatiev House. His research included the abdication of the Tsar, his arrest and the dispatch of the family to Tobolsk and their life there before the transfer to Ekaterinburg. The physical threat to the Romanovs, after all, only became apparent with the Bolshevik Revolution and the radicalizing of the Soviets of the Urals region.

For Sokolov, it was not just the Germans, or the Jews, or the democrats, but a mysterious conspiracy that had begun years before the war. As he wrote in a private letter in 1922:

> *The murder of all the members of the House of the Romanovs appears as the fulfilment of one and the same purpose, developed in one unitary plan, whose very first victim was Grand Duke Mikhail Aleksandrovich. . . . For many years before the revolution arose the murder plan, which had as its objective the destruction of the idea of the monarchy. In the midst of clerical circles the representative of this idea was in reality Rasputin. The cycle of ideas, engendered by this individual, created the phenomenon which directly brought about the death of the Royal Family and which in the person of other persons (after the death of Rasputin) existed in Tobolsk and Ekaterinburg to the moment of their death. . . . This work has not ceased even now.*

A conspiracy theory that managed to encompass Rasputin, the Orthodox Church and the Urals Soviet was no mean feat, but it was made even more elegant by Sokolov's discovery of its malevolent intent still at work. It was now directed at him, of course, because of his efforts to demonstrate that the Imperial Family was really dead and not miraculously saved, as Bolshevik propaganda would have it. The lack of support he had experienced in exile, the cold shoulder he had received from surviving Romanovs, was thus easily explained. Like the Tsar himself, Sokolov was a martyr to the truth.

Given the obsessive fear that all these chroniclers of the last days of the Romanovs had of Bolshevik disinformation, it is amazing how easily they were seduced by it. Diterikhs contended at one point in his book that a particular motivation for the Bolsheviks to hide the bodies was to sow discord and ensure false conclusions among the investigators. How well they succeeded! The best example must surely be the common boast of Wilton, Diterikhs and Sokolov that they had seen through the Bolshevik rumour that claimed that the Romanovs had not been incinerated at the Four Brothers but had been buried somewhere else. They were all also taken in by the so-called Perm Trial.

At the end of 1919 a sensational news story reported that in the Siberian city of Perm, on 17 September 1919, the Bolshevik authorities had tried 28 people for the crimes of murdering the Tsar and his family and looting their possessions. The trial discovered that the entire family had been killed, and that the person responsible was the head of the Ekaterinburg Cheka, a man named as 'Yakhontov'. He was described as a Left Social Revolutionary, who had organized the deaths in order to cast discredit for the crimes on the Soviet authorities. 'Yakhontov' and four of his associates in the Ekaterinburg Soviet were reportedly convicted and shot.

The Perm Trial gained particular notoriety when Jewish groups in the West, noting the Russian names of all the defendants, seized on the reports to bolster their assertions that the Jews had not in fact killed the Tsar. Diterikhs and Wilton both demolished the Bolsheviks' contentions, establishing that none of those names had held the positions claimed for them. Since the original report had appeared in the official Communist Party newspaper *Pravda*, the trial itself had clearly been a provocation designed to discredit the SRs and exonerate the Bolsheviks for the murders. It was a typical piece of Communist disinformation and propaganda.

There is only one shortcoming in this analysis: *Pravda* never carried the article in question, as a cursory examination of that newspaper would have revealed. The source, rather, was the *émigré* journal *Rossiia*, published in Paris. Far from being disinformation, the article was actually White Guard rumour-mongering and invention. The Perm Trial perfectly illustrates how even the foremost specialists on the Romanov murders found it difficult to navigate in a sea of speculation and false information.

Pity therefore the casual reader of a serious newspaper like *The Times* who was offered a bewildering assortment of contra-dictory reportage throughout the early years of Soviet power. In spite of – or perhaps because of – the newspaper's lack of a permanent correspondent in Moscow, it published almost any story out of Russia, no matter what the source. First reports of the royal assassinations variously stated that the Tsar had been shot on a train between Ekaterinburg and Perm, or in the riding school outside Ekaterinburg. Once the choice fell on the Ipatiev House, *The Times* reprinted accounts that contained all the melodrama of a Victorian penny dreadful.

According to a report received from the French press, the first head of the Provisional Government, Prince Georgy Lvov, had been imprisoned in Ekaterinburg in a cell next to that of the Imperial Family. On the night of the murders, he had heard the family being dispatched by bayonets, one by one, before being finished off with revolvers. Their whole cell was turned into 'a pond of blood'.

On 28 January 1919 a special correspondent reported that the family had been in bed when they heard the approach of the executioners. They had quickly risen, dressed and knelt to pray. 'The terrified Grand Duchesses clasped each other. The Tsare-vich burst into tears, tried to stand and fell, whereupon the Tsar broke off his prayers to take his sick son in his arms. The Tsarina continued in prayer.' The door burst open, and Yurovsky entered. 'With a short, devilish laugh [he] turned to the Tsar and said, "I see you are already prepared. . . . Our visit does not concern you alone. We shall exterminate your wife and your whole brood also."' As the royal party was roughly handled down the stairs to the basement, they encountered all their old servants and retainers, including Dr Botkin. '"You, too?" said the Tsar to Botkin, who bowed very low, unable to utter a word.' The entire group were then shot at close range with revolvers, one at a time. The Tsarina was first, the Tsar last.

Before long, *The Times* carried accounts of escapes, with headlines like THE TSAR LEGEND, on 17 February 1919. This highly improbable version of events, albeit from 'trustworthy authority', reported that the Imperial Family was interred in the Troisko-Sergievsky Monastery in Zagorsk, while the Tsar himself had been brought to the Kremlin. Lenin was prepared to transfer power to the monarch when the bourgeois class separating the Tsar from the people no longer existed.

Such stories kept appearing in all the world's press, for there was an insatiable public appetite for information on the Romanovs and their final destiny. Fortunately, there was an almost inexhaustible supply. Nicholas's family must have been one of the most documented of all time. All the members of the royal household were keen photographers, with the time and money to indulge their hobby. Thousands of photographic images were available to chronicle the rise and fall of this Imperial Family and its fresh-faced children. All the Romanovs kept journals, and all wrote letters, many of which were preserved and reprinted. The Soviet authorities published the Tsar's diary and his correspondence with his wife. For western readers they had the advantage of having been written in English, and the Nicky-Sunny Letters became a publishing success story. Those on the edges of the Russian court, such as Gilliard, Botkin's daughter Tatiana, or Aleksei Volkov, the Empress's personal valet, all published memoirs or glimpses of the domestic life of the Imperial Family. As the official reports of Wilton, Diterikhs and Sokolov began to appear, they provided grist for the mill of a whole generation of literary charlatans.

Thus, in Brussels a pseudonymous author, Enel, published a booklet entitled *Sacrifice*. The author was actually a Russian *émigré*, Mikhail Skariatin, who specialized in the study of astrology and cabala. His starting-point were the mysterious runes discovered in the death room by Sokolov, but not apparently seen by Sergeev months earlier. No proper record has ever been made of these figures. The photograph taken by Sokolov is presented without scale or orientation, which makes it difficult to deduce how – or if – they should be read. One need only examine the various attempts to transcribe them, in Nikolai Ross, Diterikhs, Sokolov, Enel or Summers and Mangold, to see how they have been recopied in incompatible versions. They are frequently connected with the Heinrich Heine poem about Balthazar, which is often itself mistakenly described as being in Yiddish.

Wilton could do no more than describe the scrawls as a 'cabalistic inscription which has not been deciphered', and that was enough for Enel. With a light touch, he connected the runes with the letter L in Hebrew, Greek and Samaritan, allegedly the three languages of Jewish history. Employing the Hebrew system of equivalence, whereby each letter of the alphabet has a numerical value, Enel produced a 'translation': 'Here the king (the heart of the state) has been sacrificed for the destruction of the state.' In short the murder of Nicholas was a ritual murder carried out by Jews.

Enel concluded with the pious declaration that 'we are far from including all the Jewish nation in our accusation. Such an insinuation would be false and unjust.' This was a distinction that was quickly lost when the work was published in expanded translations in German (1930) and Russian (1990).

Diterikhs's grisly description of murder and decapitation engendered a continuing literary effort to account for the missing heads. The most effective account was one published in Germany, which reads like a cross between a Gothic novel and Mikhail Bulgakov's classic *The Master and Margarita*. Lenin's whole Politburo has gathered in a tower at the Kremlin to examine and dispose of the head of Tsar Nicholas. As a storm breaks over the city, the head is brought out of a glass jar, remarkably preserved, except that the hair and beard have gone white. Trotsky's sarcastic observations are interrupted by an ominous thunderclap, which reduces the audience to silence. While the group prepares to toss the head into a stove, the sole woman present, Aleksandra Kollontai, becomes nauseous and bolts for the door, engendering sarcastic comments from her male colleagues. A red dawn accompanies the final crumbling of the Tsar's head into ash.

Equally grotesque was an account appearing in the West, which purported to be the memoirs of one of the assassins, Petr Voikov, the very Commissar for Supplies who procured the sulphuric acid for the destruction of the bodies. In 1927, while serving as Soviet Ambassador to Poland, he was assassinated by a young *émigré* monarchist, Boris Koverda. These posthumous memoirs, of very questionable provenance, described the execution as a horrible massacre, in the course of which Anastasia was bayoneted through the face. The next morning the bodies were chopped into pieces in preparation for burning. Yurovsky, who supervised the operation, was deeply perturbed. The following day he reportedly told Voikov that one of the heads had gone missing – 'the one who was stabbed through the face': Anastasia.

A public fascination for any scrap of Romanoviana, and the willingness of press and publishers to pander to this hunger with any tale, no matter how implausible or fantastic, created an environment in the West that was ripe for royal pretenders. They did begin to appear in some numbers, but none was able to make a credible case or command any sort of a following, least of all from the surviving Romanovs. The hope for a survivor was present, but before 1920 the right candidate was still absent.

Above: The Grand
Duchesses Anastasia
(left) and Maria (right).
(Luton Hoo Foundation)

Right: The official
face of the Romanov
children (left to
right): Maria, Olga,
Alexei, Anastasia and
Tatiana. (Ian Lilburn)

Right: On board the
Imperial train: Alexei
and his spaniel Joy,
the sole survivor of
the Ekaterinburg
massacre.
(Luton Hoo Foundation)

Above: The Tsar
(front) and Grand
Duke Ernst Ludwig
of Hesse, the
Tsarina's brother.
Anna Anderson's
recollection of a secret
wartime visit to
Russia by Uncle
'Ernie' was a crucial
element in her claim
to be Anastasia.
(Ian Lilburn)

Above: A rare
glimpse of the Tsarina
smiling at home with
the Tsarevich Alexei.
(Ian Lilburn)

Opposite: Pierre
Gilliard (centre), the
children's French
tutor, calls on the
Imperial Family
under house arrest at
Tsarskoe Selo.
(Luton Hoo Foundation)

From Tobolsk to
Ekaterinburg

Top: Icons protect the
Grand Duchesses'
bedroom in Tobolsk.
(Luton Hoo Foundation)

Above: May Day
1918 outside Freedom
House in Tobolsk.
(Luton Hoo Foundation)

Above: Dr Evgeny
Botkin, personal
physician to the Tsar,
who died with the
Imperial Family in
the Ipatiev House.
(Ian Lilburn)

Left: The Tsarevich
Alexei and his sister
Olga on board the SS
Russia in transit from
Tobolsk to
Ekaterinburg.
(Luton Hoo Foundation)

Above: Vasily
Yakovlev delivers the
Tsar to the leaders of
the Urals Soviet,
taken from the
famous picture by
Soviet artist V. Pchelin.

Opposite: The Ipatiev House behind the wooden pallisade (inset) and the fatal basement room where the Romanovs and their servants were executed. (The wall has been cut away to remove the bullets.)

The two chief rivals for the honour of killing the Tsar: (top) Petr Ermakov, standing by the sleepers that marked the burial site of the Romanovs; (left) Yakov Yurovsky in an informal pose. Ermakov's Mauser (centre), which he used to shoot the Tsar. (All A. Grakhov)

Above: Sokolov's desperate search for the remains of the Imperial Family at the Four Brothers site in the Koptiaki Woods in 1919.
(Luton Hoo Foundation)

Right: Guards at the Ipatiev House, some of whom joined the firing squad.

CHAPTER FIVE

The Poor Invalid

ANNA ANDERSON WAS a remarkable woman. She survived countless severe illnesses, confounding the diagnoses and expectations of numerous distinguished doctors; she weathered the combined efforts of the Romanov and Hesse families to discredit her; and her persona remained intact even ten years after her death to inspire loyal followers to continue the search for proof that she was indeed the Grand Duchess Anastasia, the youngest daughter of Tsar Nicholas II.

This woman, who first appeared as Fraulein Unbekannt (Miss Unknown), inspired hundreds of devoted supporters throughout her life. Many of the true believers made themselves bankrupt in her service. Others enjoyed the aura of royalty and mystery that she inspired, while yet more quite simply attempted to profit from her fame and notoriety. Anna Anderson spawned an Anastasia business – books and films, ballet and music – and yet she herself led a precarious existence, dependent on the goodwill of others. She was not an easy woman. Her tantrums, bad temper and frustrating ability to fall out with many of her acolytes, who had suspended their own lives to take care of her, were legendary. At the same time she could be charming, vivacious and very good company, even to the end of her life.

James Blair Lovell, who only knew her as an old woman, by

this time living in Charlottesville, Virginia, described her hypnotic strength in his book, *Anastasia, The Lost Princess.*

> When she fixed her gaze on you, she drew you immediately and completely to her. The color was as deep as her suffering, but there was also a glint, luminescence, like the innocent anticipation in the eyes of infants who have just learned to focus on the world. Indeed, even as she trained those incredible eyes on you, she was also taking in everything around her. If eyes are truly portals to the soul, then hers revealed an intense sadness and an equally profound sense of wonderment.

The power of her blue eyes has been commented on by nearly all those who fell under her spell. Precisely this physical feature appears in descriptions of Anastasia's father. Aleksandr Kerensky, who was initially Minister of Justice in the Provisional Government, was responsible for the guard over the Tsar at Tsarskoe Selo. He met with Nicholas II often at close quarters and recalled his appearance as that of 'a pleasant, somewhat ordinary colonel of the guards, very ordinary except for a pair of wonderful blue eyes'.

However, as was the case with all the witnesses attempting to prove or disprove Anna's identity over a period of 50 years, there is a jarring note, even over the conventional wisdom concerning Anna's blue eyes. The Romanov children's English tutor, Sydney Gibbes, wrote formal descriptions of all members of the family, which were given to an examining magistrate in Ekaterinburg after the assassination of the Imperial Family. He stated of Grand Duchess Anastasia, 'Her eyes were grey and beautiful', perhaps mirroring her mother, the Tsarina Alexandra, whom Gibbes described as having 'wonderful soft grey eyes'.

Gibbes, who had been appointed the English teacher for the Tsar's children in 1908, followed the family to Tobolsk after the revolution, where he attempted to amuse them in the long-standing English tradition, by putting on plays. In 1954, he was called to identify Anna when she was in Paris and declared very clearly that 'she in no way resembles the true Grand Duchess Anastasia that I had known and I am quite satisfied that she is an impostor.' Although Gibbes did not comment on the colour of Anna's eyes when he saw her in Paris, he fixed on her right ear, which he attested did not resemble that of the Grand Duchess, going by a photograph he had of Anastasia. Anna's eyes, her ears, her scars, her hands, her mouth were all subjects of intense discussion as supporters and enemies alike tried to prove their case. For her devoted partisans, it was her more intangible attributes, her character, her behaviour, her knowledge of life at the Romanov court, that drove them to her defence. For some, it was simply her presence.

One of her most devoted and loyal champions was Gleb Botkin, son of Dr Evgeny Botkin, the Imperial Family's personal physician who died with the family at Ekaterinburg. He first met Anna in 1927 at Castle Seeon, where she was staying with the family of the Duke of Leuchtenberg, who were distant relatives of the Romanovs but who had never met Anastasia before the revolution. Gleb, however, did not need proofs.

> For nine years I had believed – nay, known – her to be dead. And now she stood before me. Her luminous blue eyes looked straight into mine and her small beautiful hand, with long tapering fingers, was approaching my lips in that almost automatic gesture of hers I knew so well. So had her hand approached my lips the very first time we met, for although we were but children then, and she by eleven months my junior, she was a Grand Duchess – the daughter of my Emperor – and I a hereditary Nobleman of the Russian Empire. And so we were both observant of etiquette.

Gleb Botkin opens his book *The Woman Who Rose Again* with these words. For him that was enough. He never faltered in his knowledge that she was indeed the Grand Duchess and passed this certainty on to the next generation, for his daughter Marina Botkin – later known as Marina Schweitzer after her marriage to US attorney Richard (Dick) Schweitzer – would prove an equally doughty fighter for Anna's identity and 'rights'. Botkin was encouraged to travel from the United States to Germany in 1927 by his sister, Tatiana Melnik – from her marriage to Constantine

Melnik in 1918 – who had positively identified Anna as Grand Duchess Anastasia. The witness of the two Botkin children was crucial in furthering Anna's cause, as they had personally known the Imperial Family as children. They lived in Tsarskoe Selo from 1908 to 1914 with their father Dr Evgeny Botkin, and saw the Tsar and his family at close quarters, although the children did not mix personally. During holidays in the Crimea the Botkins did have direct contact with the Imperial Family, though, and especially with the younger children, Maria, Anastasia and Alexei, who were their playmates.

Both the Botkins wrote books about Anna Anderson and never wavered in their belief that she was truly the Grand Duchess Anastasia. Gleb Botkin, however, took on a more public role in his efforts to gain recognition for her. As he put it, 'I felt no sacrifice to be too great for me to make, provided that it tended to restore to Anastasia her identity, rights and a normal mode and manner of life.' He bravely, perhaps over-enthusiastically, took on the Romanov and Hesse dynasties in the public arena, to the dismay of other supporters of Anna, who preferred a more discreet approach.

If Gleb's articles and books and Anna's subsequent transatlantic voyage brought her fame in America, she had already become a media *cause célèbre* in Germany. Grand Duke Andrei, cousin to the Tsar, who had also known Nicholas's family personally, played a significant role in promoting Anna's identity as Anastasia, as did two personal friends of the Empress, Zinaida Tolstoy and later Lili Dehn. In America Princess Xenia, the daughter of Grand Duke Georgy and second cousin of Anastasia, believed in Anna's identity, and while she could not publicly contradict the Romanov family position, she was a loyal friend who provided testimony in Anna's defence.

While many of Anna's crucial supporters had not known the Imperial Family before the Revolution, they frequently had a Russian connection. Prominent among these was Harriet von Rathlef-Keilman, who had lived in the Baltic provinces before the revolution. She made extensive efforts during the 1920s to have Anna recognized as the Grand Duchess, sacrificing her independence to become Anna's companion and nursemaid. She wrote a book, *Anastasia*, about Anna, which was published in German in

1928 and in English the following year and which gained extensive publicity for the cause when it was first serialized in the *Berliner Nachtausgabe* in February and March 1927. This popular newspaper lapped up this new twist to the Romanov saga, following widespread publicity about the family's assassination and the last days of the Romanovs, which became a popular staple of German illustrated magazines.

Another significant supporter was the Danish ambassador to Berlin, Herluf Zahle, who was commissioned in 1925 by Prince Waldemar of Denmark to investigate the case. Prince Waldemar, brother of the Tsar's mother, Dowager Empress Marie Fedorovna, formerly Princess Dagmar of Denmark, paid for Anna's hospital bills until her identity could be verified. Zahle collected an enormous amount of information and evidence about the case and supported Anna during her numerous hospital stays, but finally had to withdraw from her side on the orders of the Danish Royal Family. His evidence has become a centre of controversy as the Danish Royal Family has never allowed public access to the files, contending that the investigation was purely a family matter.

Later, Prince Frederick of Saxe-Altenburg championed Anna's 30-year law suit through the German courts, while several 'ladies-in-waiting' helped her in her daily life despite her idiosyncrasies and bad temper. Finally, when Anna was 67 years old, the faithful Gleb Botkin found her a husband, Jack Manahan, 18 years her junior, who took care of her until she died in 1984.

She was a trying, difficult and eccentric person, and yet she successfully relied upon 'the kindness of strangers'. She attracted people and retained their intense loyalty for many different reasons. If she were not the Grand Duchess, she proved a remarkably successful pretender. And if she were the Grand Duchess, then the hackneyed cliché, 'stranger than fiction', precisely describes her story.

The deceptive Soviet announcement that only the Tsar had perished, and the rest of the family had been sent 'to a safe place', created a field day for impostors. It did not take long for rumours, sightings and witnesses to confirm that the family had survived.

The Dowager Empress Marie Fedorovna was a leading exponent of the survival theory, publicly maintaining to her death that Nicholas, Alexandra and all their children were living obscurely somewhere in Russia.

Although most of those connected with the Dowager Empress considered this fanciful in the extreme, it did have the effect of keeping the disparate Romanov family in line. While the head of the dynasty in exile did not accept the death of the last Tsar, it meant that all claimants to the throne were illegal until the Tsar's demise could be proved.

It did not take the attitude of a Dowager Empress to start the pretender ball rolling. The speculation surrounding the Sokolov investigation, alleging that one or two of the Grand Duchesses had managed to escape the firing squad, initiated the parade of impostors that persists to this day. But Gleb Botkin had been there. After the assassinations he made his way from Tobolsk to Ekaterinburg, Vladivostok and finally out of Russia to Japan in 1920. Later he was to examine the stories surrounding the death of the Imperial Family and his own father, Dr Evgeny Botkin. The pretender industry was going strong:

> To add to the general scepticism with regard to all rumours of escape, numerous Grand Duchesses and Tsareviches, all of them obvious frauds, appeared in every town in Siberia. Some of them, however, were quite successful in getting themselves believed in, especially one handsome courtesan, who for months posed as Grand Duchess Tatiana, and as such was fêted by many White regiments at the front. In Vladivostok one enterprising gentleman by the name of Solovieff [Soloviev] who was married to Rasputin's daughter, Matrena [Maria], organised a regular business of exporting rescued Grand Duchesses. He periodically informed local millionaires that he had a rescued Grand Duchess in his keeping, but had no money to send her abroad. The good-natured merchants gave him money freely, and for that were rewarded by Solovieff's permission to see the rescued 'Grand Duchess' depart on a steamer. The role of the Grand Duchess was played by some one of the local courtesans who met her benefactors on the deck of some departing steamer,

permitted them graciously to kiss her hand and before the last whistle sounded, returned to the pier by a different gangplank.

Gleb's sceptical attitude persists until he first caught sight of Anna.

Other imposters have appeared throughout the world, from Eugenia Smith of Chicago to the self-styled Prince Alexis d'Angou, Duc de Durazzo, who claims that his mother was Anastasia's sister, Grand Duchess Maria. A contemporary Australian pretender sells patents of nobility to his faithful followers.

The bravest impostors were those who appeared on Soviet soil, where their fate was not determined by the gentle indulgence of Western society. A Soviet merchant seaman, Nikolai Dalsky, claimed to be Alexei and at his death in 1965 passed his claim to the throne to his son, 'Nikolai Romanov', whose son Vladimir is styled 'the Tsarevich'. This dynasty had the good sense to await the fall of Communism before proclaiming itself. Nadezhda Ivanovna Vasileva, who claimed she was the real Anastasia, died in a mental hospital in Kazan in 1971. Filipp Grigorievich Semenov convinced some of his doctors at a mental hospital in Petrozavodsk that he was the Tsarevich Alexei.

Anna's story also begins in a mental hospital, in Berlin in 1920. On the evening of 17 February, at about 9 pm, she jumped off the Bendler Bridge into the Landwehr Canal, apparently with the intention of committing suicide. A police sergeant pulled her to shore and delivered her to the Elizabeth Hospital. She was dressed simply in a black skirt and stockings, linen blouse, boots and a heavy shawl, the typical clothes of a Berlin working woman. The police and hospital staff could find no identifying marks or papers. She refused to answer any questions about her identity and thus became Fraulein Unbekannt.

After six weeks of stubborn silence, the Berlin authorities transferred her to the Dalldorf insane asylum. She spent the next two years sharing a ward with 12 other patients, mostly lying in bed facing the wall and showing little interest in her surroundings or in conversation. During that time her health deteriorated, and her weight dropped 21 lb to an emaciated 100 lb. She was to retain this appearance throughout her life, a tiny, thin and frail woman, who suffered from serious bouts of illness.

Although she frustrated all attempts by the medical staff to ascertain her identity, a fellow Dalldorf inmate, Clara Peuthert, managed to gain her confidence. Anna's first acolyte was thus a madwoman. Anna had obtained a copy of *Berliner illustrirte Zeitung* of 23 October 1921, which carried a story claiming that Grand Duchess Anastasia had escaped the Ekaterinburg massacre. Clara had seen a similarity between Fraulein Unbekannt and the Grand Duchesses and leapt to the conclusion that she was the Tsar's second daughter, Grand Duchess Tatiana.

When Clara was released from Dalldorf on 20 January 1922, she took on the exciting mission of saving the lost princess. Her first step was to approach Captain Nicholas Adolfovitch von Schwabe, formerly a Russian officer in the Guards. He usually spent his afternoons sitting in the courtyard of the Russian embassy church on Unter den Linden, selling monarchist propaganda.

At this time there were 500,000 Russian exiles in Germany, 100,000 living in Berlin. Among the political and economic turmoil of post-war Berlin, a plethora of Russian centres, associations, political groups and organizations had sprung up. Most of the exiles did not believe that the Bolsheviks would remain in power long, and many were jockeying for position when the time came to return to their homeland. While they had to earn a living in this alien country, most maintained their Russian culture through the interlocking circles of *émigrés*. This hotbed of displaced persons thrived on gossip and intrigue.

At Clara's instigation, von Schwabe went to visit Anna at Dalldorf and later introduced other members of the Russian community to her bedside. These souls included Zinaida Tolstoy, a friend of the Tsarina Alexandra, who recognized Anna as the Grand Duchess. Anna generally refused to cooperate with the intrusive questioning and stares of these visitors, adopting behaviour that became her trademark as she endured visits from people wanting to identify her. She tended to hide under her bedclothes, cover part of her face with a cloth or her hand, with only her frightened eyes visible to show the torment that these interrogations brought her. She did not assist with Zinaida and even more crucially remained stubbornly unhelpful for the visit from Baroness Sophie Buxhoeveden, the former lady-in-waiting to the Tsarina.

It was a one-sided encounter. The Baroness stormed into the asylum. Unaccustomed to having her requests ignored by a mental patient who preferred to hide herself in her bedcovers than to answer questions, she became angry. She pulled the invalid out of bed and pronounced, 'She's too short for Tatiana'. That indeed was true, for Anna at five foot two inches could hardly claim the stature of Tatiana, the tallest daughter of the Emperor. However, she was the right height for Anastasia, the smallest of the Tsar's daughters. It is not surprising that there was this initial mix-up, for Grand Duchess Olga, the Tsar's sister, was later to say that she bore a much closer resemblance to Tatiana than to Anastasia, although she was clearly several inches shorter than Tatiana. Some days after the fiasco, Anna simply and accurately said: 'I did not say I was Tatiana.' Thus she gained her identity almost by default – Anastasia.

While Anna appeared indifferent to the consequences of these visits, they had serious implications. Baroness Buxhoeveden's repudiation of her imperial identity was enough for the Supreme Monarchist Council, which accepted the Baroness's word that Anna was merely another pretender. For Clara Peuthert and Captain von Schwabe and other members of the Russian circle, however, Anna's identity became an intriguing riddle. They saw Anna's stubborn personality and refusal to cooperate as 'proof' that she was not a simple adventuress. This was reinforced by her mischievous streak, which became more pronounced as she grew older. If her supporters were careless enough to assume she was Tatiana, then why should she correct them?

Another key figure now entered Anna's life – a former provincial police officer in the Polish provinces of Russia. Baron Arthur von Kleist and his wife Maria, in common with other Russian exiles in Berlin, had heard about the miraculous escape of Anastasia and her unfortunate domicile at the Dalldorf asylum. Although they had never seen the Tsar's children, they determined to take care of her on the basis that she might be Grand Duchess Anastasia. After frequent visits and presents, Anna agreed to be taken away to Berlin's Little Russia. It took only a few days for the von Kleists' fourth-floor apartment to become a social centre for White Russians, who came to chat, to stare and to ask questions of the former mental patient. Jealous gossip attributed unkind motives to the von Kleists' act of generosity, but at the time they shared von Schwabe's belief in Anna's royal identity.

It was at this time that the weakest link in Anna's story became commonly known. The von Kleists affirmed that Anna told them she was the Grand Duchess Anastasia and that she was the sole survivor of the massacre. She said she had hidden behind her sister Tatiana and fainted. She later came round to find herself in the care of one of the soldiers whom she named as Alexander Tschaikovsky. She said Tschaikovsky took pity on her, rescued her at the last minute and then, with the aid of his brother, took her to Romania. There she claimed she had a son, whom she named Alexei after the Tsarevich, and married Tschaikovsky. Tschaikovsky was subsequently killed in a street fight in Bucharest, and his brother then escorted Anna, crossing borders by night, to Berlin, where she hoped to find safety with her Aunt Irene, Princess Heinrich of Prussia, the Tsarina's sister. She left her son behind in a Romanian orphanage.

This fantastic tale developed many variations, which grew in the telling. Different versions of key events, such as the birthdate of her son, would never be proved or disproved. For her enemies, the implausibility of her 1800-mile flight to Romania and her journey to Berlin fuelled their scepticism. Her alleged son disturbed various Romanov camps who would not countenance such a claimant to the Russian throne. Unsurprisingly this is one pretender who has never turned up. Anna has had numerous 'daughters', and other supposed 'children' of her sisters have claimed their Romanov heritage. But Alexei of Bucharest has never surfaced.

Whatever the basis of this story, it did provide her with a name, Mrs Tschaikovsky, which she used for many years. Her stay with the von Kleists also gave her the name Anna. The von Kleists asked her what they should call her, and she proposed Anna, a shortened version of Anastasia. Anna remained with her throughout her life. While she became known to some as Anastasia, she was yet to fall into the name by which most of the world was later to know her – Anna Anderson. She adopted the surname Anderson while on a visit to America to confuse pursuing journalists and later was called Anastasia Manahan, when she married Jack Manahan.

She had only spent a short period at the von Kleists, suffering intense scrutiny and numerous interrogations from visiting Russians, when she fell severely ill. The von Kleists' physician, Dr Schiler, diagnosed acute anemia and also noted in his report that she had suffered a severe injury to the head. The doctor also observed that she talked Russian 'with good pronunciation' in her sleep. To his surprise she made a remarkable recovery and then disappeared, only ten weeks after she had begun her stay with the Kleists.

Two days later a friend of Captain von Schwabe found her near the Berlin zoo. Afterwards these missing days would be referred to in court by Doris Wingender, who stated that Anna was Franziska Schanzkowska, her former tenant. Doris said that the whirlwind life and constant questioning at the Kleists had made Franziska run 'home' to escape from all those Russians who were proclaiming her a princess. After being discovered at the zoo, accommodation was arranged for her with a wealthy police inspector, Franz Grunberg, who had the additional advantage of owning a country home at Funkenmuhle.

It was here that Anna endured a pivotal visit, resulting in the implacable opposition of the Hesse relatives of the Tsarina. Her faithful fellow patient, Clara Peuthert, had tried to help her cause by writing letters to Grand Duke Ernst Ludwig of Hesse-Darmstadt and Princess Irene of Prussia, brother and sister of the Tsarina, pleading that they visit Anna and confirm that she was their niece. Grunberg was bold enough to secure a call from Princess Irene, which went the characteristic way of other visits. Unwarned of the impending royal visitor, Anna ran away from Irene at the supper table and later in her room turned away from the Princess and refused to talk to her, with tears streaming down her face.

Princess Irene consequently wrote: 'She did not respond even when I begged her to say one word or make one sign that would show me that she had recognised me; it was even the same when, in order to neglect nothing, I said to her, "Do you not know your aunt Irene?"' Irene did, however, note that she bore some resemblance to Grand Duchess Tatiana but remained adamant that Anna was not who she claimed to be. This disastrous encounter influenced the Grand Duke Ernst, who never bothered to meet Anna and opposed her claim throughout his life.

Anna's supporters asserted that Irene privately expressed doubts about her judgement in not recognizing Anna as her niece, but if that were the case she never wavered in her public statements. For failing to acknowledge her aunt, Grunberg angrily threw Anna out of his house. This initiated a three-year period of wandering between *émigré* houses and hospitals, accumulating devoted followers and gaining more notoriety in turn. She also underwent more meetings with witnesses, most of which became the subject of bitter recriminations and conflicting recollections.

Anna then developed serious tuberculosis of the bones and came near to death on several occasions, but in her characteristic manner she confounded medical opinion time and again by her miraculous recoveries. In between hospital stays, she was shuffled between the von Kleists, Clara Peuthert and other *émigré* houses, a focus of gossip and intrigue, and above all the subject of sensational articles in the press. She lost many of her former friends, even including the faithful Clara.

Anna was a guest of a poor working-class family, the Bachmans, when Inspector Grunberg once more came into her life. His house hosted another failed encounter with the former German Crown Princess, Cecile of Prussia. Once again, Anna remained silent and refused to cooperate with the visitor or answer her questions. This infuriated Grunberg, who understandably lost patience and refused to support her further. However, it left space for the next significant 'believer'.

Harriet von Rathlef-Keilman had lived in Russia's Baltic provinces before the revolution and was now eking out a precarious living in Berlin as a sculptor and children's author. She was introduced to Anna in July 1925, acted as her chief nursemaid and companion and, perhaps more importantly, championed her cause in the German press. She also became a devious figure in the eyes of the former imperial tutor, Pierre Gilliard, who accused her of 'coaching' Anna in her reminiscences of the Russian court.

By this time Anna was seriously ill with tuberculosis of the bones, and only the expert surgery of another Russian, Dr Sergei

Rudnev, kept her arm from amputation. It is no exaggeration to say that Harriet saved her life by devoting herself to Anna's recovery and watching over her bedside round the clock. During Anna's illness she met her most significant visitors, Grand Duchess Olga, sister of the Tsar, Pierre Gilliard, the former French tutor, and his wife Shura, who had been young Anastasia's nursemaid.

Reports of the missing Russian princess had by this time reached the court in Copenhagen, where the Dowager Empress Marie Fedorovna, once a Danish princess, had set up her residence, with her youngest daughter, Grand Duchess Olga. Dowager Empress Marie had been in the Crimea and was removed by the British ship HMS *Marlborough* in 1919, just before the Whites were overthrown by the Red Army. She was rescued with 19 members of her family and a group of others and was able to bring out jewels and Romanov regalia. After a brief visit to England, she returned to her native Denmark. As head of the Romanov family, the Dowager Empress was not without her own problems. In 1924 Grand Duke Kyril Vladimirovich had declared himself the heir to his cousin, Tsar Nicholas II. Kyril had a very shaky claim to the throne because of his morganatic marriage, which was not approved by Nicholas. Kyril's claim also challenged Marie's proclaimed belief that her son and family had somehow survived. Throughout these difficult times, she was also asked to countenance reports of numerous pretenders, of whom the most persistent and credible was Anna Tschaikovsky, perilously ill in a Berlin hospital.

Her brother, Prince Waldemar of Denmark, asked Herluf Zahle, the Danish ambassador to Berlin, to examine the whole affair. He also invited the Tsarina's personal valet, Aleksei Volkov, to visit her. Olga, in her turn, asked the Gilliards to travel from Lausanne and see the patient. If there seemed to be any truth in the assertions, Olga was prepared to come from Copenhagen to meet the patient. As is inevitably the case with the Anna Anderson story, no two versions of these visits concur.

The elderly servant Volkov, who had lived at close quarters with the Imperial Family at Tsarskoe Selo, was the first visitor. The first day she would not speak to him, but he was able to see her walking in the hospital garden through a window. The second day, he actually met her face to face but was disconcerted to find she only spoke German, and his words, in Russian, had to be translated. She also said she did not know him, although Anna's few recollections of life before the revolution brought tears to the old man's eyes. Volkov later denied that she was the Grand Duchess in an interview with the Russian newspaper, *Poslednie Novosti*, published in the Baltic city of Reval, now Tallinn.

Volkov commented negatively on the people who were with Anna during his visit. 'The conduct of the people who surrounded Madame Tschaikovsky seemed to me very suspect. They intervened all the time, completed her inadequate answers and excused all her errors under the pretext that she was ill.'

Harriet von Rathlef-Keilman's continued presence at Anna's bedside was also cause for complaint by the Gilliards and the Grand Duchess Olga, and Harriet was later accused of masterminding a plot to defraud the Romanov family. Indefatigable in her care for the patient, she had no fear of approaching Anastasia's grand relations or anyone else to further her cause. Within a week of meeting Anna, she had followed in poor Clara Peuthert's footsteps and written to Grand Duke Ernst, only to be snubbed in a way that could leave no room for doubt. In her efforts to gain recognition for the 'little girl', as she always called Anna, Harriet stumbled on evidence that Anna's supporters considered the decisive reason for Ernst's refusal to acknowledge his 'niece'.

In conversation Harriet asked Anna when she had last seen her Uncle Ernie, as he was known in the Imperial Family. She was astounded by the reply. Anna affirmed that Ernst had made a secret trip in 1916, in the middle of the war, in order to persuade his brother-in-law, the Tsar, to conclude a separate peace treaty with Germany. Harriet, naturally thinking that Anna's knowledge of this trip would prove her authenticity, sent a friend to visit the Grand Duke. She never got to see the Grand Duke himself but had to make do with Count Kuno Hardenberg, Grand Marshal of the Hesse court. She reported that his polite attentions utterly changed when she repeated Anna's assertion that Grand Duke Ernst had made a secret trip to Russia.

The evidence, as with so much concerning Anna's plight, comes down to the Scottish verdict of 'not proven'. Anna's protagonists insist that the Grand Duke actually made such a visit, without the sanction of the German High Command, but with the discreet approval of Kaiser Wilhelm II. They have hearsay reports to back their claim but no documentary proof. They argue that the fall of the monarchy in Germany made it dangerous for the Grand Duke to acknowledge that he had carried out this mission, which could have been seen as treasonous. He was therefore determined to quash the testimony coming from Anna's lips.

The evidence in favour of Anna's story includes a statement from Crown Princess Cecile in a formal deposition in 1953. She said that she heard from her father-in-law, the Kaiser, that 'this visit was already known in our circles at the time.' It is also common knowledge that the Kaiser favoured a separate peace with Russia throughout 1916, which culminated in the unanswered letter that he sent to the Tsar. A formal peace offer was made to all the Allied powers by the German chancellor, Theobald von Bethmann-Hollweg, on 12 December 1916. Unsubstantiated evidence takes the form of undocumented sightings as well as eyewitnesses who say they saw the Grand Duke on his journey through Norway and Finland to the Imperial Court. But no concrete proof of his visit has surfaced either in Russian or German documents.

Although the approaches to the House of Hesse had led the claimant up a blind alley, this did not prevent Olga fulfilling her intention to come from Copenhagen. The Gilliards had tried to see Anna in the summer but found her too ill to respond to any of their inquiries. They returned in October, with Olga. The resulting series of encounters produced accounts that have become legendary for their mutual contradictions and incitement of family feuds. Both sides in the battle for Anna's identity have been so acrimonious that families have become divided over the question, blighting both the hopes of Anna's devoted supporters that she be recognized, while strengthening the resolve of her opponents.

Witnesses to the meetings say there is no doubt that both the Gilliards and Olga initially recognized Anna when they first arrived in Berlin. The visitors themselves subsequently denied this and said they were moved by compassion for the poor woman, whomever she might be. The fact is that the callers were clearly hesitant at first. Gilliard had last known Anastasia in Tobolsk, when, in the words of her mother, writing to her friend Anya Vyrubova: 'Anastasia is very fat like Maria used to be – big, thick-waisted, then short legs – I hope she grows more.' By 1925 Anna was emaciated and had had most of her front teeth extracted; she had just begun to recover from a severe illness and was still under the influence of morphine.

In addition Anna conducted the meetings in her customary manner. She was largely silent. This prevented false statements, but did not make a positive impression. Her reactions were later described by Gilliard as 'apathetic'. Their puzzlement at the apparition in the Berlin hospital was aptly summed up by Olga in a letter to the Danish ambassador to Berlin, Herluf Zahle: 'I can't tell you how fond I got of her – whoever she is. My feeling is that she is *not* the one she believes – but one can't *say she* is *not* as a fact – as there are still many strange and inexplicable facts not cleared up.'

Olga later categorically denied that she had recognized her and blamed the confusion on Anna's disappointed supporters, who point to the fact that Olga sent five sympathetic letters from Copenhagen and made Anna a gift of a silk shawl – evidence that she did feel Anna might be her niece.

In January 1926 the Danish newspaper *National Tidende* published an article stating that Olga did not recognize Anna and that the visitors could not find the 'slightest resemblance' in Anna to Grand Duchess Anastasia. In December of that same year, Olga wrote to Princess Irene of Prussia, saying that she did not recognize Anna. She also stated that the people surrounding Anna made more of her sympathy towards the patient than was in fact the case.

> They pretend that she recognized me, but I want to tell you how it all happened: they had warned her of my visit. She herself acknowledged that they had said: 'On Tuesday you will be very happy. Someone is coming from Denmark.' Then, obviously, she could imagine the rest and wait for 'her aunt'. She was unable to reply to any of the small and intimate questions which I put to her.

Olga said she felt great pity for 'this poor creature', enough to suspend her initial doubts, but as time went by she became sure that Anna was a pretender.

Anna's supporters generally cast Pierre Gilliard as the villain of the piece and have alleged that he was paid to discredit Anna by Grand Duke Ernst, who wished to hush up the revelation of his 'secret mission' to Russia. Had they known of his secreting of the Romanov treasure in Tobolsk and of the 'Gilliard List', Pierre Gilliard's itemized record of the jewels and valuables, they would have had an even stronger motive. The jewels were the personal property of the Romanovs and would be the inheritance of any real Anastasia. For Olga's betrayal, they point to fortune hunting of a different sort. Anna told her supporters that she disclosed details of a fortune deposited in a bank in England by the Tsar for his daughters. Olga and her sister, Grand Duchess Xenia, were thus aware of the wealth that awaited them if all the Tsar's children were dead. This mysterious bequest has never appeared, but it caused a great deal of indelicate bickering and mudslinging.

At first, Harriet von Rathlef-Keilman directed most of her displeasure at Gilliard, who returned the feelings in equal measure. He wrote articles denouncing Anna and later admitted that he had urged Olga to condemn her in the *National Tidende* article. Harriet published a book, *Anastasia*, the first of many that related Anna's life, and argued her case. This was later angrily denounced by Gilliard in his book, *La Fausse Anastasie*, published in Paris in 1929, where he ran through an impressive amount of 'proof' that she was a mere impostor. He particularly blames Harriet's hard work for the fact that Anna was taken seriously by anyone.

The problem was that the testimony from both sides is largely unprovable. For every piece of evidence against Anna, such as the fact that she appeared to speak neither Russian nor English, her supporters cite psychological explanations. They have not been slow to blame Anna's precarious existence and lack of acceptance by her royal relatives on a variety of unwholesome motives on the part of her detractors, rather than on the more simple explanation that she was seen as an unbalanced pretender. For instance, the Tsar's cousin Grand Duke Andrei expressed his opinion in no uncertain terms to the president of the Berlin Russian Refugee

Office, Sergius Botkin: 'Gilliard has at last exposed himself as a petty man capable of lying, but incapable of understanding that it is his own lies which betray him.' Anna's adversaries came up with many pernicious stories of their own.

What is more astonishing is the sway this 100-lb woman held over highly placed members of several royal families. For instance Grand Duke Ernst of Hesse had not been on speaking terms with Grand Duke Kyril of Russia since Victoria, Princess of Saxe-Coburg and Gotha, had left her German husband, brother of the Tsarina, to marry Kyril, cousin to the Tsar. They were, however, united in condemning Anna's claims. Meanwhile Ambassador Zahle, who had earlier held the prestigious post of President of the League of Nations, put his credibility on the line with the Danish Royal Family by continuing to support Anna, despite the displeasure of the Dowager Empress. All unknowingly, Anna would continue to divide friendships and families alike.

By March 1926 Anna was sufficiently recovered from the operation on her arm to go to Lugano to convalesce – with her expenses paid by the Danish Prince Waldemar through Ambassador Zahle. After difficulties in obtaining the necessary passport for Fraulein Unbekannt, she was accompanied there by the ever-faithful Harriet. Here another of Anna's infamous rows developed, with led Harriet to beg Baron Vassily Osten-Sacken, private secretary to Sergius Botkin at the Berlin Russian Refugee Office, to relieve her of her charge because the situation had become intolerable. Osten-Sacken concluded that the two women had simply got on each other's nerves. Harriet returned to Berlin, and Anna was put in the Stillachhaus Sanatorium at Oberstdorf, her sixth hospital in six years.

This famous quarrel with Harriet symbolized the pattern of Anna's existence. She managed to lose many of her most influential friends and 'ladies-in-waiting' throughout her life, treating them often with cruelty. Despite this despotic, tyrannical side to her nature, she possessed something in her personality that forever drew new followers, moths to the fame.

It was at this time that one of the few witnesses about whom no one appears to have said a bad word came into Anna's life. Dr Evgeny Botkin, the Tsar's personal physician, had been killed in Ekaterinburg with the Imperial Family. His daughter and son,

Tatiana and Gleb, escaped to France and the United States respectively. They became crucial attestants given their childhood acquaintance with Anastasia. Sergius Botkin, who was Tatiana's cousin, encouraged her to travel to Oberstdorf to identify Anna. It required only 24 hours for Tatiana to assert that Anna was the Grand Duchess. She never wavered in this conviction. Like many others she spoke of Anna's 'unforgettable eyes'. But she was also convinced by the way Anna behaved. When Tatiana mentioned an album containing pictures of the Imperial Family: 'She asked to be allowed to look at the pictures. Anyone who had seen her bent over those photographs, trembling and crying, "My mother! My mother!" would not have been able to doubt any longer.'

Tatiana attempted to interest the Romanovs in her new-found Grand Duchess. But all she achieved was the implacable hostility of nearly all the Romanov clan. She was put off with claims that the Dowager Empress must not be upset or that Anna was at the centre of a 'powerful, secret organization' that hoped to put her and her son on the Russian throne. This identification did coincide with the serialized publication of Harriet von Rathlef's book in *Berliner Nachtausgabe*. The high level of publicity led to photographs of Anastasia being on sale in kiosks all over Germany, and her plight became the stuff of general sympathy. The Romanovs could not ignore the fact that Anna had caught the public imagination.

Then, just as Ambassador Zahle announced the discontinuation of Anna's funding from Copenhagen after Grand Duchess Olga had decided she was not Anastasia, luck once more shone brightly. Duke George of Leuchtenberg, who was distantly related to the Tsar, invited her to stay at his home, Castle Seeon in Upper Bavaria. At first Anna was reluctant to accept his offer, but eventually did so on condition that Tatiana Melnik should accompany her. It was during her time there that Anna's opponents produced evidence that she was actually a Polish factory worker named Franziska Schanzkowska, who had been reported missing in Berlin during March 1920. This allegation was first made by a private detective, Martin Knopf, in the pay of the Duke of Hesse. Anna's supporters noted wryly that his discovery took a few weeks, while the Berlin police had failed to make this identification over seven years. This 'discovery' was countermanded by Harriet von Rathlef, who made the improbable assertion that the real Schanzkowska had been killed by a notorious criminal gang. Harriet later retracted that charge.

Anna's stay at Castle Seeon was a significant juncture in her life. The Duke of Leuchtenberg believed implicitly in her claims, although his wife wavered, and the children were divided on the issue. Her year with the Leuchtenbergs proved trying for the family, who had to endure Anna's increasingly volatile temperament. She spent much of her time locked up in her room, often suffering from severe headaches or from other emotional disturbances. The castle attracted those inevitable interlopers and curiosity seekers who wished to gawk at the 'princess'. A number of more exalted visitors did come to identify Anna, including Rasputin's assassin, Prince Felix Yusupov, who had married the Tsar's niece Irina. He categorically denounced Anna's claims.

In May 1927, three months after she arrived at Seeon, Anna had a visitor from the other end of the social scale: Franziska Schanzkowska's brother, Felix, was sent to identify her. Different characters, but the familiar inconclusive plot. The Duke of Leuchtenberg and his son Dmitry were both present at the meeting, which took place in nearby Wasserburg at an inn. The Duke said Anna did not recognize Felix, while his son was adamant that she did. Another version of events claims that Felix did identify Anna as his sister and initially said so. But later, according to this report, the two of them walked around the garden, and when they returned Felix was unwilling to sign an affidavit to that respect.

The document he did sign conceded that: 'There does exist a strong resemblance between her and my sister. The resemblance is strong when you look from the front, but not when you look from the side. ... Frau Tschaikovsky's speech as well as her general manner of expression is totally different from that of my sister Franziska.'

He then went on to say that unlike Anna, his sister had no deformities of the feet, had no scars or birthmarks, had a full set of teeth and spoke 'little Polish and good German'. This testimonial followed an earlier visit by Franziska's former landlady, Doris Wingender, who positively identified Anna as the Polish worker. Doris's testimony was subsequently muddied by accusations of bribery and payment for the story coming from the newspaper *Berliner Nachtausgabe*. Doris Wingender and her evidence became yet another cause of bitter acrimony between Anna's supporters and detractors.

While these scenes enacted in an attempt to establish Anna's identity once and for all did at times descend into farce, there was a far more serious current behind the bitter squabbling over Anna's claim to be Anastasia. The police could have arrested Anna for fraud, could have taken her identity papers or at least questioned her. There was also the danger that they would lock her up in an asylum as incurably insane. They did nothing. Officially, Anna remained Frau Tschaikovsky. There were reports that influence 'from above' stopped the police from doing this. There was also the added pressure from the Romanovs, who were encountering quite sufficient publicity for their taste from Harriet von Rathlef's pen in *Berliner Nachtausgabe*.

It is ironic that Anna's excursion to the inn to meet Felix Schanzkowska also afforded the opportunity for Gleb Botkin, Tatiana's brother, to catch what he considered to be his first glimpse of Anastasia since she had waved to him from the window of the governor's house in Tobolsk. Gleb had arrived from his new home in the United States, his expenses paid by the North American Newspaper Alliance in New York. Anna refused to meet with Gleb for several days, fearing that he would write about her in the newspapers. She had previously denied that she knew Harriet von Rathlef was writing a book about her and claimed to abhor the uproar and headlines that her case was attracting.

After the initial 'casual meeting' arranged by Grand Duke Georgy, Anna agreed to see Gleb Botkin. This encounter was the real turning-point in Anna's life as a pretender. The fact that Gleb earned a precarious living as a writer and designer to support his wife and five children did not deter him from putting his duty to Anna first. In his book, *The Real Romanovs*, he was remarkably critical of the Imperial Family and the world of the Russian court, which he likens to that of the Sleeping Beauty:

A sort of enchanted fairy-land to which only a small number

of people had the right of entry. . . . Ostensibly everybody in Tsarskoe Selo adored the Imperial family, and I myself, being only a child, naturally believed the Sovereigns and their children to be superhumanly perfect in every respect. Later I had of course to give up that illusion, but keen as my eventual disappointment was, I still feel that the world at large has never been very just towards the last rulers of the Russian Empire.

He criticized his father for his obeisance to court etiquette, and yet he called Anna 'Your Imperial Highness' throughout her life. This extraordinary zeal, matched by his disillusion with the fate of Russia under the last Tsar and his wholehearted embrace of America and evident admiration for his new country's democratic institutions, may have led him to inappropriate actions on Anna's behalf. While the Romanov family tended to prefer that publicity be kept as low-key as possible, Gleb outraged many of Anna's other supporters, including his sister Tatiana, by his headstrong and public approach to solving her affairs. And yet, while he acted the perfect courtier, he also had a close personal relationship with Anna. His wife, Nadine, never met her. 'She was kind of never invited,' commented his daughter Marina Schweitzer. Anna and Gleb would go to the cinema together and share long-standing private jokes. Marina Schweitzer said Anna dominated her father's life, with her mother's tolerant understanding: 'He had to, she was the Grand Duchess.' This close friendship did not prevent his banishment when Anna quarrelled with him, and there was a period of ten years when Gleb and Anna had no communication.

At this time paranoia, which was to become part and parcel of both Anna's life and those of her defenders, increasingly came to the fore. Anna took seriously alleged threats to her life. Gleb became convinced that Anna would only be safe from her enemies if she moved to America. His articles there had attracted considerable attention to her cause, and consequently he returned home to the United States, determined to find the finance necessary to bring her over. He finally found a sponsor in the attractive shape of Xenia Leeds, the princess daughter of Grand Duke Georgy. Princess Xenia had married the wealthy industrialist, William B.

Leeds, and despite difficulties she encountered when Anna stayed with her and also with her friend, Annie Jennings, she remained faithful to Anna.

Anna's departure was greeted with relief by the Leuchtenbergs, who by this time had become exhausted with the task of looking after her. Pierre Gilliard, in contrast, was almost hysterical at the thought of losing the lady to America, just when he was poised to unmask her as the fraudulent Franziska Schanzkowska.

Just as Anna's enemies were fortified by the allegation that she was Franziska Schanzkowska, Grand Duke Andrei met Anna in Paris and positively identified her. As the case gained notoriety, the Romanov family had to suffer more and more family disputes, many of which were brought into the public domain by Gleb. His accusations against the apparent indifference of the Romanovs were motivated by his desire to expose the base motives of family members regarding Anna, for he considered it self-evident that she was the Grand Duchess Anastasia.

Anna arrived in New York to be met by Gleb and a hustling scrum of journalists demanding an answer to their shouted, disingenuous question: 'Are you the Grand Duchess or just a phoney?' Anna spent the first few weeks of her visit with Annie Jennings, at her residence on Park Avenue, and became a celebrated guest among Long Island's rich and famous and wannabees. She met a wide number of people, including the pianist Serge Rachmaninov, who was to help her in the future. She then went on to spend a quieter six months with Princess Xenia, at her residence at Oyster Bay.

Xenia was another witness who had played with Anastasia as a child. Her approbation of Anna's claim never wavered. In an affidavit prepared for the German court case she said: 'One of the most convincing elements of her personality was a completely unconscious acceptance of her identity. She was herself at all times and never gave the slightest impression of acting a part. I am firmly convinced that the claimant is, in fact, Grand Duchess Anastasia of Russia.'

Xenia's faith in Anna's authenticity was reinforced by two incidents. She recognized the voice of Prince Dmitry, son of Grand Duke Aleksandr Mikhailovich, as a member of the

Romanov family. She heard him playing tennis without being able to see him and accused Xenia of breaking her promise not to invite the Romanovs to the house while Anna was staying there. The second incident involved Xenia's four-year-old daughter, Nancy. Anna burst into tears on seeing her, saying that, dressed in a sailor's cap, the little girl reminded her of her lost brother, the Tsarevich.

During the early stages of her American tour, Anna avoided Gleb, convinced with Princess Xenia that he had given too much publicity to the case. Pressure mounted with the tenth anniversary of the Romanov assassination in July 1928, the date by which lawyers advised that Anna should put in a claim for the tsarist fortune allegedly lodged in British, German and American banks. Distribution of the money to surviving relatives could not be undertaken until ten years after the assassination, as the deaths of the Tsar and his immediate family had never been proved. However, Anna was engaged in one of her inevitable quarrels, this time with Xenia. Supposedly, Xenia broke a promise to take Anna to visit the Dowager Empress in Copenhagen. Gleb claimed that Xenia, together with the Tsar's sisters, Grand Duchesses Xenia and Olga, offered to support Anna for life if she dropped her claim. Princess Xenia denied ever saying this and would later only say that lies and confusion had mixed up the issue.

Almost by default, Anna fell to the charge of Gleb. The pianist Rachmaninov paid for her to stay for four months at the Garden City Hotel, Long Island, where she was registered for the first time under the name of Anna Anderson, a subterfuge designed to confuse local journalists. Gleb assumed the identity of her brother, in order to be able to visit her more freely at the hotel. He also retained a lawyer, Edward Fallows, and set up the Grandanor Corporation, which would raise funds to pay the attorney, who would investigate and seek to obtain her alleged fortune. Grandanor, an acronym of Grand Duchess Anastasia of Russia, supplied ammunition to Anna's enemies, by giving them the pretext of labelling her as an adventuress, while tarnishing Gleb with the same brush. In fact Anna's childlike nature meant that she took little interest in legal or financial affairs, while Gleb, to prove that he had no mercenary intent, announced that all revenues derived from this enterprise would go to the Red Cross.

Anna had spent two months at the Garden City Hotel, when the Dowager Empress died on 13 October 1928. Within three days of her death, 12 members of the Romanov family (out of a total of 44 who were living scattered around the world) formally recognized the assassination of the entire Imperial Family. Members of the Hesse family had published their declaration just two days earlier. The statement went on to denounce Anna as an impostor, saying 'our sense of duty compels us to state that the story is only a fairy tale. The memory of our dear departed would be tarnished if we allowed this fantastic story to spread and gain credence.' The indecent haste with which the statement was put out left a very bad taste in the mouths of Anna's supporters.

For Gleb it came as a bitter pill. It served to reinforce the suspicion that Anastasia's aunts, the Grand Duchesses Xenia and Olga, refused to acknowledge Anna because they wanted exclusive access to the alleged bank accounts. Gleb's rebuttal, which he sent to the Associated Press for publication, is extraordinary for its imprudence and strong language.

> Twenty-four hours did not pass after the death of your mother . . . when you hastened to take another step in your conspiracy to defraud your own niece . . .. You obviously knew that her late Majesty would not have permitted the issuance by you of such a statement and only waited for her Majesty's death to make it public. It makes a gruesome impression that even at your mother's death-bed your foremost worry must have been the desire to defraud your niece and it is appalling to see that you did not even have the common decency of waiting if only a few days after your mother's death before publicly resuming your ignoble fight . . . .
>
> I refuse to believe that you are actually convinced that . . . Mrs Tschaikovsky is not Grand Duchess Anastasia. You know very well that she remembers the slightest details of her childhood, that she possesses all her physical signs including birth-marks, that her handwriting is at present the same as it had been in her youth . . .. That you are personally convinced of her real identity . . . is evident enough from the fact that in the course of your whole fight against her you have never

made a truthful statement nor mentioned a single fact, but resort exclusively to the vilest slander and most preposterous lies.

Before the wrong which Your Imperial Highness is committing pales even the gruesome murder of the Emperor, his family and my father by the Bolsheviks. It is easier to understand a crime committed by a gang of crazed and drunken savages than the calm, systematic, endless persecution of one of your own family – an unfortunate, suffering and perfectly innocent young woman – the Grand Duchess Anastasia Nikolaevna . . . whose only fault is that being the only rightful heir to the late Emperor she stands in the way of her greedy and unscrupulous relatives.

This extraordinary public attack was met by silence on the part of the Romanovs. But it was not forgotten. When Anna's tissue sample was being disputed in court in Virginia 66 years later, the name of Gleb Botkin was nearly sufficient to induce the Romanovs to enter the case. In justification of his action, Gleb said he had been advised that if the Copenhagen Statement were left unanswered, then the United States government would have to accept it as true and deport Anna back to Germany as an impostor. He also claimed that he had been recommended to make his reply libellous so that the Romanovs would have to sue him if what he said was untrue.

Gleb's heightened nerves may have also played a role. Anna and her entire entourage were afraid of conspiracy, attempted murder or kidnap, either by their enemies, by the authorities or by the Bolsheviks. While some of these fears were paranoia, Marina Schweitzer recalls her parents telling her that sometime during the 1930s someone did come to their house with the express intention of murdering her father, Gleb. It is perhaps not surprising that Anna's supporters saw conspiracies round every corner.

It is also indicative of the whole affair that both sides accused the other of harbouring base motives. While Gleb attacked the Romanovs for having their eyes on the fortune, Anna's enemies cast the aspersion back to Gleb and Anna, an allegation fuelled by the foundation of the Grandanor Corporation. Under the articles of the Corporation, Fallows, who was working unpaid, would receive one-quarter of all the monies recovered under $400,000 and then 10 per cent of all the rest, while the shareholders were scheduled to recoup five times their original investment. While such an arrangement clearly left the protagonists wide open to ridicule, the idea was to raise money by subscription in order to be able to take the case to court.

Shortly after the Corporation was established Anna quarrelled with Gleb and returned to live with Annie Jennings in January 1929. Gleb wrote, in *The Woman Who Rose Again,* that Anna demanded his complete devotion and attention, which he was finding increasingly difficult to give, and when he contracted a severe bout of influenza, she suspected that the 'illness was a diplomatic one . . . felt deeply hurt and decided to move to Miss Jennings' house'. Gleb's description of their rift echoes an earlier encounter he described in *The Real Romanovs* between his father and the Tsarina. In the period before the war his father, Evgeny, then personal physician to the Tsar, contracted typhoid fever and was ill for some time. 'Happily he recovered and we went on a trip abroad, but for a long time he remained weak and irritable; moreover he was worried by a sudden coolness on the part of the Sovereigns who, although very attentive and solicitous at first, later grew to begrudge him his prolonged illness.'

Anna's second stay at Annie Jennings' house was not fortuitous. She behaved tyrannically and treated everyone in the household as though they were her own personal servants. By the spring of 1930 Anna herself was taken in by a true impostor, Jill Cossley-Batt, who claimed she was really the Dowager Countess of Huntingdon, currently on special assignment for *The Times.* In fact Cossley-Batt set out to 'capture' Anna by attempting to turn her against her hosts. By the time the scam was revealed, Anna was at her wits' end and, after accidentally killing one of her parakeets, she became hysterical and was forcibly interred in a mental institution. By August 1931 her American friends bundled her back to yet another asylum, this time in Germany, at Ilten, near Hannover. In such ignominious circumstances, Anna's first New World adventure came to an end.

CHAPTER SIX

No Mere Adventuress

ANNA'S PATHETIC RETURN to Europe in 1931 heralded the start of a new life in Germany. She may not have been blessed by wealth or the glamorous life of New York, but she did find a new protector. This time he came in the shape of another distant relative of the Romanovs, Prince Frederick of Saxe-Altenburg. His sister had married Prince Sigismund of Prussia, the son of Anastasia's aunt Irene, who had failed to recognize Anna in 1922. Prince Frederick was also distantly related to the Romanovs – his mother was a cousin of the Dowager Empress, while his aunt Elizabeth had married Grand Duke Constantine of Russia. Frederick was interested in archaeology and mystic philosophy, a lively mercurial person about whom his sister commented: 'Oh Frederick, he might be upstairs or there again, he might be in Istanbul.'

He first met Anna when undertaking a mission for his brother-in-law, Prince Sigismund, who had last met the Romanov family before the war. Prince Sigismund devised a list of 18 'test questions', which he said could only be answered by the authentic Anastasia. In typical fashion, Anna became difficult about the proposed meeting and wondered humorously how she could know that he was indeed a prince of Saxe-Altenburg and not, perhaps, a Polish factory worker. She finally agreed to meet him, took five days to think about the questions and finally answered them all correctly.

This was enough for Prince Frederick, who then served her devotedly for the next 50 years. He was instrumental in finding her new friends, protectors and allies and was also the lynch-pin in seeing her through the German lawsuit, the longest-running civil legal action in German history. Litigation began in 1938 and continued intermittently until 1970. Ostensibly, the lawsuit was filed contesting the distribution of tsarist funds held in a German bank to Romanov relatives. Underpinning the entire suit was the need to provide legal proof of Anna's Romanov identity.

The question of Anna's inheritance and the prospect of the alleged tsarist riches had run through the disputes about her identity like a silver thread. Her own attitude to the law courts was similar to her attitude towards the various 'courtiers' and visitors who wanted to help her and prove her identity. She would alternately be indifferent and obstructive, followed by bouts of intense activity, firing her lawyers, re-employing them, cooperating or not as the mood took her. This behaviour, although frustrating to her supporters, tended to reinforce their faith that she was Anastasia. If she were merely a fortune hunter, they argued, surely she would have exerted herself more purposefully, just as they thought she would have attempted to make a more favourable impression upon her royal visitors, such as Grand Duchess Olga and Princess Irene.

It is not surprising that various witnesses thought there must be money deposited in overseas banks by Tsar Nicholas II, who before the revolution was one of the richest men in the world. The opulence of the Romanov court had become the stuff of legend; the Grand Balls attended by the Imperial Family and a mere 3000 guests; the exquisite and fabulously expensive Fabergé eggs, which the Tsar presented to the Tsarina every Easter; the yacht called the *Standart*, which King Edward VII of England coveted when he met the Tsar at Cowes on the Isle of Wight; and the family jewels, some of which were found sewn into the underwear of the Grand Duchesses when they were murdered at Ekaterinburg.

Despite the fact that the Tsar was an autocratic ruler, he did not own everything in Russia. As William Clarke, who has written numerous financial books on the City of London, details in his book, *The Lost Fortune of the Tsars*, there was a strict division between the wealth of the state and the private resources of the family. On abdication, the Tsar had lost many of the trappings of royalty, including state jewels, the royal cars and the royal palaces, which strictly speaking belonged to Russia, for use by the Imperial Family as head of state. The family's personal fortune was still significant. In 1917 Prime Minister Aleksandr Keremsky and Prince Georgy Lvov, as first head of the Provisional Government, had estimated the family's private wealth at some 14 million roubles or £933,000, while Count Pavel Benckendorff and Count Rostovtsev, on behalf of the Tsar, had stated that the family's total resources amounted to between 12.5 million roubles and 17.5 million roubles or between £833,000 and £1,666,000. These estimates included accounts and investments both at home and abroad, but it had proved impossible to verify these figures. By the time the family arrived in Ekaterinburg, the Bolshevik government had vastly reduced this fortune. Their personal accounts, in common with other 'rich' people, had been nationalized, and on 13 July 1918, a few days before the massacre, the government had passed a decree converting the properties of the Romanov family back to the nation. By the time of their deaths, the family wealth consisted of the jewellery they had managed to smuggle with them and any monies or property held by them abroad.

The Romanovs who managed to escape Russia, especially the Dowager Empress Marie, brought jewellery and other effects with them, but by the standards of the pre-revolutionary Imperial Court, they lived in relative poverty. The Dowager Empress and her youngest daughter, Grand Duchess Olga, lived in Copenhagen relying on the goodwill of the English and Danish royal families. Grand Duchess Xenia lived at Frogmore Cottage in Windsor as a permanent resident and received an allowance from the English Royal Family. Xenia had reached such a low financial ebb during the war that Queen Elizabeth, the Queen Mother, sent her food hampers, although on Xenia's death in 1960, she left an estate worth more than £100,000. Olga later moved to Canada and died in poverty above a barber shop in Toronto.

In contrast to their previous lifestyle, these close relatives of the Tsar had fallen on hard times indeed. Accusations have been levelled that Queen Mary and others swindled the Romanovs out of the true value of their jewels, as they were gradually sold off to meet their bills. Many of the Romanov gems are worn by members of the English Royal Family to this day, but if they acquired them through sharp practice, there is equal evidence that they helped their Romanov cousins financially. In these circumstances, it would be surprising if the Tsar's mother and two sisters did not do everything in their power to recover money and property deposited outside Russia by the Tsar. In fact there were only two successful cases lodged by these immediate relatives of the Tsar. Other members of the Romanov family had varying success in trying to be recompensed for property they owned before the revolution.

In 1928 Grand Duchess Xenia brought an action against the Finnish state – Finland, formerly a province of Russia, had become an independent state in 1917. In 1892 her father Tsar Alexander III had paid 100,000 roubles for property in the village of Halila, including the Halila sanitorium, which had subsequently been handed over to Empress Marie's Foundation in 1900 by Nicholas. After six years and following the intervention of the Bank of England, Finland wrote a cheque to Xenia and her relatives covering the value of the property.

The second case involved deposits held by the Mendelssohn Bank in Germany. In 1934 the Central District Court in Berlin granted the Romanovs access to the Tsar's remaining assets in Germany, comprising deposits held by the Mendelssohn Bank, which before the First World War had enjoyed long-standing business with the Russian government. The heirs were recognized as the Grand Duchesses Xenia and Olga, Countess Brassova, widow of the Tsar's brother Mikhail, the Marchioness of Milford Haven who was Princess Victoria of Hesse, the Tsarina's sister and her other siblings, Princess Irene of Prussia and Grand Duke Ernst of Hesse. The original value of the investments in Berlin remains unknown, but estimates put it between 7 million and 14 million roubles. However, wartime inflation and the hyper-inflation of the early 1920s had taken its toll. By the time the certificate of inheritance was issued in 1938, the value of the account was put at between £20,000 and £25,000.

This was not the fabled fortune discussed and dreamed of by Anna's friends and enemies alike. If this was all that the advisers and lawyers of the Romanov family were able to find in the West, what had happened to the rest of the Tsar's gold? Is it still entombed in the Bank of England as some of Anna's biographers believe, or did the stories of the Tsar's fabulous wealth become exaggerated fables, its worth multiplying with the years?

The litigation to gain the money from the Mendelssohn Bank provided Anna's supporters with the key they needed to establish her identity. She finally contested the certificate of inheritance in court on 17 August 1938. As the sums involved were relatively small, it can be asserted that the litigants were not particularly interested in cashing in on Anna's potential wealth. Indeed Grand Duchess Xenia, who has in many accounts been portrayed as avariciously seeking to defraud her 'niece', did not even bother to collect her share of the Mendelssohn account.

The question of the remaining missing fortune occupied the minds and imaginations of many of Anna's partisans. The fact of the matter may be that it simply did not exist outside Russia. At the outbreak of the First World War in 1914, the patriotic Tsar Nicholas II announced that he would be withdrawing all his funds deposited in banks overseas to help pay for the war effort, and he ordered all Russia's aristocratic families to do the same. He could not withdraw funds from the Mendelssohn Bank as it was located in Germany, the enemy power. Gleb Botkin confirms this premise in his book *The Real Romanovs*:

> During our exile in Tobolsk, the Emperor told my father that he had used up all his personal funds in England paying for the munitions bought in England for the Russian Army – a patriotic sacrifice for which the Emperor had been highly praised at the time by the few people who were aware of it.

Grand Duke Alexander, husband of Grand Duchess Xenia, wrote in the 1930s that 'beginning with the summer of 1915, there was not a farthing left in the Tsar's name in the Bank of England, nor in any other bank outside Russia.'

There are many independent reports that not only did the Tsar carry this out but also many of Russia's richest families followed suit. Prince Felix Yusupov, a member of one of Russia's richest families before the war, writes that after the revolution they found themselves left with a London apartment and a villa in

Switzerland. 'At the beginning of the war, my parents had transferred back to Russia all the money they had had abroad. With the house on Lake Geneva, all that was left of our wealth was the jewellery and valuables that we had been able to take with us when we left the Crimea, and the two Rembrandts.'

Despite this evidence that the funds had been siphoned back to Russia in 1914, Anna's supporters believed her tale about the special bank account in England set up by the Tsar to provide dowries for his four daughters. Prince David Chavchavadze, a former CIA agent who is also a descendant of Nicholas I of Russia and the last Georgian king, has written recently in his book, *Crowns and Trenchcoats* (1990), a recollection that sounds uncannily similar to Anna's testimony on the existence of an account dedicated to the four Grand Duchesses. Chavchavadze is reporting an anecdote told by his father, Prince Paul Chavchavadze, based on a conversation with the Tsar's last Finance Minister, Peter Bark:

> Bark told my father the following: there had been an account in England under the code name OTMA (Olga, Tatiana, Maria, Anastasia). During the war Nicholas II ordered Bark to withdraw this account and bring it back to Russia as an example to society to do the same thing. Bark tried to talk the Emperor out of this, and he said it was the only time he ever saw Nicholas II lose his temper. The withdrawal was accomplished, and most, but not all, of society followed suit.

Gleb Botkin implicitly believed Anna's tale of a special account at the Bank of England, or in a bank in England, depending on which account is retold. When Gleb told Anna that his father had reported the Tsar had no money in England, she replied that: 'My father had used all his own money to pay for the munitions Russia bought from England during the War. The money he told us about was our money. He had it deposited shortly before the war for my sisters and myself.'

Gleb could only explain the apparent indifference shown to Anna by the Tsar's sisters, Grand Duchesses Xenia and Olga, by asserting they wanted to keep the Tsar's money for themselves. Anna herself said she had told Grand Duchess Olga, during her visit in 1925, that the Tsar had opened an account either in a bank in England or in the Bank of England. Some of Anna's supporters say that Olga's attitude towards her 'niece' changed at that time. Others report that she first mentioned this account in 1925 to Herluf Zahle, who followed up the information by contacting representatives of the Bank of England. Anna later signed a statement, dated 15 December 1928, asserting her knowledge of the account.

> After our family had left St Petersburg and were in exile at Ekaterinburg in Siberia, very shortly before the deaths of the other members of my family, my father told my three sisters and myself that before the World War in 1914, he had deposited in the Bank of England five million roubles each for my three sisters and myself.
>
> In 1925, when I was in Berlin, the Danish Ambassador Zahle at Berlin whom I had told of this deposit of monies made official inquiries and very shortly afterwards informed me that he had received an answer to his inquiry, that there were monies on deposit for my sisters and myself in the Bank of England, but the Bank was unwilling to state the amount.

If Zahle was the first on the money trail, he did not leave many clues behind him. In response to all the enquiries made to the Bank of England, officials have drawn a blank. They have no record of correspondence from Zahle and have denied repeatedly that such an account exists. Zahle prepared an extensive report of his enquiries into Anna's case for the Danish Royal Family, but this file has never been opened for public perusal, as the crown states that it deals purely with personal family matters. Philip Remy, the German television producer, claims to be the first to examine the section of Zahle's papers lodged with the Ministry of Foreign Affairs, Copenhagen, but says that it contains little that is new. He says it includes documentation that Zahle first believed in Anna's imperial identity but later changed his mind. The rest of Zahle's report will presumably remain a secret until well into the next century when the 100-year rule on crown papers expires.

● ● ●

Zahle was not the only investigator on the trail of the Tsar's millions. In America they were also busy. Edward Fallows, hired by Anna as her attorney under the terms of the Grandanor Corporation, made detailed enquiries about possible tsarist deposits and received what he considered to be equivocal responses from the Bank of England. An American lawyer, Fanny Holtzmann, who had successfully advised Princess Irina Yusupov, the Tsar's niece, in her suit for damages against Metro-Goldwyn-Mayer over their film about Rasputin, was employed by Irina's mother, Grand Duchess Xenia. Holtzmann also could find no convincing evidence that any of the Tsar's personal fortune remained in banks outside Russia.

Gleb had poisoned the atmosphere by accusing the Romanovs so blatantly and publicly of persecuting Anna for pecuniary motives. In the climate of the times it is not surprising that he would have thought there had to be money somewhere. The *New York Times* reported in 1929 that the Tsar had been worth between $10 billion and $30 billion, and estimated there could still be properties and investments worth up to $1 billion. At the time of Tsar Nicholas's abdication in 1917, the *New York Times* asserted that the Tsar's annual income was $42 million. This was officially refuted, but the newspapers a few weeks later put his wealth at $9 billion, including investments in US railway stock. These figures can be seen, especially in hindsight, as 'guesstimates', but the number of noughts after them certainly was sufficient to fire imaginations and to spark the assumption that 'there is no smoke without fire.'

The investigations of Edward Fallows did little to cast any light on the matter. On his first visit to Europe in 1929, Fallows met with Arthur Gallop, a partner in Freshfields, Leese and Munns, solicitors to the Bank of England. Fallows encountered the normal rejoinder of any applicant to the Bank, that 'we are not permitted to disclose the existence or amount of a deposit except to an accredited depositor.' This non-committal reply was enough to encourage Fallows that the funds did exist. What was necessary was to prove Anna's identity as a legal claimant. His visit to Berlin was more fruitful. A director of the Mendelssohn Bank, Dr Paul Kempner, confirmed that the Tsar had deposited several million roubles before the war to invest in German securities. Fallows later pursued various leads in American banks, but these all came to nothing.

During his various enquiries Fallows was subject to numerous approaches from White Russians, who claimed to know about secret bank accounts in England, Germany, Switzerland and America. For instance Aaron Simanovitch, Rasputin's former secretary, said he could reveal the source of $17 million lodged in a New York bank, if Fallows would do a deal with him. In Europe a Russian lawyer tried to persuade Fallows to share the proceeds of various accounts, an offer he had previously made to the Grand Duchesses Xenia and Olga.

The fact that Grand Duchess Xenia was not tempted by any of these dubious deals and profit-sharing schemes can most likely be put down to the judicious advice of the tsar's finance minister, Peter Bark. He had been instrumental during the war in providing shipments of gold bullion and other financial commitments to pay for needed war supplies. His professional conduct in negotiations during the war made him known and respected by officials at the Bank of England, who set him up as head of the newly reconstructed Anglo-Austrian Bank in London. He was also appointed as adviser to various Central and East European banks, which the Governor of the Bank of England, Montagu Norman, saw as vehicles for rehabilitating the economies of Central Europe, and was consulted over the complex series of debts incurred by the break-up of the Austro-Hungarian Empire. Finally in 1926 the Bank of England set up the Anglo-International Bank, and Peter Bark was appointed managing director.

The name of Bark became anathema to Anna's supporters because of her veiled accusations that he knew of the existence of the special account set up by the Tsar for his four daughters. Gleb Botkin reports that she came close to naming him when she told him about the special account in 1928.

> He [the Tsar] told us that he had not felt it his right to touch that money because it was ours. And he also told us that it was a camouflaged account of which nobody knew anything, except the man who had deposited the money, and which could not be found by simply examining the bank's books. He told us the name of that man who knew about it, and the

amount . . . I do not remember the man's name. I tried and tried to remember it, but never could. All I do remember is that it was not a Russian name, but a Germanic name – a very short name . . . a one syllable name.'

James Blair Lovell, author of *Anastasia The Lost Princess*, claimed that in tape recordings Anna said the accounts could only be accessed through a password, which was a man's name, 'a short, perhaps Germanic name with an "a" in the middle, and that it had "something to do with a tree".' This rather disingenuous and heavy hint, clumsily pointing the accusatory finger at Bark, led Lovell to believe that Bark had siphoned off funds from the account to set up the Anglo-International Bank. Lovell proceeded to accuse the British Royal Family and the Bank of England of colluding with Bark's supposed use of the dowry money and of paying an allowance to Grand Duchess Xenia to ensure her silence.

In these claims Lovell was following the path set by Fallows. The basic allegation of Anna's powerful relatives conspiring to rob Anna of her inheritance was certainly on the mind of Fallows as he diligently continued his work on behalf of Anna. His work mainly contributed to the paranoia and flood of accusations emanating from Anna's 'court', for there was no hard evidence to substantiate these theories. As William Clarke details in his book, Peter Bark purchased only 200 shares, when the Anglo-International Bank was set up, in order to qualify as a director. He later bought more, but the bank's initial capital came from a variety of City firms and partly from the Bank of England. Peter Bark was paid a salary for his services. When he first arrived in England he had had to approach his former banking contacts for loans and later had to raise a loan to pay for hospital expenses. When he died in 1937, his will noted that his entire estate came to £14,126, hardly the estate of a man who had siphoned off the Grand Duchesses' fortune.

By the time Edward Fallows died in 1940, his family were destitute. During the 1930s they had resorted to appeals for him to leave Anna's business in Europe and come home. He had only succeeded in formally establishing the Tsar's accounts in Germany, which in any case became public knowledge when the

Tsar's relatives claimed the residue of the account in the Mendelssohn Bank. He had also suffered the indignity of being fired and then rehired by Anna, all of which just seemed to have stiffened his resolve to pursue what he considered her rights. Although he had signed the terms of the Grandanor Corporation, which would have given him ample remuneration if the fortune had been found, he worked for Anna for more than ten years without pay. Further controversy was to surround his work even after his death. His daughter later refused to hand over his dossier of evidence on Anna's case, perhaps hoping to sell the information, or possibly as some sort of revenge on the fortunes of the woman who had occupied her father's time and energies for such a long period.

There were, of course, banks, such as Barings in London, which held Russian deposits, and possibly banks in Switzerland, but all attempts to locate the Tsar's private funds have come to nothing. There were indeed deposits from the tsarist government, which successive Soviet governments have claimed as belonging rightfully to them. Western bankers have generally responded to Soviet requests for recompense that no funds can be disbursed without the Soviet government taking on responsibility for tsarist debts, a stalemate that was to be resurrected during various discussions on trade expansion and other developments during the succeeding years of Soviet power. What is undeniable is that these funds belonged to the government rather than to the Imperial Family.

While Edward Fallows was attempting to solve the conundrum of the tsarist accounts, Anna was ensconced in the nursing home at Ilten near Hannover. Annie Jennings and other Americans were paying for her stay there, during which time she recovered from her New World experiences. Initially she besieged the poor Fallows with letters demanding the arrest of Miss Jennings for forcibly sending her back to Europe. She also sent a conciliatory note to Princess Xenia, coming as close as she ever would to apologizing for quarrelling with her former protector. By this time, Princess Xenia was divorced from William Leeds and had moved to a small house at Syosset.

During her time at Ilten she was examined by Dr Hans Willige, whose psychiatric assessment echoed those made by German doctors in the earlier sanitoria. His report, kept with the Fallows papers, now in the Houghton Library, Harvard University, and quoted in writer and historian Peter Kurth's *Anastasia: The Riddle of Anna Anderson*, gives one of the clearest intimations into her psychology.

> The lack of any symptoms of insanity was proved so conclusively during the very first examination that we were already able to tell Frau Tschaikovsky on the second day that she was not insane and not in need of treatment in an institution . . .. Hers is, however, a personality of unique character, consisting to a high degree of a strong willfulness, a highly egocentric outlook and an interior haughtiness. [I cannot] entirely abandon the diagnosis of a psychopathic condition; after all, one might well designate so peculiar a personality as Frau Tschaikovsky obviously is . . . as psychopathic . . .. She had good reason to assume she was being persecuted. To be able to [impersonate another] would require a surpassing intelligence, an extraordinary degree of self-control and an ever-alert discipline – all qualities Frau Tschaikovsky in no way possesses.

This assessment confirms that of most of her admirers, who speak, often in coded terms, of her 'eccentricities' and the difficult side of her nature. It also attempts to explain the causes of her paranoia, which come into play throughout her life, although it is at times difficult to know whether she fuelled the corresponding pathological fears expressed by her supporters or whether they added to hers.

As her most ardent supporters generally believed her assertions, it is understandable that Gleb Botkin's impetuous assumption that the Grand Duchesses Xenia and Olga were attempting to defraud her of her fortune stems from her account of the Tsar's conversation to his daughters in Ekaterinburg. The doctor's assessment of her 'strong willfulness' is also interesting in that as time went on, particularly in her old age, she does appear to have played with the beliefs of her supporters, changing details in her story, perhaps unconsciously, but nonetheless seeming to test their fidelity or credulity.

The last part of the psychiatric report assumed that Anna was incapable of deliberately impersonating the Grand Duchess Anastasia. There is no evidence that even her most implacable enemies believed that – even Pierre Gilliard in his book refers to the 'poor invalid' and instead vents his spleen on Harriet von Rathlef. It is safe to assume that she herself believed she was Anastasia. There never seems to have been any discussion among the Romanov or Hesse families that she should be charged with fraud, despite Prince Yusupov's assessment that she was 'just an adventuress, a sick hysteric and a frightful playactress'. Most of her opponents who met her were puzzled by her air of authenticity and struck by her knowledge of the Imperial Court and Russia, but rarely did they see her as deliberately out for what she could get, a significant corollary to the long search for the tsarist fortune. And while the doctor may say that she was not intelligent enough to carry out a role, the numbers and dedication of her supporters indicate what a fascinating personality she possessed. They clearly loved being in her company and helping her in any way, despite the 'storms' that the downside of her nature would invariably bring about.

Her time at Ilten brought her increasing fame as yet more articles, speculation and material were published about her, and they in turn brought her a greater following. Apart from Prince Frederick who played a major role in her life, she made other significant friendships. Paul and Gertrude Madsack, who published a sympathetic article about her life in their newspaper, the *Hannoverscher Anzeiger*, were later to befriend her to the extent of paying for an apartment where she lived for many years. She was not lacking in visitors from high society either. Empress Hermine, the second wife of the deposed German Kaiser Wilhelm II, came to see her. This was a significant meeting, not only because the tacit acceptance of Anna's claim by the Kaiser meant that many aristocratic German doors became open to her. It also, by implication, reinforced Anna's assertion that Germany had helped her during her time in Bucharest after she had escaped from Russia. Many assumed that the Kaiser would have known about this and that is why he indirectly endorsed her claim. During the next five years she was to stay with many aristocratic families:

Prince William of Hessen-Philippsthal; Baroness Monica von Miltitz; Baron von Kleist Restov; and Princess Reuss.

After leaving the Ilten sanatorium in 1932 she enjoyed uncharacteristic prosperity, visiting German aristocrats and well-wishers alike. Her return to Germany had been greeted by widespread publicity, resulting in offers of help from friends and strangers. However, her first foray into the outside world ended ignominiously. She stayed a few weeks with the Heyden-Rynsch family in Eisenach, but then quarrelled, walked to a telephone box and called the devoted Harriet von Rathlef. After being sent packing from Lugano six years earlier, Harriet was only too pleased to bring Anna back to Berlin and find a suitable place for her to live. Their renewed friendship only lasted a year as Harriet died unexpectedly from a ruptured appendix at the age of 44. Anna was also taken up again by the Zahles, who proved as kind and caring to her as they had in the past.

She was, however, still dogged by controversy. Her relative security was shattered by an article on 4 September 1932 in the London tabloid, *News of the World*, under the headline IMPOSTOR UNMASKED! 'PRINCESS' CONFESSES SHE IS FRAUD. The sensational article alleged that Anna was a Romanian actress who had been hypnotized to play the role of Anastasia by a 'former manservant in the Romanov household'. The article concluded that the Romanovs would not take criminal proceedings against her, so long as she signed a full confession before entering a convent. Far from the Romanovs suing her, the newspaper found itself slapped with a libel suit, brought by Fallows. Suspicion for planting the story fell on the Grand Duke Kyril, but the libel case dragged on, only to lapse finally during the Second World War, when as a resident of Germany Anna could not sue in England. Shortly after the *News of the World* article's appearance, Anna was summoned to a meeting in Berlin, which involved an offer of an allowance from Grand Duke Kyril and Prince Yusupov in return for dropping her claim to the title of Grand Duchess Anastasia.

While Anna was not overtly concerned about the lawsuit, it never occurred to her to drop her claim as Grand Duchess. Despite her precarious existence, she was not tempted by the consideration of a regular allowance and apparently lived her life much like Mr Macawber in Charles Dickens' novel, *David*

Copperfield, in the belief that 'something will turn up.' Her friends reported that at times she expressed the desire to earn her own living and not be dependent on others, but that was clearly impossible for someone with a temperament like hers. It was also, at the end of the day, not necessary. Something or someone did indeed turn up.

Fallows, having sold his house and his life-insurance policies and probably having also ruined his health, had just about decided to give up on Anna's case by this time. The *News of the World* article served an unforeseen purpose of rekindling his interest and faith in the case. This did not make it all plain sailing for him. She rehired him as attorney only in the summer of the following year, 1933, just before the Berlin court listed the members of the Romanov and Hesse families as the beneficiaries of Tsar Nicholas II's property.

Although this was a relatively happy and calm period of Anna's life, that did not make Fallows' task simple. In 1935 he rushed to Hannover, where Anna lived for much of the 1930s, having been told that her life was in danger. Anna defied the doctors yet again to recover completely for many years, despite a month in 1936, when, angered, she shut herself in her room, refused food for three days and promptly disappeared. She was found more than a month later, wandering in the countryside, having survived on berries and mushrooms.

By 1938, however, many of the parameters of Anna's life changed. A year earlier Grand Duke Ernst of Hesse had died of cancer, and within a month a plane crash took the lives of many of his family. As a result Lord Louis Mountbatten, uncle to the future Prince Philip, Duke of Edinburgh and husband of Queen Elizabeth II, effectively became head of the Hesse family. Lord Mountbatten, a wealthy man from his marriage to the granddaughter of Sir Ernest Cassel, one of the richest men in England, took on Grand Duke Ernst's mantle. Anna reserved her strongest vitriol for this man who financed the opposition to her in court and who would come to condemn her claims quite publicly.

In addition, on the instructions of the Nazi government, the Hannover police were instructed to determine once and for all whether or not Anna was Franziska Schanzkowska. If it could be proved that she was an impostor, then she would be incarcerated. A meeting was arranged with the Schanzkowski family. It was, however, not to be that easy. Anna locked herself in her flat for a week, obliging Fallows to fly in from the United States to use his best powers of persuasion. He was in despair, when he remembered the subterfuge that had been used to persuade her to move to Castle Seeon, despite her strong reluctance.

His only method of communicating with her was through the front door of the apartment. She did not open his letters nor let down the barricades. Shouting through the door, he asked her if she would meet the Schanzkowskis if accompanied by Tatiana Botkin. Anna replied that Tatiana had abandoned her. Fallows had earlier asked Tatiana to come to Hannover to teach Anna Russian, but Tatiana had replied that since her divorce she was unable to leave her children in Nice. Just as Tatiana's brother Gleb had found that his bout of influenza cost him – temporarily – his friendship with Anna, so Anna construed Tatiana's family commitments as betrayal. Fallows was not to be deterred, however. He then shouted through the door to ask whether she would consent to see the Schanzkowskis in the company of Gleb. After a long silence, Fallows was admitted, and Gleb was on his way to Hannover. Together they went to meet the Schanzkowskis on 9 July 1938.

Anna was to be looked over by Franziska's two brothers, Valerian and Felix, the latter having already met her in 1927, and her two sisters, Gertrude and Maria. Fallows was also present, but as he was American and thus unqualified to practise law in Germany, he had to be content with the simple role of witness. Valerian and Felix were first to deny that Anna was their sister. However, their calm assessment was soon to be pierced by a scream from Gertrude.

'Can you deny that you are my sister? Go on, say it. You cannot fool me.' The Hannover police then engaged the furious Anna in close questioning, with the constant chorus coming from Gertrude. Anna was regally successful. She finally swept out of the police station, and not one of the Schanzkowskis was willing to sign an affidavit against her, despite Gertrude's hysterical assertions. The success of this encounter encouraged Fallows to pursue her identity in court. He persuaded Anna to appoint two German lawyers, Paul Leverkuehn and Kurt Vermehren, to take her case to court.

During the war Anna suffered Allied bombing, in common with the rest of the German population, and was also often hungry, until she fled East to escape the worst effects. She spent part of the war years at Schloss Winterstein, the home of another aristocratic supporter, Louise von Saxe-Meiningen, and stayed there until the autumn of 1946. It was from Schloss Winterstein, which was now in the eastern part of Germany and under Soviet occupation, that Prince Frederick came to her rescue and helped her escape to the West. He and his family had lost all their property, which was now in the Eastern zone, and he himself had walked 500 km to reach the Allies' occupied zone of Germany. He was able to gain the services of the Red Cross to help Anna cross borders to arrive in the French zone at Bad Liebenzell.

Prince Frederick then helped set up Anna in a former barracks at Unterlengenhardt in the Black Forest, a beautiful if isolated village, where Anna was to live for about 20 years. Baroness Monica von Miltitz accompanied her there and devotedly served her well into her nineties. Many of Anna's circle at Unterlengenhardt were Anthroposophists, whom she had met through her friendship with Harriet von Rathlef. Rudolf Steiner had earlier set up a colony of Anthroposophists in the village. Anna was more than welcome in their midst, where several devoted elderly women eagerly became her 'ladies-in-waiting'. Baroness Monica von Miltitz, an impressive and intelligent woman, would take care of Anna's extensive correspondence, but it would be the telephone calls that vexed her beyond endurance. Anna would pick up the phone day and night, calling distant locations with no thought of the cost. When the bill did arrive, the Baroness would put her head in her hands, 'It's enormous. How are we going to pay this?'

Despite the relative isolation of the village, journalists swarmed there to write articles about Anna. They were generally unsuccessful in their attempts to interview her, but that did not prevent the stories from being written. An indication of her popular fame can be judged by the fact that a picture postcard was printed in Germany showing the 'Residence of Grand Duchess

Anastasia'. Gradually, enough visitors came to stare at the 'tragic princess' that some entrepreneur found it worth his while to set up coach trips aimed at catching sight of Anna, much as contemporary tourists go to Africa in the hope of spotting the rare white rhinoceros. Some of the tour operators even promised afternoon tea with the 'Grand Duchess'.

It is thus hardly surprising that Anna became more and more reclusive and eccentric. She gradually built impenetrable barriers of barbed wire and other booby traps around her modest hut and finally kept four fierce hounds, half German Shepherd and half St Bernard, that terrified her visitors, invited and uninvited. In this way her eccentric personality was reduced to something approaching a freak show for the visitors, a situation that naturally reinforced her paranoia. Her rare appearances did not disappoint the gawkers. Dressed winter and summer in a long overcoat and strange headgear, she generally hid the lower part of her mouth behind a handkerchief as she strode off, accompanied by her dogs.

Tatiana Botkin – as Tatiana Melnik became known again after separating from her husband in 1929 and their subsequent divorce – went to visit Anna in 1957, the first time they had met for 30 years. She describes finding Anna in her Black Forest hut, in her book *Anastasia retrouvée*.

> Through a small window nearly blocked by vegetation, the dull day barely illuminated a veritable Aladdin's Cave. Picture frames, knick-knacks, postcards, photographs were piled up everywhere, a bizarre quantity of objects among which I recognised official portraits of the Emperor and Empress, old epaulettes, a Cossack officer's belt decorated with tarnished silver ornaments and everywhere unopened letters. Envelopes invaded everything and stamps in all colours bore witness to the most exotic parts of the world . . ..
>
> And then, when my eyes had finished taking in this baffling spectacle, I perceived at the end of the room a large wooden bed, with covers, piled one on top of the other, concealing a human form. I approach. Anastasia is there. She is hiding the lower part of her face with a handkerchief. An expression of terror fills her eyes.

Anna's fortunes improved when the movie *Anastasia*, released in 1956, became a blockbuster. The French authoress, Marcelle Maurette, had written the original play not knowing that Anna was still alive. She had read the first two books about the Anastasia phenomenon, by Harriet von Rathlef and Pierre Gilliard, and had not attempted to make the script an accurate portrait of her life, giving Anastasia a lover and a happy ending when she meets her grandmother, the Dowager Empress. On hearing that Anna was still alive, Maurette was persuaded to share the royalties from this fantastically successful film. Under the jurisdiction of Prince Frederick, one-third of the sum went to the lawyers, Kurt Vermehren and Paul Leverkuehn, who had worked on her behalf without pay, one-third went to building Anna a new house, and the last third was saved to provide a regular income. A nicer and larger 'dacha' was built for her, which gradually degenerated into the sordid mess of her previous dwelling.

Anna remained controversially in the public eye, even without the adoration that the film *Anastasia* bestowed upon her. The lawsuit, which she had originally thought would establish her identity in six weeks, was still on-going. The petition to withdraw the certificate of inheritance from the benefactors of the Mendelssohn bank account continued in the courts until 1957, becoming a Teutonic *Bleak House*, even though most of the money had long been disbursed to the named relatives. The legal process was not made any easier by the fact that evidence papers collected in Anna's favour and kept in Leverkuehn's office had been destroyed by fire during the war. The Fallows' papers were not available as his daughter continued to hang on to them. While this petition got nowhere, one of the judges at the Berlin Court of Appeal made a suggestion. He said that in his opinion there was sufficient evidence for Anna to sue for recognition as Grand Duchess Anastasia, rather than suing for the withdrawal of the certificate of inheritance.

Thus started a new and lengthy quest for the lawyers Vermehren and Leverkuehn. In order to prove Anna's imperial identity, the lawyers decided to sue a beneficiary of the Mendelssohn account as someone who had asserted that Anastasia was dead. By this time many of the benefitting relatives had died or moved, but the lawyers decided to keep the case within national, German frontiers and chose the granddaughter of the Tsarina's sister, Irene. Barbara, Duchess of Mecklenburg, was not even born until 1920, but it was assumed that she had benefitted from the Mendelssohn money awarded to her grandmother. However, as if to emphasize the tangle the Anastasia affair had brought on the Hesse family, Barbara's father was Prince Sigismund, who acknowledged Anna, while her uncle was Prince Frederick, Anna's champion. Prince Ludwig of Hesse volunteered his services to his cousin, Barbara, as co-defendant.

Defence costs for the Duchess of Mecklenburg were largely met by Lord Mountbatten. This has given rise to speculation that he had something to fear from Anna winning verification of her identity in court. His involvement encouraged many of Anna's supporters to see the English Royal Family as willing to go to extreme lengths to extinguish Anna's claim, largely by association, because Lord Mountbatten was Prince Philip's uncle. Of course, Lord Mountbatten was a potential defendant as his mother was the Tsarina's sister, Victoria, Marchioness of Milford Haven, as were Mountbatten's sisters, Princess Andrew of Greece, mother of Prince Philip, and Queen Louise of Sweden. Mountbatten spent thousands of pounds on the case. He was also influential in preventing the BBC from researching a film in 1958 that would have included an interview with Anna. There is no question that Mountbatten passionately wanted Anna to lose her lawsuit, but there has never been any proof that there were darker forces at work.

Acquaintances of Mountbatten have simpler explanations. Barbara of Mecklenburg was destitute at the time, says one friend of the family, and Mountbatten merely offered to cover her legal costs, because he could afford to do so and especially as it could just as easily have been he himself facing the lawsuit. Others attributed Mountbatten's opposition to his mother's implacable hostility to the claim. He was merely following the family line, and in 1977, shortly before his death at the hands of Irish assassins, a friend reported that he was considering a change of mind. He was studying the latest forensic evidence, a comparison of Anna's ears with those of Grand Duchess Anastasia, conducted by Dr Moritz

Furtmayr. Furtmayr, one of Germany's leading forensic scientists, had developed a new identification test, comparing the anatomical points of the ear in cases where fingerprints and dental records are not available. Furtmayr concluded that Anna's claims were genuine. 'Is it possible . . . after all this time,' Mountbatten had apparently muttered, studying the newspaper reports. Be that as it may, Mountbatten represented a powerful force against Anna's legal claims and was more openly critical of her than most of the Romanov and Hesse family members.

A full dossier enumerating her physical features, her forensic evidence, such as ear tests, facial structure and blood tests, and many affidavits in her support was compiled for the lawsuit. There was also important evidence from the other side, including very damaging testimony from a man who was to prove a charlatan. Hans Johann Mayer, an Austrian who had been a prisoner of war in Russia in 1918, approached Anna's defence team to offer his services. He said he was at the Ipatiev House at the time of the assassination, and he would swear in court that Anastasia had escaped.

In consideration for his trouble, he thought it reasonable to ask for an allowance of £250 a month for life or, in the event of a settlement in Anna's favour, a lump sum of £200,000. After his offer was refused, he wrote a series of articles for the news magazine, 7-Tage, stating that he had seen the entire family dead. To back up his claims he had 'documentary evidence', including the draft of the official statement by the Bolshevik government that the Tsar was killed. The draft showed the words 'and his family' crossed out by hand, putting it in line with the Bolshevik announcement that declared the Tsar alone had perished.

He was also called in by the prosecution as a witness against Anna. Anna's counsel did find two witnesses who managed to limit the damage. The first stated that Mayer was a simple forger. The second witness pointed to various spelling mistakes in the Russian and mistakes in the use of titles. However, Mayer was not acknowledged to be the fraud he was until 1964, when the prosecution, now in the Hamburg Court of Appeal, acknowledged that Mayer had committed perjury. Mayer's documents, unfortunately, claim readers to the present day, and his account has even been published in Russian translation.

It was also at this court session that Pierre Gilliard was nearly reduced to incoherence by the persistent badgering questions of the judge. On the second day of interrogation, Gilliard dropped a bombshell. On being asked about material used in his book *La Fausse Anastasie*, Gilliard finally admitted that he had burned all his documentary material. There was uproar in the court, leaving the former imperial tutor, whose wife had recently died, to return to Lausanne, where he had a car crash from which he never recovered.

The Franziska Schanzkowska allegations naturally surfaced once again, and Doris Wingender and her sister testified that Anna was the Polish factory worker who had lodged at their house. The judges travelled the world to hear testimony from the many witnesses involved, including a sad interview with Grand Duchess Olga in Toronto, where after a few hours of close questioning she arose and declared the interview was over. Anna was later to do the same, when the judges finally tracked her down in Unterlengenhardt, but in this case the 'interview' only lasted ten minutes.

This and the subsequent court cases were well covered at the time by Dominique Aucleres, a French journalist writing for *Le Figaro*. She attended all the hearings and presented comprehensive reports for her readers. She became convinced of Anna's authenticity and later wrote an influential book, *Anastasia, qui êtes-vous?*, published in Paris in 1962. There were other witnesses in Anna's favour, such as Felix Dassel, an officer who spent several months in 1916 in the hospital patronized by Grand Duchess Anastasia. Anna herself never appeared in court. At first she categorically refused to have anything to do with the court case, but was finally persuaded when she understood that its outcome could hinge on her cooperation.

One of the main arguments used against Anna in her quest for recognition was her idiosyncratic knowledge of languages. She did not seem to know any language very well, which some experts have attributed to partial amnesia from blows she may have suffered to her head. Grand Duchess Anastasia herself was not a brilliant scholar. As her French tutor Pierre Gilliard wrote in his book that when she reached the age of 12 it became very difficult to turn her attention to serious study. Her English tutor Sydney Gibbes put it more graphically: 'It seemed as if her mental development had been suddenly arrested; and though she played the piano and painted, she was only in the first stages of either accomplishment.'

The Grand Duchesses' first language was naturally Russian, which Anastasia would have spoken with her father and her nursemaid Shura, who was later to marry Pierre Gilliard. She studied French with Gilliard and English with Sydney Gibbes. The Tsarina's favourite language was English, which she had learnt as a child when staying with her grandmother, Queen Victoria. Alexandra's letters and diary are written in English, and although she learnt Russian, she was embarrassed by her poor accent and hesitant about speaking it. Anastasia would have spoken English with her mother, although her notebooks preserved by Gibbes reveal many errors in her written knowledge of the language.

When Anna was first found in Berlin and known as Fraulein Unbekannt, she spoke very little, but the language she did speak was poor German. Gilliard in his books attacks her on the grounds that the Grand Duchess did not know German, although this accusation was an own goal. He had preserved timetables of the Imperial children's lessons, which clearly delineate German lessons twice a week for Anastasia and the other Grand Duchesses. Her German accent clearly puzzled everybody who met her and has been described as 'Bavarian', 'Schwabian' or merely a mass of incorrect grammar and syntax hidden by an exotic accent. During Anna's early illnesses nurses and doctors reported that she spoke Russian while under the influence of the various drugs she had to take, but it is possible that the German nurses would not be able to distinguish between Polish and Russian. The suspicion that she did speak Polish rather than Russian reinforced the case for her being Franziska Schanzkowska.

As for Anna herself, she said that she would not now speak Russian, but there are well-documented instances of her speaking Russian words and phrases. Her opponents alleged she had picked up scraps of the language by living with Russian *émigrés* in Berlin. Her supporters naturally welcomed her Russian interjections as evidence that knowledge of Russian was lodged deep in her subconscious, it just took the right moment and atmosphere for her to be able to articulate it. As time went on, she also began speaking English, albeit in a very idiosyncratic manner, but here again it is known that Faith Lavington, an English governess with the Leuchtenberg family, gave her some English lessons during her stay at Castle Seeon.

The riddle of her knowledge of languages was not made easier by Anna's personality. One of her friends noted that in later life she tended to speak a language that those around her would not understand – a symptom of her extreme paranoia towards strangers. Thus in Germany she would speak in English, while in the United States her preferred language was German. Her idiosyncratic and incorrect use of the English language is very hard to quantify. Another of her friends remarked that her English did not sound to him as though she had learnt it in childhood, but rather picked it up later in life. But, here again, language experts have said she could have learnt it as a child.

As is the case with most of the facts surrounding Anna's life, it is hard to come to a definite conclusion. What is certain is that her language knowledge was a key point for her opponents and supporters alike. Thus, when Judge Backen decided to visit Anna in the Black Forest, one of the most crucial aspects of this hearing was for Anna to convince him that she knew Russian. Under the German legal system, judges hearing a case can take evidential statements *in camera* for witnesses who are unable to attend the court. Thus they met with the Grand Duchess Olga in Toronto, and as there was clearly no possibility of persuading Anna to appear in court, the judge also had to go to her. He took with him a designated expert in Russian.

On 20 May 1959 a group from the court laid siege to Anna's fortress. She refused to have anything to do with them for three full days, despite the entreaties of her 'ladies-in-waiting', her attorney Kurt Vermehren and other supporters. Finally Baron Ulrich von Gienanth, who had been brought in to handle the earnings from the *Anastasia* film in 1957 and who looked after her finances and became a trustee of her will, arrived and won a hard-fought concession: 'He can stare at me for ten minutes.'

After minimal cooperation, the utterance of a single Russian word and precisely ten minutes, the judge was dismissed. 'And now I say goodbye.'

After this treatment, the judge came out and told the waiting group, 'I don't know who she is, but she is a lady.' The protocol written by Judge Backen after the meeting gives a clear indication of Anna's manner of behaviour, which persuaded so many people that she was indeed 'a lady'.

> [The plaintiff] gives the impression of a very self-confident and energetic lady. She seems . . . to be thoroughly clear and mentally competent. She speaks in a regal manner, with a deliberate distance. Sometime she will look her conversation partner directly in the eye, while burying the lower part of her face in a high collar; sometimes the face turns all the way to the left side and is hidden entirely in the collar of her coat.

This habit of hiding the lower part of her face remained with Anna to the end of her life, a practice that probably began when she had many of her teeth removed in the early 1920s. The description of her style of speech gives a serious clue as to her power over the various 'ladies-in-waiting' and other well-wishers. She was eccentric and demanding, but she was also very good company, 'self-confident and energetic'.

In the subsequent law case, it was the fate of Prince Frederick and his friend Ian Lilburn to prepare Anna for a second hearing, designed to test her knowledge of Russian. This time it was a different judge, by the name of Bathge, together with Russian language expert Irene Neander who arrived at Anna's hut in the Black Forest in September 1965. The meeting went on for one-and-a-half hours, with questions posed in Russian, to which Anna replied in English. Anna was asked to read Russian poetry and join in the judge's rendition of Russian folk songs, but although she let slip a few words of Russian, her testimony remained stubbornly in English. Finally, when all the participants were exhausted, and the judge prepared to leave, Anna simply asked when the questioning about her case was to start.

In addition to these subjective appraisals of Anna's claims, several scientific studies of her physiognomy were addressed to the hearing, including a 60-page report by Professor Otto Reche, founder and president of the German Anthropological Society, an expert in genetics and an experienced court witness. This document compared photographs of Grand Duchess Anastasia with Anna and concluded that she was the Grand Duchess. Other forensic evidence, particularly studies of the shape of her ears, had over the years come to differing conclusions, but the similarities were easily sufficient to make them at the least uncannily close and, at best, proof of her identity. However, the court did not accept them as proof positive. On 15 May 1961 it ruled that her claim was unfounded. It also threw out the counterclaim that Anna was in fact the missing Franziska Schanzkowska as 'irrelevant' although, in the judge's opinion, it was quite likely. On the same day, Anna lodged an appeal.

After three-and-a-half years, the court had left Anna in exactly the same position as when she started. She may or may not be Grand Duchess Anastasia. She may or may not be Franziska Schanzkowska. Because of various anomalies in the way the expert witnesses had presented their material, the High Court of Appeals in Hamburg admitted the case in 1962. Shortly afterwards, Kurt Vermehren was killed in a car crash, and Prince Frederick and his friends had to find her a new attorney. There was no money available to pay fees, but, as luck would have it, Carl-August Wollmann offered his services free of charge and in the nick of time. He had read the published verdict of the first tribunal and joined that dogged band of Anastasians. Prince Frederick and Ian Lilburn travelled all over Europe to find evidence, new witnesses and above all to deal with an increasingly fractious Anna. They were joined once again by Dominique Aucleres, who covered the case for *Le Figaro*.

New witnesses were found, and fresh anatomical evidence presented, but it all appeared to make no difference. On 27 February 1967 the judges ruled that the plaintiff had failed to provide sufficient proof that she was the Grand Duchess, or it could be called 'not proven'. After the ruling Anastasia's friends were forced to scatter, although there was never any question that her case would go up the ladder to the Federal Supreme Court at Karlsruhe. A new attorney was found, Baron von Stackelberg, who had to attack the ruling on the case based on examining the procedures undertaken in the lower courts. The Supreme Court made its final ruling on 17 February 1970, which was 'neither established nor refuted'. The judge confirmed that it had taken no stand on Anna's actual identity. The Supreme Court had only decided that the Hamburg High Court of Appeals had made its decision 'without legal mistakes and without procedural errors'.

The 1967 judgement had pushed Anna into a deep depression. During the lengthy court trials, she had written regularly to Gleb Botkin, very dissatisfied with her surroundings and deeply disillusioned with the people around her at Unterlengenhardt. She did travel to Paris in connection with a new film being made about her life, a sign that despite the court judgement, she had not been forgotten. It was during this visit that Tsar Nicholas's former mistress, the ballerina Mathilde Kschessinska, who had married Grand Duke Andrei, told a television interviewer that she recognized Anna as the Grand Duchess.

In May 1968 Anna appeared in public at Unterlengenhardt for the last time, for the 100th anniversary of Nicholas II's birth. Towards the end of that month she locked herself inside her decaying house and refused to open the door. After four days her friends forcibly took her to hospital at Neuenburg, Baden-Württemberg, but were unable to find out her condition as the nurses refused to discuss her case on Anna's orders. The crisis was probably precipitated by orders from the mayor of Unterlengenhardt and the district board of health to clean up the premises. While she was in hospital, Prince Frederick and Ian Lilburn took on this Herculean task, which included supervising the destruction of her cats on the orders of the local authorities. 'It seemed there were always two or three more of them until in the end there were over 60 we dealt with,' said Lilburn.

Local farmers had already been destroying her animals when they found them half-starved in their fields. The cats had also taken over inside the house. Anna gave up her bed that had been slept in by Queen Victoria to the cats, preferring to sleep on a couch. Anna did not forgive Prince Frederick his action for many years. She also accused him and Ian, in collaboration with the long-suffering Baroness von Miltitz, of stealing documents and artifacts worth more than $10,000. They, for their part, found money, cheques and postal orders never cashed, despite the fact that Anna's house had been mortgaged twice and that all her supporters had freely given well beyond their means to her cause.

All this meant nothing to Anna. Prince Frederick was designated the 'new Yurovsky'. Yurovsky had murdered her parents and family. The new Yurovsky had murdered her cats.

CHAPTER SEVEN

Religious Fervour

IN JULY 1968 Baron von Stackelberg submitted his brief to the Federal Supreme Court contesting the decision reached by the Hamburg High Court of Appeals. In the same month Anna was released from hospital and flew to America. Her mental affliction, in tandem with the grinding disappointments of the legal processes, had caused her to turn against the society of the Anthroposophists in Unterlengenhardt and take up Gleb Botkin's offer to visit the United States. Gleb's wife Nadine had recently died, and he was now living on his own in Charlottesville, Virginia. A friend of Gleb, Jack Manahan, a wealthy and eccentric resident of Charlottesville, paid for her flight and that of her travelling companion Alexis Miliukoff, another Russian *émigré* espoused to her cause and enthralled by her charisma.

Gleb had made Anna's life-story known to Manahan, who was a history buff and an authentic expert on genealogy, especially that of European royal and aristocratic families and prominent Americans. Jack was well known in the university town of Charlottesville, where his father had been the Dean of Education at the University of Virginia and had also become rich through successful real-estate ventures. This made him a member of the town's Country Club set, a position Jack inherited as a well-heeled member of Charlottesville's upper-middle classes. He had earlier held posts teaching history in various American universities, but by this time he did not need a paid appointment and lived in his parents' elegant house near the University of Virginia and took care of lands he had inherited in nearby Scottsville.

Jack, sensitive to gossip that might damage Anna's reputation, installed his 67-year-old guest at his farm in Scottsville, while he stayed in his Charlottesville house. Miliukoff had entered her circle in Unterlengenhardt and stayed in Charlottesville only a few days. Despite being tagged a scoundrel by Anna, he had managed to win her confidence. He persuaded her to make a series of tapes, which would later form the basis for the James Blair Lovell biography. This was not the first book based on her words, for Roland Krug von Nidda had written a well-publicized work in 1957, consisting of her verbatim recollections and interspersed with passages of explanation, partly provided and composed by Prince Frederick. Anna's other attempts at autobiography foundered, including one assisted by Gleb Botkin, because her words were not considered sufficiently interesting or, at times, coherent enough to support a commercially viable work.

The tapes used by Lovell are not uninteresting, although they are at times confused. The problem is that they are too intricate and overdone. There are moments when Anna appears to be deliberately mischievous. She gives two separate scenarios for the death of the Imperial Family. The first echoes the Sokolov investigation, with the obvious addition that Grand Duchess Anastasia manages to escape. The second version derives from the ingenious story told in *The File on the Tsar*, which asserts that the Tsarina and her daughters were separated from the Tsar and Tsarevich and sent to Perm, rumours of which had been published earlier based on contemporary local testimony. Anna even suggests that her 'sister' Grand Duchess Olga is perhaps living near Lake Como. There is a pretender Olga, Marga Boodts, who lives at the lake, but very few believe in her claims.

Anna's other fantastic reminiscences include an alleged attempt on her life by Prince Felix Yusupov, while she lived at Castle Seeon, and her meeting with Adolf Hitler, at which she says the Führer promised to restore the Romanov autocracy after he had conquered the Soviet Union. Even making allowances for her age – the tapes were recorded while she lived at Unterlengenhardt when she was in her sixties – it seems there are times when she deliberately wants to test the credulity of her acolyte. This playful turn of mind was captivating to her supporters, even if they did not believe everything she said. Equally it is difficult to know which versions of events she believed.

Anna's arrival in the United States started auspiciously. She was in sufficiently good humour to give a number of interviews to journalists, which touched on the German court case. But now that she was 67 – but seemed considerably older – and always wore eccentric clothes, the media's ability to turn her into a fairy-tale princess was stretched to breaking-point. There was certainly interest in her story, but it was not the moblike exposure she had suffered when she first came to the USA in 1928.

It was not long before Anna was to tumble into a pitfall, partly of her own making. Shortly after she set foot on American soil, Maria Rasputin, daughter of the Tsarina's notorious spiritual adviser, contacted her and later arrived in Charlottesville from Los Angeles. At first Maria acknowledged the 67-year-old woman as her long-lost childhood friend and on her return to Los Angeles arranged for a Gala Tea to be held in her honour there. Anna accepted the invitation but, on the night before her scheduled departure to the West Coast, arbitrarily changed her mind. The Gala Tea was off and with it Maria's recognition: 'I've been bluffed by her,' she said. Gleb regarded the whole débâcle, which had attracted considerable press attention, with a cynical eye, writing to Miliukoff after the initial meeting between the two women:

> As she [Maria] proceeded to expand on her ardent love for and devotion to Anastasia, I asked her where she had been all these years. My question embarrassed her visibly, and she mumbled something to the effect that she had been very busy and had not heard about Anastasia until recently, which was, of course, a lie. I cannot help but suspect that Maria's acknowledgement of Anastasia was just a publicity stunt to advertise [her] book [about Rasputin].

This incident was one of the most blatant attempts to cash in on Anna's fame and would not be the last.

As in previous times of need, Anna was to find another

protector to take care of her – Jack Manahan, whom she married on 23 December 1968. Jack, who was 18 years her junior, implicitly believed in Anna, even going so far as to call himself 'son-in-law to the Tsar'. For Anna it solved her visa problem. She had entered the United States on a six-months visitors' visa and had announced that she would not return to Germany. In addition Jack had sufficient means to support her financially. Despite his extreme eccentricities, he stood by Anna to the end.

The remaining Anastasians were grateful to Jack for providing security and care for Anna. There was a price to pay for this though, as Marina Schweitzer, Gleb's daughter, acknowledged. Jack had wanted to be royal all his life, and now he had achieved his ambition – he was a member of the Romanov and Hesse families. He loved to expound on the genealogy of his new royal 'relatives' and would overwhelm visitors with his detailed knowledge of European royal families, their marriages, their children and their possessions. He was also in the habit of telling visitors, 'Go on, ask her some questions', a request with which Anna rarely complied.

These frequent demands for Anna to perform upset some of her supporters. Royal etiquette requires that casual visitors do not ask them questions – guests have to wait for the exalted person to talk to them and then only discuss those matters raised by the princess. Jack, however, encouraged journalists, fielding their questions, showing them the Romanov memorabilia stacked up in the Manahan house, while he reminisced about a long-forgotten royal intrigue or scandal. His knowledge was formidable, but as time went on his grasp on everyday reality began to fade as, in return for his exalted status as a royal person, he struggled to cope with his demanding wife.

Jack's belief in Anna's authenticity was total, and he found an astounding number of reasons to confirm it. During the 1920s in Berlin Anna had amazed Russian after Russian, aristocrat and more humble *émigré* alike, by her knowledge of Russia and the Imperial Court. Sergius Botkin, president of the Russian Refugee Office in Berlin, told his cousin Gleb: 'Well, Madame Tschaikovsky is either Grand Duchess Anastasia, or else she is a miracle; and you know that I do not believe in miracles.' Sergius helped Anna considerably during the 1920s, but he would only have been persuaded to acknowledge her publicly if her royal identity had been legally proved.

Sergius Botkin was one of many who wanted to believe in Anna but, knowing the strength of feeling she inspired among both supporters and critics, diplomatically clung to neutral ground to avoid splitting the *émigré* community. Her case was strong enough to attract the attention of European royalty and aristocrats, so it is not surprising she still has her adherents today.

Even the Hesse family, which led the public opposition to her claims, contained adherents of Anna. Prince Sigismund, son of the Tsarina's sister, Princess Irene of Prussia, believed in Anna implicitly despite his mother's opposition to her claims. Irene's husband Heinrich had gone so far as to ban Anna as a topic of conversation in the house because it upset Irene so much. Prince Sigismund, however, also believed in the Grand Duchess Olga of Lake Como, a faith that attracted far fewer adherents than Anna. His public espousal of Marga Boodts embarrassed the Anastasians, as it cast doubt on his credibility as a witness.

The present generation of Romanovs are mostly sufficiently removed from Tsarskoe Selo not to entertain dreams that they will once again host Grand Balls for 3000 guests. But the division, started by Grand Duke Kyril Vladimirovich's declaration of himself as Tsar-in-exile in Berlin in 1924, persists into the late twentieth century.

Kyril's great-grandson, 14-year-old Georgy, born in Spain, is being groomed by his mother, Grand Duchess Maria, to take over the Russian throne, should it be restored. The rest of the Romanovs, under the leadership of Prince Nicholas of Rome, who is from a remote branch of the family, oppose this claim and set up the Romanov Foundation in 1992 to provide financial assistance to a new democratic Russia. They have deliberately excluded Kyril's descendants. Prince Nicholas, the elder statesman of the family, follows the edict established by the Dowager Empress in Copenhagen. She felt there should be no claimants to the throne and that this was a question that could not be settled in exile. Prince Rostislav, a London banker and grandson of Tsar Nicholas's sister, Grand Duchess Xenia, is not concerned about the restoration of the Romanov throne. 'This is up to the Russian people,' he says.

When the so-called Copenhagen Declaration was published in 1928, only three days after the Dowager Empress's death, some thought it was the last word on the subject to come from the Romanov family. In fact, out of a total of 44 surviving Romanov relatives, only 12 signed the document. Nine of the signatures were from Grand Duchess Xenia's family – she had seven children. The tenth was that of Grand Duchess Olga, the only one who had actually seen Anna. The last two signatories were the Tsar's cousins, Grand Duke Dmitry Pavlovich and Grand Duchess Maria Pavlovna. The unity of the family was paper thin. Most of the Romanov clan would have been in Copenhagen for the funeral and could have signed the document at that time.

The motivation behind the Copenhagen Declaration, published with such indecent haste after the death of the Dowager Empress, remains a mystery. Many of the Romanovs were light-hearted about it, or perhaps simply lax. For instance, Grand Duke Boris, cousin of the Tsar, used to slam the table and shout, 'Give the girl a chance.' With this laissez-faire attitude towards the pretender, perhaps it is not surprising that the Copenhagen Declaration appears to have emanated from the more serious Hesse family, who published their condemnation of Anna two days before those members of the Romanov clan gathered in Copenhagen were able to issue their own declaration.

Although the family line was negative, there were Romanovs who did support Anna, most notably Grand Duke Andrei, another of the Tsar's cousins. He became interested in her case and sought the Dowager Empress's permission before embarking on his inves-tigation of Anna's claims. He had met the Imperial Family regularly before the revolution as an aide-de-camp to the Tsar and therefore knew the authentic Anastasia. He recognized her at a meeting in Paris in 1928 and wrote to Gleb Botkin:

> For two days I had occasion to observe the invalid, and I can tell you that no doubt remains in my mind: She is Grand Duchess Anastasia. It is impossible not to recognise her. Naturally, years and suffering have marked her, but not as much as I would have imagined. Her face is striking in its

profound sadness, but when she smiles, it is she, it is Anastasia, without a doubt.

After that encounter much of Andrei's energy was directed towards trying to persuade other Romanovs to accept her, while also working hard to keep the family divisions out of the public eye. He wrote an impassioned letter to Grand Duchess Olga, attempting to convince her to reconsider her dismissal of Anna's claims, but it is not known whether he even received a reply. With the exceptions of the Grand Duchesses Xenia and Olga, however, most of the Romanovs did not take a great deal of interest in the case. The fact that only 12 members of the family signed the condemnatory Declaration did not mean that the other Romanovs supported Anna. They may have just preferred to stay out of the picture.

Grand Duke Andrei's widow, Mathilde Kschessinska, at the age of 95 was filmed by a French television crew. Kschessinska, the ballerina who had been Tsar Nicholas's mistress before either of them was married, recalled meeting Anna, whom she identified as Anastasia. Her son, Vladimir, immediately ordered the film crew to edit out that answer, as he feared upsetting the Romanov family. It was a difficult balancing act trying to please all the disparate Romanovs.

While Anna's supporters are convinced that her knowledge of the Imperial Court came from her childhood, Pierre Gilliard attempts in his book to attribute her reminiscences to the infor- mation she picked up during her stays with Russian *émigrés* in Germany in the 1920s. One such story was that she knew her aunt Olga called her 'Schwibs'. Grand Duchess Olga was unhappily married for years to Peter of Oldenburg and finally in 1916 was allowed to marry a commoner, Colonel Nikolai Kulikovsky, a cavalry captain in the Cuirassier Regiment. The Kulikovskys had two sons. During the childhoods of Tsar Nicholas II's children she had been their closest aunt and was Grand Duchess Anastasia's godmother. Her role as a childless aunt in the lives of her nieces and nephew, always ready to play games with them and bring them special treats, was well known, taking on special piquancy when Olga was finally allowed to marry for love and have her own family.

Before visiting Anna in 1925 she had heard that Anna knew about the Schwibs nickname, thus arousing her deep curiosity. However, Gilliard attempts to destroy this 'evidence' of Anna's authenticity by publishing a letter Olga wrote to Princess Irene of Prussia, the Tsarina's sister.

For nearly four years, they stuffed the head of this poor creature with all our stories, showed her a large number of photographs etc., and one fine day she astonished everybody with her memories.

Mr Gilliard, his wife and my husband, and before us, the elderly Volkov [former chamberlain to the Tsarina], have all seen her and conversed with her, they do not believe that she is our Anastasia. On the contrary, they state that we all recognised her and that we then received an order from Mama to say that she is not Anastasia. This is a great lie! I believe that this story is fraudulent, but I think there are many people who believe it, but they are those who never knew Anastasia.

During the four days that we spent in Berlin, Mr Gilliard and my husband saw all the Russians with whom she had stayed and they learned in this way many things of great importance. Here is one: they told them that she had learned the nickname 'Schwibs' from an officer I met in the Crimea, who later came to Berlin. He was interested in the invalid and asked her if she knew this nickname and who gave her the name; naturally she was unable to reply. But later, she suddenly said: 'My aunt Olga called me 'Schwibs'! Everybody was astonished and made enquiries to find out if this was true.

This letter, written a little more than a year after the Grand Duchess Olga visited Anna, is fair evidence, not only of Olga's negative attitude towards Anna but also that her 'niece's' special 'knowledge' must have come from Russian *émigrés*. However, Olga was writing to Irene, who had denied Anna's claims out of hand, and this could have hardened Olga's attitude in the letter.

Anna's supporters still claim, however, that the Gilliards and Grand Duchess Olga did recognize Anna during their visits. At first her believers attributed the visitors' reluctance to acknowledge Anna to deference for the feelings of the Dowager Empress, but darker motives were later ascribed – money. Pierre Gilliard in his book reserves his most vitriolic attacks for Anna's companion, Harriet von Rathlef, and the evidence she produces in Anna's favour in her book *Anastasia*. Gilliard's attitude points to the strength of Anna's character, that even when seriously ill, he saw her as a victim either of her supporters or of her own delusions, but he did not accuse her of being a wicked charlatan or a fortune hunter. He saw her as a sick invalid, who had been coached in the role of Anastasia by her supporters. Even though Gilliard blames Harriet for the situation, as Grand Duchess Olga said in her letter, there is no question but that her supporters, especially Harriet, truly believed in her identity.

Gilliard states in his book that on the second day of his first visit, Anna mistook Mme Gilliard, who had been Anastasia's nursemaid, Shura, for Grand Duchess Olga. This incident is omitted in Harriet von Rathlef's book. On the other side of the coin, Gilliard also ignores incidents that support Anna's claims. For instance, on her first visit, Shura looked at Anna's feet and found they had the same bone deformation as those of Grand Duchess Anastasia – a fact Gilliard chose to forget. Shura exclaimed that the malformation known as *hallux valgus* was worse in the right foot than in the left, as was the case with Anastasia. He also chose not to discuss Anna's assertion that Grand Duke Ernst had made a secret trip to Russia. His deliberate omission of all references to 'Uncle Ernie's' secret trip reinforced claims by Anna's supporters that Gilliard was working for Ernst and being paid for his trouble.

Anna's supporters also contest Gilliard's dismissal of another of her revelations. Anna said that her mother the Tsarina had liked the symbol of the swastika, which of course at that time had not been tainted by its adoption by Adolf Hitler. She said the Tsarina had the ancient Indian image on her car, a memory that impressed her supporters. In his book Gilliard printed a picture of the Tsarina sitting in a vehicle that has a swastika displayed prominently on the bonnet. Gilliard alleges that a Russian officer had given Anna this picture. Friends of Anna claim, however, that Gilliard painted in the swastika on the photograph before publication. Anna's veracity is supported by Ambassador Zahle, who had heard her story about the swastika. He told Harriet that only

The very model of the
modern Grand
Duchess: Anna
Anderson in New
York society, 1930.
(James Blair Lovell)

The Anastasia myth

Right: The young
Anna Anderson in
Berlin. (James Blair Lovell)

Below: Anna with
faithful supporter
Prince Frederick of
Saxe-Altenburg.
(James Blair Lovell)

Above: In old age,
holding court as
husband Jack
Manahan looks on
approvingly.
(James Blair Lovell)

Right: The
Hollywood version:
Helen Hayes, Yul
Brynner and Ingrid
Bergman in
Anastasia.
(20th Century Fox)

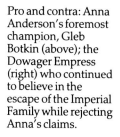

Pro and contra: Anna
Anderson's foremost
champion, Gleb
Botkin (above); the
Dowager Empress
(right) who continued
to believe in the
escape of the Imperial
Family while rejecting
Anna's claims.

Above: On the eve
of the revolution: the
Dowager Empress
Maria, Grand Duke
Mikhail, the Tsar for
a day, and his sister,
Grand Duchess
Xenia. (Ian Lilburn)

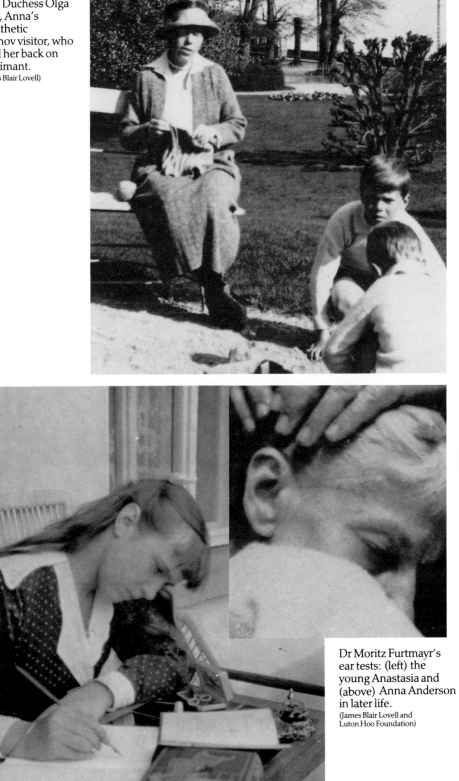

Grand Duchess Olga (right), Anna's sympathetic Romanov visitor, who turned her back on the claimant.
(All James Blair Lovell)

Dr Moritz Furtmayr's ear tests: (left) the young Anastasia and (above) Anna Anderson in later life.
(James Blair Lovell and Luton Hoo Foundation)

The paths of glory lead but to the grave

Top: The purported remains of Nicholas and Alexandra on display in Ekaterinburg. (A. Grakhov)

Above: The mass grave on the Koptiaki road. (A. Grakhov)

Right: The memorial at the grave-site. (A. Grakhov)

Above: The experts
report on the
investigations at the
Koptiaki grave
(extreme left, Dr
Aleksandr Avdonin,
and extreme right, Dr
William Maples).
(A. Grakhov)

Left: Deputy State
prosecutor Vladimir
Soloviev with
Ermakov's bayonet,
which was used to kill
Anastasia. (Fen Montaigne)

Bottom right:
Amateur sleuths seek
Romanov remains in
the Koptiaki Woods.
(A. Grakhov)

The last daughter of the Tsar. Grand Duchess Anastasia Nikolaevna, 1901–18, lives on in the 1995 production of the ballet *Sleeping Beauty* at the Bonn Opera House. (Ian Lilburn, top)

with the help of a magnifying glass had he been able to distinguish such a mascot in a photograph that was published long after Anna had asserted the Tsarina's attachment to the swastika.

The other error that Gilliard indisputably makes is his scoffing at Anna's memories of a 'green room', which he said never existed. In fact the malachite room is well known and was used by the Imperial Family exclusively to rest before receptions. Perhaps Gilliard was never admitted to this private room. By the same token, however, Gilliard is correct when he asserts that Anna mistakenly described the Tsar and Tsarina as having separate bedrooms. They always slept in the same room. From her account of the Tsarina's chamber, Gilliard surmises that Anna is describing a room shown on a postcard and described as 'the Tsarina's bedroom'. The problem is that the postcard fails to name the Tsarina. It was in fact the bedroom of Catherine the Great.

Gilliard's book was also discredited by its association with the co-author Constantin Savitch, former president of the Court of Assizes at St Petersburg. He joined the Anastasia business, and having gained Harriet von Rathlef's confidence, he took her extensive notes and then used them selectively to denounce Anna's authenticity on the lecture circuit. He proposed various fanciful conspiracy theories relating to her claims, contributed a small portion of Gilliard's book and then disappeared at the end of the 1920s, never to be heard from again. He was joined on the lecture circuit by Captain von Schwabe, whom Clara Peuthert had first approached in 1922, but who later changed his attitude towards Anna, and by Nikolai Markov, who headed the Supreme Monarchist Council. They all proclaimed various negative versions of her story, including conspiracies headed by Jews, Masons and Bolsheviks to seize the throne.

There are many other stories of Anna's recollections that seem to verify her claim, notably one that involved Dr Sergei Rudnev, the surgeon who saved Anna's arm. He recalled that on the day war was declared in 1914, he was walking by the palace in Moscow with a friend when he saw the Grand Duchess Anastasia and Tatiana throwing paper balls from a window down at people walking by in the street below. When Rudnev and his companion looked again towards the palace, the two girls quickly disappeared. In 1925 the doctor asked Anna what she was doing on that historic day. He reported that she acknowledged, 'My sister and I were playing the fool, and were pelting the passers-by with little paper balls.' Rudnev was to become one of Anna's believers and later said that she had a reading knowledge of Russian, as well as speaking Russian and English while under the influence of drugs, during her various illnesses.

These allegations and counter-allegations are largely anecdotal. They are used, often in paraphrased form, or simply forgotten as it suits the purpose of the supporter or opponent. Anna inspired in her followers almost a religious fervour, which made them see themselves as a reviled sect. Their tormentors, in the form of the Romanov and Hesse families, were depicted as evil or, as Gleb Botkin inferred, worse than the Bolsheviks. Some of this fervour rubbed off on the so-called persecutors, such as Lord Mountbatten, who spent thousands of pounds to prove Anna was an impostor.

When Gleb Botkin was forced to wait several days before seeing her, she sent him a message asking if he had brought his 'funny animals' with him. The Leuchtenbergs, with whom she was staying, could not understand this request. But Gleb had indeed brought his 'funny animals', a series of drawings depicting animals in military uniforms that he had sketched throughout his childhood in Russia. She later confirmed his positive identification of her by picking out those he had completed in Tobolsk and those he had done later. Although Gleb himself considered this as happy proof that she had indeed seen his drawings before, at least some of them bear the date of composition underneath Gleb's name. The cynical might attribute her knowledge of the animal drawings to the fact that Gleb's sister, Tatiana, had already visited her, although the Leuchtenbergs said that Tatiana had not discussed these drawings with her. Gleb's daughter, Marina Schweitzer, has now obtained permission to lodge these same drawings as historical documents at the Library of Congress in Washington D.C.

Harriet von Rathlef's notes do reveal Anna's large accumulated knowledge of the personnel, rooms and events surrounding the everyday life of the Tsar and his family. If she had picked up all this knowledge from Russian *émigrés*, then that was a prodigious feat in its own right. Her supporters, of course, argued that she could not have done so, and in any case why should anyone have wanted to coach her into the part? The only explanation for them was that she was the Grand Duchess.

There is one considerable hole in the arguments of Anna's supporters. They say her memory was sadly impaired by the head injuries she received from the rifle butts of the soldiers during the assassination. They attribute her inability to speak any language well, particularly those of her childhood, to this amnesia. But at the same time they point to detailed memories of trips on the imperial yacht the *Standart*, swastikas, paper balls and other incidents as proof of her identity. There is no question that the psychological ramifications of head injuries coupled with such a great shock as the assassinations would produce inestimable injury to the victim's mentality and recall. But no one seems to have connected the essential contradiction of her memory loss for languages, running parallel with her childhood reminiscences, some of which are trivial in the extreme and would be forgotten by anyone, with or without heavy blows to the head.

Prince Sigismund of Prussia first ascertained Anna's identity by relying on her essentially correct answers to the series of questions he posed to her in 1932 through the offices of his brother-in-law Prince Frederick of Saxe-Altenburg. At this time Sigismund was living in Central America, so he asked Frederick to carry out this mission. Frederick would not reveal Sigismund's questions or Anna's replies for many years, to avoid being accused of having supplied Anna with the answers. He later said she correctly identified her last meeting with Sigismund as being at the hunting lodge at Spala, in what was in 1912 the Polish provinces of Russia. Anna also recalled that Sigismund had stayed in the quarters of Count Fredericks, the minister of the court, and answered the 16 other questions quite accurately. While this was enough proof for Sigismund and by extension for Frederick, who had never met Anastasia as a child, it is very curious that anyone would recall such details 20 years after the event.

Lili von Dehn was another significant supporter of Anna, as she had known Anastasia as a girl through her close friendship with Tsarina Alexandra. Dehn did not meet Anna until 1957 because she had been living in South America, but she was also impressed by Anna's knowledge of court affairs. Her deposition includes how:

> She spoke of an occasion when the empress was very displeased, even angry with Anja [Anya Vyrubova]. That was only known to the Empress, Anja, myself and the little Grand Duchess who was present, but too young to understand the meaning and only remembered the fact. We spoke of the officers we mutually knew, and she never made a mistake.

Anna underwent numerous psychological tests during her many stays in German hospitals. All her examining doctors agreed that she was not insane. But they were generally at a loss as to how to explain the mental condition they found. Friends say she was certainly 'mentally affected', particularly in her behaviour, which ranged between lively, intelligent banter and extreme, rude abuse. She also had a reclusive side to her nature, which made her quite passive, staying in bed for long periods and taking very little interest in her surroundings. At other times her paranoia would prompt her to take bizarrely protective actions, such as barricading her house in Unterlengenhardt. This paranoia, though extreme, is explicable, given her goldfish-bowl existence. The constant curiosity of doctors and onlookers in her life is documented clearly in various medical reports and was recorded in Harriet von Rathlef's book, *Anastasia*. Dr Lothar Nobel, head doctor of the exclusive Mommsen Nursing Home, Berlin, where in 1925 Dr Rudnev had performed surgery on Anna's arm and where Grand Duchess Olga visited her, reported:

> To questions relating to her past she gives slow and hesitating answers, considers for a long time with a strained expression on her face, and finds difficulty in calling to mind the names of persons and places. After a very long time, she ceased completely to be suspicious of me, and, when occasion arose, she told me without hesitation about her early life; it is better to approach her by means of indirect questions . . . . Her manner of speech is, of course, absolutely free of all theatrical gesture and is natural. It also happens that she herself forgets many things she has narrated, and, on my referring to them

again, she wonders where I have learnt about them . . .. It can hardly be definitely decided how far the loss of memory is connected with the head injuries, since it is not possible accurately to ascertain the severity of the injuries. This form of disturbance of the memory is peculiar, and does not fall under any recognized category, particularly as it extends equally over the past as a whole. Only in relation to things which have occurred in the immediate past is her memory normal . . . . It appears to me impossible that her recollections depend on suggestion and that the knowledge of many insignificant details may be attributed to anything other than to her own experiences. Further it is hardly probable, psychologically, that anybody, who for some purpose or other is playing the part of another, would act as the patient is doing and show so little initiative in the realisation of her plans.

Thus Dr Nobel was puzzled by her condition, but he did not attribute her memory gaps and knowledge of 'many insignificant details' to coaching or reminiscences by the patient's companions, because Anna was so lethargic about trying to prove her identity. Her general behaviour also struck him as quite spontaneous and genuine. Thus while he cannot assert whether or not Anna actually is the Grand Duchess, he does accept the general premise that she is not deliberately perpetrating a fraud. At the same time he acknowledges that her memory is normal when it comes to events in the immediate past.

A leading psychoanalyst, Professor Karl Bohnhoeffer, also examined her in Berlin in 1926, and came to a similar conclusion:

The patient is not suffering from a mental disease in the ordinary sense of the word; but she shows the signs of a psychopathic constitution, which makes itself apparent in her emotional irritability, in her susceptibility to changes of mood, in especial to depression and in the peculiar disturbance of her memory . . . . There are disorders of the memory which depend more or less on the conscious suspension of the will . . . .. In connection with the remaining facts ascertained regarding the power of recollection, it is probably a case of loss of memory by auto-suggestion growing out of the desire to drive away the recollection of her experiences. It has been asked whether there can be any hypnotic influence exerted on the patient by a third person. This is to be denied as is also the supposition that the whole affair is a deliberate fraud.

Professor Bohnhoeffer also puzzles over Anna's amnesia, but he puts it down to Anna's overwhelming need to forget. He too dismisses Gilliard's basic assertion that she developed her memory of court life from others.

The leading physicians of the day were clearly unable to reach a conclusive diagnosis of Anna's peculiar mental condition. Their reports are also wide open to different interpretations, inviting the arguments between her supporters and detractors that raged throughout Germany at that time. Their testimonies do point, however, to a general sympathy for the woman's plight, which was to be echoed in the acceptance and fascination her story held for the general public. Interestingly, Grand Duchess Olga also felt a general sympathy towards her, as shown in the five notes she sent to Anna after her visit in 1925.

In view of the subjectivity of such reports, although the physicians were attempting to determine her mental condition through objective scientific observation, it is perhaps more worthwhile to study the physical evidence. Here the parallels are breathtaking. For Gilliard her only similarity to Anastasia was her blue eyes, remarked upon by nearly all those who knew her. Even this physical attribute is open to dispute, for as discussed earlier, Sydney Gibbes described Grand Duchess Anastasia's eyes as grey. Ian Lilburn recalled that Anna's eyes were generally bright blue but would darken if she became angry or upset. While her eyes were clearly reminiscent of one of Tsar Nicholas II's most distinguishing features, they were probably most arresting because of the strength of Anna's character. Her life, filled with illness, controversy and insecurity, showed that, whoever she was, she certainly had a very powerful and charismatic character. Such were the efforts to discover how she could have acquired her knowledge of Russia if she were not the Grand Duchess, that Dr

Osty was brought in by Duke George of Leuchtenberg in an attempt to hypnotize her in 1937, while she was staying at Castle Seeon. He failed.

Her feet, as noted by the nursemaid Shura, suffered from the congenital malformation called *hallux valgus*, which was worse in the right foot than in the left, just as in Grand Duchess Anastasia's case. This condition, where the big toe bends right in over the middle, causing a bunion, is not unusual and can be developed by women who wear ill-fitting shoes or spend too much time on their feet. Dr Rudnev, who operated on her arm, said, however, that Anna's condition was so extreme that it must have been present from birth.

Other identifying marks included a small scar on her right shoulder blade. Grand Duchess Anastasia had had a mole cauterized in that position so that it would not show when she wore ball gowns. Anna also had a small blemish on her forehead, similar to the Grand Duchess Anastasia, which was generally covered with a fringe when she was a girl. Anna had a scar on the base of the middle finger of her left hand, which made her finger stiff and which Harriet von Rathlef attributed to an accident when a footman closed a carriage door too early and trapped the hand. This incident did indeed happen, but according to Grand Duchess Olga, it was Anastasia's sister, Grand Duchess Maria, who suffered from having her finger trapped in this way.

Anna had many of her teeth removed during her stay at the Dalldorf asylum and thereafter found it difficult to obtain dentures that would fit her. Her subsequent embarrassment over her teeth was apparent from her life-long habit of covering her mouth with a handkerchief or paper tissue. Film of Anna as well as many photographs show this obsessive trait, which also contributed to her sense of mystery, as visitors often could not see her face properly. This habit was so pronounced that Gertrude Madsack, owner of the *Hannoverscher Anzeiger*, would joke about it, calling her Miss Paper. She often told Anna that she would not take her out unless she put in her false teeth.

Anna said that she had her teeth removed because the blows from the Bolshevik rifle butts had loosened many of them. The nurses at Dalldorf say that 16 teeth were removed in Germany after her almost constant complaints of toothache. The nurses surmised she could have wanted to change her appearance in this way and said they also saw her plucking out her hair, apparently in a vain effort to change her hairline.

Her opponents naturally told a different story from Anna's, to the effect that she deliberately wanted to alter the shape of her jaw, which did not look like Anastasia's. The faithful Duke of Leuchtenberg, ever ready to help Anna, had had a plaster cast of her upper and lower jaws made and took them to Paris so that the former dentist of the Imperial Household, Sergei Kostritsky, could come and look at them. He had earlier refused to examine Anna's teeth in person. He declined to remark on any of their peculiarities and only commented: 'As if I should have left the teeth in that condition.' He was later ready to join Gilliard in testifying against her.

Other marks on her body include a triangular scar on the top and bottom of one foot, disfigurements that would be consistent with accounts that the triangular blade of a Russian bayonet had pierced right through her foot during the massacre at Ekaterinburg. She also had a groove, one inch above her right ear, that could have been a bullet scar.

Throughout her life Anna was subjected to handwriting analyses, which were later used as evidence in the German court cases. In the 1920s various claims about her handwriting and its similarity or dissimilarity to that of the Grand Duchess became extremely controversial, echoing the heated disputes over her knowledge of languages. Harriet von Rathlef says that when she first knew Anna, she had considerable difficulties with any kind of writing. 'When I came to know her, she could neither write nor read,' she commented. She also reports that Anna first wrote her name 'Anastasia' in 1925 and did so in Roman letters, without having any signature taken from the Grand Duchess's hand to imitate. She then sent a Christmas card to the Gilliards in Lausanne, which they studied intently to see if the writing matched that of the Grand Duchess. They were struck by its similarity to Anastasia's signature when she was about 15 years old.

Gilliard later alleged that Anna had taken great pains to copy the signature from existing documents, assertions that he backed up by printing a photograph in his book of her repeated attempts to 'copy' the signature. Harriet von Rathlef, however, attributes Anna's difficulties in writing to this partial memory loss that so afflicted her knowledge of languages. In her book she states that Anna started writing in English quite naturally, at the request of an Englishwoman they met in Lugano, who simply assumed Anna had written knowledge of English. This description of Anna's half-remembered knowledge of languages echoes testimony from the diary of Faith Lavington, the English governess at Castle Seeon, who gave Anna English lessons during her stay there.

The science of graphology came to play a significant role in the German trials. The Hamburg High Court of Appeals appointed their own independent handwriting expert, Minna Becker, who found 137 identical characteristics between Anna's handwriting and that of the Grand Duchess Anastasia. She told the court that in her opinion no two people could write with such consistent similarity and concluded that the claimant was the Grand Duchess. She also compared the writing of Anastasia with that of Franziska Schanzkowska at the instigation of the prosecution and found no similarity.

In the absence of fingerprints and until very recently the scientific proof of DNA fingerprints, ears were considered very reliable indicators of identity. Scientists say that the structure and pattern of ears remain essentially the same throughout a person's life from the age of four months. They may become more 'fleshy' with age, and the lobes may drop, but the essential shape remains the same. Ear analysis has legal standing and has been accepted in courts, particularly in the United States, for identification purposes. The comparison of Anna's ears with photographs of the Grand Duchess has exercised the minds of a number of anthropologists over the last 70 years, work that has consistently foundered on the problem of comparing Anna's ears in photographs taken at the same angle and in the same lighting conditions as those pictures depicting the Grand Duchess.

Pierre Gilliard was the first on the anthropological hunt and commissioned his friend and colleague at Lausanne University, Professor Marc Bischoff, to make a comparative study. He came up with a categorical no. Other studies followed, but all the results were overturned by Professor Baron von Eickstedt of Mainz University. He showed that Bischoff had compared only six photographs taken from different angles and with different lighting, which had the effect of distorting the comparison. Eickstedt took the trouble of personally visiting Anna, carefully taking similar photographs of Anna's ears to those in existing photographs of Grand Duchess Anastasia. As far as the evidence pertaining to the ear was concerned, he concluded that 'this ear does not count clearly against, but altogether for the identity,' and he strongly condoned Anna's claims. His report was altogether more thorough than earlier studies, using as many as 300 photographs, including some members of both the Romanov and Hessian families.

However, none of these examinations was sufficient for the Hamburg High Court of Appeals. The judges appointed the anthropological expert, Professor Otto Reche. He visited Anna in Unterlengenhardt, took exact measurements of her face, studied hundreds of photographs, dismissed all the earlier reports and ended his investigation with the words:

'The general conclusion is therefore: proof that Frau Anderson is the Grand Duchess Anastasia.' His study concentrated on the width of the cheekbones in relation to the face and to the lower jaw, and the height and width of the eyesockets and of the forehead.

These tests echo the more modern comparison using computer technology, employed by Geoffrey Oxley, who compared the faces of Anna Anderson and Franziska Schanzkowska in this way for Julian Nott's television programme on Anna Anderson, shown on Britain's Channel 4 on 5 October 1994 as *The Mystery of Anastasia*. He came to the conclusion that they were probably one and the same person. Computer technology does not convince everyone, however. Russian scientists have used similar research techniques on the skulls of the Tsar's daughters at Ekaterinburg and come up with the definitive assertion that Grand Duchess Maria is the missing daughter – not Anastasia.

The scientist who probably had the most effect on the case was Moritz Furtmayr, who had long worked as an identification expert with the West German police. He based his testing on the premise that the relationship between the key points of the skull do not change after birth, a system that has been used in German courts and is considered very reliable. He applied other tests, including a comparison of the ears, which matched at 17 anatomical points, five more than is considered admissible for evidence in the West German courts. Anna also passed other forensic tests, causing Furtmayr to affirm in 1971: 'It can be considered proven and verified that Mrs Anderson now living in the United States is without doubt one and the same as the Grand Duchess Anastasia.' Anna's attorney, Baron von Stackelberg, was ready to reopen the case in the German courts on the basis of this new evidence, but Prince Frederick urged against the possibility as he could see no useful purpose in returning to the legal battlefield.

More recent testimony has confirmed the astonishing similarity of Anna's ears to those of the Grand Duchess. Julian Nott commissioned Professor Peter Venezis, Regius Professor of Forensic Medicine at Glasgow University, who also assists the police in identification work, to make a comparative study of Anna's ears with those of the Grand Duchess. A team of five people looked 'completely blind' at a number of pictures portraying Anna Anderson, Grand Duchess Anastasia and others. They were not told who they were trying to match as they submitted the various images to a video superimposition technique imprinted on computer monitors. There was one dissident in the team who did not agree, but four members matched Anna's ears with those of the Grand Duchess.

'There was a remarkable similarity,' said Venezis. 'I wanted to give them a 5 [the highest match] but I couldn't because they were taken at different angles. We were also looking at vastly dissimilar ages.' Venezis is merely the last in a long line of scientists to confirm that if Anna is an impostor, then she is a very lucky one. In the absence of fingerprints and, until recently, DNA evidence, ears were considered the best scientific test available. The similarity of Anna's ears to those of the Grand Duchess is no longer disputed.

Throughout the long saga, physiological evidence has formed another basis of dispute between Anna's friends and foes, as scientists have discovered similarity and dissimilarity, like a regular drumbeat over the years. Very late in the day, Moritz Furtmayr discovered a farcical mix-up, which added to the confusion.

Earlier experts had reversed the negative of a photograph taken of Anna at the Dalldorf asylum, which meant that some scientists had been comparing her left ear with the right ear of the Grand Duchess.

By this time it was too late to speculate on what 'might have been'. Anna was living in Charlottesville with Jack to take care of her, meeting the press and enjoying a degree of celebrity. Gleb died one year after she married Jack, almost the last of her supporters who had known the Grand Duchess in Russia. While Anna seemed to enjoy baffling those who came to question her by producing more and more exotic stories about the Romanovs, she and Jack also became more isolated as their lives became more eccentric. Much of the attention focused on the couple by journalists was courted and fielded by Jack, whose fascination with the royal houses of Europe never abated. He was always willing to supply information and photographs to visitors and discuss the myriad details of his wife's case, as Anna predictably often refused to meet anyone.

Meanwhile, their living conditions deteriorated, in a fashion similar to the decline in Anna's house in Unterlengenhardt. The front room of the house for some reason had a tree stump in its centre, and the various Russian treasures and bric-à-brac that she had collected through her life began to disappear behind the piles of rubbish, such as newspapers, fast-food containers and empty catfood tins, that were rarely cleared out. Neighbours report that as the lawn at the front of the house grew out of control, Anna began placing booby traps to discourage visitors, postmen and city officials alike. She also once more started collecting animals, with as many as 30 cats and the usual quota of large, fierce dogs. The Manahans did not clean up after the cats, so that visitors reported a terrible stench emanating from the property. As for the dogs, they became well known in Charlottesville. Dick Schweitzer, Gleb Botkin's son-in-law, recalls one visit they had from the Manahans, where Marina was smart enough to run back into her house and shut the door against the dogs. Richard, playing the role of a good host, went out to greet them and was bitten by one of her dogs for his pains.

The state of the property naturally brought complaints from the neighbours, who filed court cases to have something done about this obvious health hazard. Jack was ordered to clean up and would do so, but the house would quickly deteriorate again. He would then be hauled back into court.

In 1977 Jack invited Prince Frederick and Ian Lilburn to visit Charlottesville and give a talk on Anna's case to a university audience. Ian said he thought Jack wanted to effect a reconciliation between Anna and Prince Frederick, after her abrupt dismissal of him following the 'Yurovsky-style' murder of her cats in Germany. Ian recalls the visit with good humour, including the cockroaches in the apartments owned by Jack next door to his house, where Ian and Frederick stayed. Jack made a good attempt to look after them: 'He would bring us breakfast across from the main house, but we just couldn't eat it because of the cats all over the kitchen.'

In August 1979 Anna developed a blockage in her lower intestine, which was removed by Dr Richard Shrum at the Martha Jefferson Hospital in Charlottesville. Part of the obstructive tumour was gangrenous, and a sample was stored at the hospital. At the time Jack and Anna's friends were grateful that the operation was not more serious, although Anna was never to walk again. She spent most of her time sitting in her wheelchair or in the front seat of their very old car. Two years later she presided over celebrations for Anastasia's 80th birthday party. Seventy-five people attended, testimony to the power still exerted by this frail old lady. Meanwhile, the writer Royce Ryton was the latest playwright to find enough magic and sympathy from her life-story to turn it into the play, *I am who I am*, which opened in New York in September 1982. A new made for television movie would be filmed a few years later, and even into the 1990s ballets and films continued to use the Anastasia theme.

By the turn of the decade Anna's life was nearly over. Her last year was a sad testament to the woman who had been the guest of aristocrats all over Europe and the toast of Long Island's wealthy community, and someone who had continually attracted willing 'ladies-in-waiting' to care for her. The deterioration of the house and of Jack's health were so extreme that the circuit court appointed local attorney William Preston to act as guardian. In November 1983 Preston had Anna committed to a local hospital, as he determined that Jack was no longer able to care for her. Jack attracted more bizarre publicity to her case when he 'kidnapped' her from hospital for a three-day spree around Virginia. Police finally tracked them down, and Anna was placed in an old persons' home. She appeared to have a stroke in January and died on 12 February 1984 of pneumonia. Jack was to live on, suffering increasingly from diabetes and mental instability, until his own death six years later.

Anna's funeral proved to be a bizarre ending to her unusual life. Jack Manahan followed his wife's express wishes that her remains be cremated and then held a memorial service at the University of Virginia Chapel, on St Valentine's Day, 14 February. The service, attended by the world's media, was highlighted by Jack's rambling account of Anna's life, her royal claims and his very evident grief, causing his 30-minute oration to degenerate into incoherence. He then took the urn containing her ashes back to his house and started a new controversy in his attempts to honour her specific request that her remains should be interred at the cemetery of Castle Seeon. Some members of the Leuchtenberg family were against this but, after the intervention of Prince Frederick, the town council finally gave permission for her to be buried there. The ceremony was carried out on 18 June, on what would have been Grand Duchess Anastasia's 83rd birthday. Jack defended her claim to be Anastasia to the waiting press and then returned to Virginia, a lonely man, who had sacrificed his health and peace of mind to take care of his 'royal' wife.

CHAPTER EIGHT

First-Finders

THE DAY FOLLOWING the initial burial of the Romanovs, Filipp Goloshchekin addressed a group of workers in the municipal theatre. When he announced that the Tsar was dead, a cry went up from his listeners: 'Show us the body!' Interest in the case did not wane through the 1920s. Party propagandists, taking questions after a party-political propaganda speech, were often asked to explain the strange circumstances of the Tsar's execution.

The city of Ekaterinburg itself, retaken by the Red Army in 1919, developed the events of the Ipatiev House into a virtual civil cult. The Square of the Ascension Church was renamed the Square of the People's Vengeance. In the 1920s the Ipatiev House was transformed into the city Museum of the History of the Revolution. Delegations from home and abroad delighted in having their pictures taken in front of the fatal wall. A special painting, commissioned from the artist V. Pchelin in 1927, depicted Nicholas, Alexandra and Maria being handed over by Vasily Yakovlev to the leaders of the Urals Soviet in April 1918. Major participants in the events, such as the local man Petr Ermakov, had streets in the city named after them. Also in the 1920s the city's name was changed from Ekaterinburg to Sverdlovsk, to honour Iakov Sverdlov, the secretary of the Central Committee who had advised the Urals Soviet that their regicide would receive the ready approval of Lenin and his associates.

Most of all, it was the living participants who kept the events fresh in the minds of locals. The murder of the Tsar was the most important event in the life of Petr Ermakov, who was already boasting about it within hours of the burial of the family. When in his cups – which was often – he would regale listeners with stories of the execution. As a local hero, he was on display to the young, brought in to inspire them with the tales of an old revolutionary. There are still residents of Ekaterinburg who recall sitting around a campfire with other Young Pioneers and listening to Ermakov's tales of derring-do. He was not just an old drunk or a blood-thirsty murderer, but a glorious hero, who inspired young boys' dreams of becoming Chekists themselves and pumping bullets into the evil counter-revolutionaries.

Ermakov's boasting grew more and more uncontrolled. He promoted himself not just to the role of the Tsar's assassin but also as the official responsible for every aspect of the execution. In so doing he had to usurp the role of others, especially Yurovsky. He went beyond this and actually denigrated his boss's actions. In his memoirs, written in 1947, he sets the execution far too early in the evening. It is Ermakov who tricks the family down into the basement room with a story of firing in the city. He then goes out to the courtyard and commands driver Sergei Liukhanov to start the engine in order to cover the sound of gunfire. Returning to the cellar room, he personally hands to Yurovsky the execution order of the Urals Soviet. When Yurovsky nervously demurs – 'Why do we have to shoot them all?' – it is the resolute Ermakov who announces that: 'I said *all*, and I don't have time to argue with you – get on with it!'

Ermakov stands at Yurovsky's right hand while he reads the order (although he is unable to present a coherent account of Nicholas's last words). He is the one who is delegated to kill Nicholas, Alexandra, Alexei *and* one of the daughters. Finally, it is Yurovsky's Mauser that kills the Tsar instantly. Like Bottom in *A Midsummer Night's Dream*, Ermakov can play every part: he dumps the bodies in the mine in the Koptiaki Woods, and he later is the man who pulls them out; he secures the petrol and sulphuric acid, and he burns the bodies, destroying every trace. As he sums up, 'I had anticipated everything.' To clinch his claim, in 1927 Ermakov donated his tsar-killing Mauser to the Museum of the Revolution in Sverdlovsk. Nor could he stay away from the site. In the early 1920s he went to the pit, still marked by the rotten railway ties, and had his picture taken.

Yurovsky was not slow to stake his own claim, and with his Moscow connections they had a higher profile. He gave both his Colt revolver, which helped to kill the Tsar, and the Mauser that delivered Alexei's *coup de grâce*, to Moscow's prestigious Central Museum of the Revolution. In 1920 Mikhail Pokrovsky, the doyen of the new Soviet historical science, was engaged in collecting the life-stories of prominent actors in the revolution. Yurovsky was an obvious candidate, and he provided Pokrovsky with a copy of the report he had penned for his superiors. In the course of his life Yurovsky left other accounts, all designed to assert his priority over any pretenders.

The interest generated by the murder inspired a number of books, but the most popular was the account of P. M. Bykov, *The Last Days of the Romanovs*, which went through two editions in the 1920s. The title of the 1926 edition is formed by smoke from a smouldering bonfire, illustrating the cremation of the royal remains. But a careful reading of the text, which was presumably based on at least some interviews with local people, reveals that this was not the end of the story. Bykov clearly stated that there was something left after the cremation, and that these remains were taken some distance away from the Four Brothers site and 'buried in a bog', never to be found. As time passed, Bykov's book became virtually the only text available to those with an interest in the fate of the Romanovs, especially in provincial Sverdlovsk, where it was published. The book's intimation that *something* survived the destruction of the bodies gave encouragement to amateur local sleuths. Had they had access to the conclusion offered by Sokolov in any of his published reports, for example, they would never have taken up the search.

In 1928 the tenth anniversary of the execution arrived. The celebration of revolutionary anniversaries was a major preoccupation of the young Soviet regime as part of the process of creating a new civic myth, which replaced Tsars with revolutionaries. The Soviet civic poet Vladimir Mayakovsky visited Sverdlovsk and, in search of inspiration, asked to see the burial site. He described the scene in his 1928 poem 'The Emperor':

Was it really here?
No, not here.

Further on!
Here the cedar
Is marked with an axe,
The notches
on the bark
above the roots,
near the cedar
a road,
and in it
The Emperor is buried!

Plans were mooted for a new publication, which would collect documents and testimony from participants. The project suddenly stalled. Apparently Stalin one day announced, 'that's enough of this Romanov business,' and that was that. There were problematic aspects to the anniversary. Several of the participants had connections with Lev Trotsky, whom Stalin had just bested in the political struggle for leadership, and whose memory he was eager to blacken. Trotskyites could do nothing positive for the revolution. Indeed, Yurovsky's daughter, Rimma, was sent to the camps in the 1930s. Beloborodov, Goloshchekin, Didtkovsky and Safarov, the leaders of the Urals Soviet, were unluckier still: they were all shot as 'enemies of the people'.

Nonetheless, events conspired to keep alive the memory of the Romanovs in Siberia. In his memoir on the execution, Yurovsky recalled complaining regretfully in his report to the Urals Soviet that he had not had time to search all the members of the family thoroughly. On the day that he took over from Aleksandr Avdeev as commandant of the House of Special Purpose, Yurovsky forced the Romanovs to give him their personal jewellery 'for safekeeping'. The search party that ransacked the Ipatiev House on the morning after the execution was looking for more than silk shirts and samovars (although they took these as well). Plenty of jewels showed up – two suitcases full, by one account – but the Bolsheviks were still convinced that many of the Romanov jewels had been hidden somewhere. The only possible location was Tobolsk, but all who might have provided the necessary information had been shot or, in the case of the valet Terenty Chemodurov, simply forgotten. Interrogations of the nuns revealed nothing since their prioress ordered them to perish rather than reveal the hiding places. She herself died in police custody.

The secret police remained alert, and in 1933 a portion of the Romanov treasure materialized. The breakthrough in the investigation came during the interrogation of a former servant at Freedom House, Paulina Mezhans. During her time as a servant, and afterwards when she was imprisoned by the police, she had seen or heard of the dispersal of the Romanov treasure. She gave the police two leads. One was a former nun, Marfa Uzhintseva, who had brought eggs and milk to Freedom House from the nearby Ivanovsk Convent. The other was a priest, Father Alexei Vasiliev, who had conducted religious services for the family.

The police immediately arrested the hapless Marfa, who confessed all. She had indeed served as a courier, filling her egg basket with jewels, which she delivered to the prioress. A substantial hoard of treasure was accumulated before the Romanovs were moved to Ekaterinburg. Anticipating arrest herself, the prioress entrusted the treasure to Marfa, with the instruction that she should surrender it only to the 'real authorities'. Marfa wrapped the valuables in several tablecloths and hid them in a well in the convent courtyard. She was soon arrested herself as a former nun and was distraught with worry that the treasure would be lost.

Upon her release, she recovered the jewels and began to bury them in the convent cemetery, moving them about from grave to grave. This brought her no relief, because she was well aware that the Communist authorities often dug up churchyards in the hunt for valuables. She decided to throw the package into the River Irtysh, but first sought the advice of a friend of the convent, the local fish merchant Vasily Kornilov. When Kornilov heard her story, he cried out: 'What are you doing?! When the real authority comes back they are going to call you to account, and you are going to tell them that you threw the valuables into the Irtysh!' Marfa begged Kornilov to take the treasure, and after some hesitation he agreed. They buried the jewels in two glass jars in his basement. Soon after Kornilov moved away to Kazan. The wretched Marfa continued to worry, especially when the Irtysh flooded basements in the town. And now the secret police had found her out. Worse still, they grew very angry when she was unable to find the spot where the treasure was hidden.

It did not take long for the secret police to catch up with Kornilov, and he was brought back to Tobolsk. He quickly located the jars. As the two investigators, Masksevich and Borodin, unwrapped the tablecloth, they must have seen promotion glittering among the contents on the table. Before them lay more than 200 pieces of fine jewellery, including a diamond brooch of more than 100 carats, a diamond half-moon, which had been a gift from the Turkish sultan, and bracelets and pins carrying the monogram of the Empress and her daughters, as well as their diamond diadems. The total value of the haul was estimated at more than three million rubles.

This astounding discovery only whetted the appetite of the Organs, as the secret police were euphemistically known. Uzhintseva and Mezhans set them on the trail of an ever more glittering prize. They knew that Father Alexei Vasiliev had also taken things out of Freedom House in a leather satchel, including the personal effects of the Tsar, as well as the golden ceremonial sword of the Tsarevich. At the end of 1929 Father Vasiliev had set out for Omsk, but he died on the journey. His wife and sons were still living there. When arrested, they confessed, as best they could, what Vasiliev had done with the treasure. He had buried it in the ground and then hidden it in the rafters of his church. What had happened to it between then and his death on the road they were unable to say, even under repeated interrogation.

Meanwhile, the Organs spread the net wider, arresting a former valet, Aleksandr Kirpichnikov, who had served in Freedom House, and the widow of the Tsar's captor, Colonel Evgeny Kobylinsky, who had himself been shot by the Bolsheviks several years earlier. A few jewels, given as presents to her husband, were found in the flat of Klavdia Kobylinskaia. More importantly, both she and Kirpichnikov told a similar story. The overall dispersal of the jewels had been carried out by the French tutor Pierre Gilliard, and he had kept a list of the items and to whom they had been given. The list apparently included some of the Russian crown jewels. Thereafter, every interrogation in the case was sure to demand of its victims information about the 'Gilliard List'. It is unknown whether Gilliard left it in Russia, or took it with him when he emigrated.

What is certain is that the list's full contents were never recovered, even though Klavdia Kobylinskaia set the police on another likely target, Konstantin and Anila Pechekos, friends of her former husband. She had actually seen her husband pass a small box over to them in their house. The Organs again pounced. Heretofore, they had dealt with persons who were elderly, alone, afraid and easy to break. The Pechekos had taken a vow never to reveal the location of the treasure that Kobylinsky had given them, and they were determined to keep it.

The couple were threatened, as had been the others, with severe retribution on themselves and their families if they did not cooperate. Nonetheless, they continued to deny any knowledge of the Romanov wealth, even when personally confronted by Klavdia Kobylinskaia. At last Konstantin led police inspectors, including agent Borodin who had helped to recover the earlier hoard, to the former home of his brother, who had emigrated to Poland in the early 1920s. On the sixth floor he pointed to a section of the wall and said, 'There, that's the place.' A thorough search, which involved tearing down most of the wall, revealed nothing.

The agents decided to try an identical flat on the fifth floor and left Pechekos under guard. As Borodin was hammering away at the wall, he heard rapid footsteps descending the staircase. It was the guard he had left in charge of Pechekos. 'Sir, come quick! The bugger's jumped out the window!' From his hospital bed the badly injured Pechekos refused to answer any more questions about the treasure.

His wife Anila was equally courageous. She continued to repeat her husband's story that the valuables were hidden in her brother-in-law's former flat through several weeks of interrogation. Then, alone in her cell, she broke up an aluminum spoon and swallowed the pieces, dying in agony two weeks later, but without revealing her secret. The methods of the Organs worked only with people who were afraid to die, and the Pechekos, fortified by their solemn oath, proved impossible to break. The investigation petered out, and the crown jewels, together with Alexei's miniature sword, remained lost in Siberia.

If the hunt for Romanov treasure kept their memory alive in the

Soviet Union in the 1930s, the intervening years and the Second World War caused the historical thread to be lost by all but a few. At the end of the 1940s the Museum of the History of the Revolution in the Ipatiev House was closed. A resident of Sverdlovsk remembers, as a small boy in the early 1950s, receiving a box on the ear from a secret policeman for announcing to friends, as the limousines of a visiting foreign delegation passed by, 'They've come to look for the grave of their relatives.' The great event of the city's revolutionary history was no longer considered fit for foreign consumption.

A renewal of interest in the Romanovs did come from the West. In 1967 the American author Robert Massie published *Nicholas and Alexandra*, a popular history of Nicholas's reign, which reached the bestseller lists and spawned a Hollywood movie in 1971. The book's appeal stemmed in part from its sensitive treatment of the family pressures created by Alexei's haemophilia. Massie was well equipped to address this issue since he and his wife Suzanne also had a son afflicted by the disease. Massie's sympathetic treatment of Nicholas, and the widespread publicity that the book received, forced the Soviets to address what had become a blank spot in their history. In 1972, the literary magazine *Zvezda* published the series *Twenty-three Steps Down*, by M. K. Kasvinov. He accused Massie, 'a hireling of the anti-Soviet industry', of making Nicholas a sympathetic figure in order to emphasize the bloodiness of the Russian revolution. Kasvinov made no such mistake, and followed the official line that the last Tsar was limited and ignorant, cruel and hypocritical.

Illustrating the dictum that bad publicity is better than no publicity, Kasvinov's literary hatchet job helped to revive interest in the last Tsar. The Ipatiev House even became a place of secret pilgrimage for lovers of Russia's past. A memorial candle or bouquet of flowers occasionally appeared outside it. Even such modest tributes seemed a dangerous revival of monarchism. In Moscow the ruling Politburo met in closed session to discuss the matter, and a decision was reached to have the house destroyed. The appropriate order, signed by Leonid Brezhnev himself, arrived on the desk of the First Secretary of the Sverdlovsk Region, Boris Yeltsin. Yeltsin was perplexed. In his estimation Ipatiev House represented no ideological danger, and it even bore a plaque announcing that it was a architectural monument of the turn of the century and protected by the state. 'What I am to tell people?' he asked Moscow. 'Whatever you like, only get rid of the building,' was the reply.

Early on a September morning in 1977, a work crew arrived at the Ipatiev House. Before the citizens of Sverdlovsk had finished their breakfast, the wrecking ball had begun to swing. Working with a haste and efficiency not often seen on Soviet construction sites, they levelled the building completely, hauled away all the debris and paved over the site with asphalt. The adjacent square, which had been renamed Square of the People's Vengeance, was renamed again, this time in honour of the Young Communist League, and a typically bland monument was erected, depicting young Communists rushing towards the glorious future. The past, in this instance, was to be obliterated.

Not all residents of Sverdlovsk viewed this destruction of Russia's national heritage with equanimity. Aleksandr Nikolaevich Avdonin had special reason to be concerned, since he himself was actively investigating 'the Romanov business'. If the Communist Party were uneasy about a few candles and a bunch of flowers outside the Ipatiev House, what would they say to efforts to find Tsar Nicholas's long-hidden grave?

One need only walk into Aleksandr Avdonin's flat on Pervomaiskaia Street in today's renamed Ekaterinburg to appreciate what fired his interest in the fate of Nicholas II. His study has a panoramic view of the bell-tower of the Church of the Ascension, which fronts the square, where once stood the Ipatiev House. The flat gives other clues to Avdonin's qualifications for discovery work. The book shelves share space with clusters of crystals and polished stones. Avdonin is a well-known geologist, a common career in the Urals with its rich mineral wealth. Each summer hundreds of geologists, both students and old hands, descend upon Ekaterinburg to participate in geological expeditions. It was a perfect cover for a secret search, since nobody in the Urals would ever be surprised to encounter a small team, armed with geologist hammers, digging in the woods.

Avdonin is a native of Sverdlovsk and had absorbed its legends before Moscow put them off limits. As a boy in the Young Pioneers he had actually heard Petr Ermakov boast of his role in the executions. As he completed his education and training, and settled into a successful career, he continued to be drawn to the mystery of the Romanovs. 'Call it inquisitiveness rather than curiosity,' he now says, while conceding that forbidden things are always more exciting and desirable. By the early 1970s Avdonin developed a stronger interest in the Romanov burial, motivated by the fact that the older generation that had witnessed these events was now dying out, and a gigantic gap was being left in Russia's national history. He decided to search actively for Nicholas's remains.

But were there remains? In this instance the secrecy and limitation of information, imposed as the 'Romanov business' moved off limits, was beneficial. Any researcher starting work in the West instinctively reaches for Nikolai Sokolov's authoritative report of his investigation, which was published in a number of languages. As Avdonin began his searches, virtually the only account available to him was P. M. Bykov's tendentious official version of events, *The Last Days of the Romanovs*. Whereas the definitive conclusion of Sokolov is that all the bodies were burned and dissolved with acid at the Four Brothers mine, leaving only a few charred fragments which the investigators carried away, Bykov's account offered more hope.

'They [the White Guards] did not find the grave of the Romanovs,' he wrote, 'because the remains of the bodies after they were burned were transported from the mine to some distance away and hidden in a bog in an area not explored by the White Guards and the investigators. There the bodies rotted away undisturbed.'

This meant, concluded Avdonin, that there were still traces of the corpses that Sokolov had not found. He also recognized the inaccuracies in this account. The remains could not have been disposed of as Bykov claimed, because, as any geologist knew, 'You can't bury anything in a bog.' At this point Avdonin decided that the grave must exist and that he would find it. When further information became available, he simply fitted it into his presuppositions. When he finally secured the Sokolov report, he understood that the unidentifiable bones that Sokolov found at the site were the remains of the burial detail's dinner. When Petr Ermakov, in his written memoirs, noted that all the bodies were 'burned', Avdonin recalled that the Russian verb that Ermakov used can mean either 'burned by fire' or 'burned by acid'.

As Avdonin continued his investigations through the middle 1970s, he began to attract kindred spirits, including young trainee-geologists who worked with him in the summer. He planned his annual hunt for the Romanovs just as he would the search for a deposit of ore. In the winter, together with a gifted young associate Mikhail Kochurov, he would examine maps and plan out the summer's search area. The small Avdonin group gave little thought to what they would do if they actually found the remains. There would certainly be no possibility of publicity, for this was a discovery that could put them in prison for 'anti-Soviet activity'. It would suffice to mark the site in their records and leave some identification for future discoverers in order to prevent this historical milestone from being totally lost to future generations.

Avdonin's explorations had been going on for several summers when, on an August evening in 1976, there was a knock at his door. He opened it to find a police colonel in full uniform standing before him, accompanied by a man sporting the formal dress of a Special Consultant to the Ministry of Interior with a prestigious Soviet service decoration in the lapel. This is it! thought Avdonin. I'm going to prison! The two men stepped into the room. 'Comrade Avdonin,' announced the colonel, 'May I introduce you to Comrade Gelli Trofimovich Ryabov? He wants to talk to you about the Romanovs.'

Gelli Ryabov needed no introduction to any Soviet citizen. He had begun his career in the regular police, or militsia. After many years of service, he became a writer whose personal experiences enabled him to create gripping stories of the travails of the Soviet 'cop on the beat', engaged in an unending struggle with criminals and bureaucrats. He provided the script for a film version of his work. On evenings when the series was screened on Soviet television, the streets were empty. His creative work earned him the prestigious State Prize. He had very high level connections in the Ministry of Interior, which was responsible for the militsia, including the Minister himself, Nikolai Schelekov.

In 1976 Ryabov arrived in Sverdlovsk to present a personal

screening of his new film on the militsia, *Born by the Revolution*, to a select group of local police big shots. He was met at the railway station by an official minder, who wanted to show him the city. 'I don't know what came over me,' Ryabov recalled later, 'but right from the station I asked to be taken directly to the House of Special Purpose.' The guide was not at all surprised: this was a typical request from visitors to Sverdlovsk, including many 'important guests' from Moscow. Within minutes Ryabov stood in the basement room of the Ipatiev House. In an interview, later published, he said:

> It is hard to say how I felt at that moment . . . I felt resting on me a responsibility for all this horror that has not been eradicated from our national history, for everything that accompanied the great cataclysms suffered by Russia. I quickly became convinced that I was obligated to learn and tell others the truth about the murder and burial of the Romanovs . . . In a word, I travelled to Sverdlovsk as an ordinary human being, with the usual psychology born of a policeman's experiences, and I left with the feeling that a mission rested upon me.

Fired with this new enthusiasm, Ryabov struck up a conversation about the Romanov burial with one of his hosts. 'The man you want is Avdonin,' he was told. 'He is a local geologist with an interest in local history. I'll take you to his flat.' Thus did Ryabov meet Avdonin.

If Ryabov had hoped to impress Avdonin with his uniform and his connections, he succeeded only too well. The intimidated geologist denied everything. There could have been no burial. The site would now be in a built-up paved-over area. He had no interest in the subject and didn't know anything about it. Ryabov was a former police investigator, and as the conversation meandered into the early hours of the morning, he recognized that Avdonin knew far more than he was letting on. Finally Ryabov's escort, the police colonel, went home, and Ryabov went to work. He had already noticed on the wall of Avdonin's study a picture of the extraordinarily popular Soviet singer and actor Vladimir Vysotsky.

'You like Vysotsky?' Ryabov asked. 'I know him well. Would you like to meet him?' The ice was broken. Avdonin admitted to more than a passing interest in the Romanov burial, but continued to hide details of his own active investigation. If Ryabov, with his Moscow connections and *blat* [influence], wanted to be 'the Boss', that was fine with Avdonin. The humble provincial would be able to hide his activities in the glow of the bigwig from the capital. Avdonin was aware that up to this point all his research had been done 'at his own risk'. The two men reached an agreement. Avdonin would share information with Ryabov, who in turn would use his police connections to seek out material from confidential state and Communist Party archives. At some point this information would be used to conduct a formal search for the grave site.

Through Avdonin, Ryabov made contact with family members of some of the principal actors in the drama, such as Yurovsky's daughter Rimma, and his son Aleksandr, then living in Leningrad. The latter was more than forthcoming: he provided Ryabov with a detailed report his father had written about the Romanov burial. There was no longer any doubt that a burial of corpses had taken place.

It also became apparent that the Moscow–Sverdlovsk axis had a rival. The Moscow author Edvard Radzinsky was also working in the archives – although without access to the Spetskhrany, or closed sections – and was interviewing and making contacts with family members and acquaintances of those involved in the deaths of the Imperial Family at Ekaterinburg. When glasnost permitted, he was able to rush into print with the tale of his own investigations, *The Last Tsar: The Life and Death of Nicholas II*. While the book was a mine of information, it had an unfinished air – boasting an epilogue, an afterword and two additional supplements – as Radzinsky struggled to incorporate late-breaking information about the discovery of the grave and DNA testing of the remains. Not for nothing is the motif of his work the despairing query: 'Will I never finish this book?'

Ryabov was able to send a steady stream of information to Avdonin, including the reports of Sokolov and Diterikhs and the testimony of Yurovsky and others. Of special interest was the photographic evidence that Sokolov included in his book, especially views of related sites in the Koptiaki Woods. Sokolov had recorded them merely as physical proof that Yurovsky's burial squad had been here or there in the woods. With the information provided by Yurovsky's memoir, it was evident that one of the photographs – of the small bridge the Bolsheviks had constructed out of old railway sleepers – might show the actual location of the burial. Then another decisive piece of evidence surfaced, the photograph that Petr Ermakov had taken of himself standing on the site of the Tsar's burial with the caption: THE TSAR IS BURIED HERE. The two pictures showed the same scene.

It was not simply a matter of walking to the site, however. The location was low-lying, marshy and on the edge of a bog, and there had been a great deal of subsidence in the intervening years. During these same decades the meandering forest road varied somewhat. The old course had to be found, for Yurovsky specified that the burial was 'right in the middle of the right of way'. At one time construction work on the nearby railway might have impinged on the site. Exploratory walks along the old Koptiaki Road, where there were many low-level areas, failed to produce any obvious candidate sites for investigation. Avdonin now knew what he was looking for, but not where to find it.

Avdonin and his young colleague Mikhail Kochurov drew up a plan of investigation for the environs of the Koptiaki Road. They were aided by Kochurov's talents as a trekker and his resultant skill at kenning the course of the old path. They used the time-honoured Soviet skill of improvising equipment, building a probe that resembled a large corkscrew. In the late autumn of 1978, test bores near the Koptiaki Road encountered evidence of buried sleepers. All the participants recognized the significance of this finding. Upon reading Avdonin's report, Ryabov recalled later, 'a chill went down my spine'. In summer 1979 Avdonin and Kochurov carried out several probes into the ground of the site they had identified. They found blackened soil, which appeared to be ash, and a very high concentration of sulphuric acid. The moment for a complete physical examination of the site had clearly arrived.

The morning of 31 May was the start of a perfect summer's day in the Urals, with cloudless skies and a temperature in the low 20s. The six people on the platform of the Sverdlovsk railway station awaiting the train to the suburban village of Shuvakish, near the Koptiaki Woods, seemed a typical group of picnickers, off for a pleasant day in the country. Along with their sandwiches, they carried a canvas bag filled with equipment not usually needed for a stroll in the woods: an axe, a saw, a sledge-hammer, two shovels, an auger and permission to conduct a geological dig. The party boarding the suburban train were Aleksandr and Galina Avdonin, Gelli and Margarit Ryabov with their friend Vladislav Pesotsky, as well as Gennady Vasiliev, a geophysicist. Over the next several days they excavated a site, just off the old Koptiaki Road, near railway crossing No. 184.

Summer in the Urals has one disadvantage, and before any work could be done, a bonfire was lit to ward off mosquitoes, just as Bolshevik work gangs had done earlier, almost 62 years to the day. Then, after a few more exploratory probes, the searchers began to dig. At a depth of 35 cm they discovered old railway sleepers. When they pulled them up, a rush of swamp gas burst into their faces. There was a layer of old twigs and brush, stones from the roadway and brick fragments. They soon reached the water table, and the hole began to fill up with water. By the time they reached 80 cm, the pit was a muddy soup, through which gas bubbled to the surface. Then, groping in the water, one of the crew found the fragments of a shattered hip bone, blackened by some kind of chemical action.

Gelli Ryabov could hardly contain himself. He shook with excitement, and his voice quivered as he asked everyone to realize the significance of this find. Bones and other artifacts now appeared with every scoop of the shovel into the water: vertebrae, the bones of a hand, shards of a ceramic jar, such as those used to store acid. Pesotsky, feeling along the bottom of the pit with his hands, made the most important find – a human skull, to which still clung bits of dark brown hair, and within which were small bits of brain tissue. Avdonin and Vasiliev, working together, brought up another skull, with golden dental work. Pesotsky was deemed to have 'archeologist's luck' when he discovered the third and final skull to be located that day.

As the skulls and bones were washed, some of them were found to have fractures, which had apparently been caused by bullets. The ten bullets that were also discovered gave eloquent confirmation. That evening the little party, who christened themselves the First-Finders, held an impromptu, but very Russian memorial service. Avdonin poured out glasses of vodka and then proposed a toast to the last Emperor of Russia. None of the First-Finders doubted that they had held his skull in their hands.

Over the next ten days the First-Finders explored the burial site without further dramatic discoveries and also investigated the open mine at the Four Brothers. They then planned their future course of action. Ryabov was given two skulls to take to Moscow and, using his official connections, seek professional expertise. Officially, the 'Romanov business' was still a taboo topic – after all, less than two years before the authorities had destroyed the Ipatiev House. Everyone that Ryabov approached preferred security to fame and absolutely refused to provide any assistance. It soon became apparent their work really had been 'for future generations'. Their own wishful thinking – rather than any expertise – concluded that they had found the skulls of Nicholas II – note the gold teeth! – and either Tatiana or Anastasia and Alexei.

The following September, after making casts of the skulls and photographing them from different angles, the First-Finders encased the remains in a box and returned them to the burial pit. They enclosed in the box a bronze Russian Orthodox crucifix, on which they inscribed a verse from the Gospel of St Matthew: 'He that endureth to the end shall be saved. Taken 01.06.79. Returned 07.07.80.' The pit was filled in and covered with boulders and earth to prevent a casual rediscovery. Avdonin agreed to monitor the area to ensure that it remained untouched. All the participants gave their solemn word that they would never reveal the existence of the burial site without the permission of all the other First-Finders.

CHAPTER NINE

'Our Kennedy Assassination'

ON 19 APRIL 1989 the telephone in his flat rang for Aleksandr Avdonin. On the line was the Sverdlovsk stringer for the Moscow newspaper *Izvestiia*, Aleksandr Pashkov. 'So, Aleksandr Nikolaevich, what can you tell me about Gelli Ryabov's discovery of the grave of Nicholas II in Sverdlovsk?'

Avdonin was stunned, but still managed to gasp out, 'I can't talk about it on the phone.' Old habits die hard. Avdonin was soon to have a bitter conversation with Pashkov. Ryabov had not only broken faith but also had done so at the most inconvenient time. Avdonin was in the midst of the amazingly complex bureaucratic preparations required for the award of his Doctor of Sciences degree, the highest rung of the Soviet scientific ladder. Now, he was inundated with a flood of unwanted visitors: monarchists, nationalists and assorted adventurers. Every Sunday the Koptiaki Woods were filled with searchers, all looking for Romanov relics. It was only a matter of time before somebody rediscovered the grave.

Although it meant breaking a promise, it is easy to appreciate the temptations that led Gelli Ryabov to break his pact with Avdonin. After four years of perestroika and the international reforms pioneered by Communist Party chief Mikhail Gorbachev, there were precious few topics that were not fair game for revisionist historians and publicists. It was only a matter of time before Edvard Radzinsky would succeed in getting his own investigations into print. The official taboo on the 'Romanov business' was about to fall, and only one man could be the first to break it. Ryabov picked up the phone.

Fatherland (*Rodina*) was a staid, illustrated monthly supplement, billing itself as a 'popular social-political-scientific illustrated magazine'. It confined itself to upbeat stories from around the Soviet Union illustrated with cheery colour illustrations. Its treatment of historical events never went beyond the rubric of 'our glorious national heritage'. *Fatherland*'s editors were not used to breaking scoops, such as the one that landed on their desk, written by the popular Gelli Ryabov. Even its title was problematic: 'And So We Have to Shoot You . . .'. The story had been passed by the censor, but how best could it be handled? In particular, how could all concerned protect themselves if something went wrong, if the unfamiliar limits offered by glasnost were somehow transgressed, and the editors were called on to the carpet?

Never was a scoop so well disguised. The authors commissioned a companion piece by the respected historian and Romanov expert Professor Genrik Ioffe, who provided a justifying context for the story. They prefaced it with a careful editorial, designed to prepare the readers for a trip to this 'tragic, complicated time':

'The Romanovs were, if not the banner of the old world, then its symbol, and perished along with it. People, plunged by history into this terrible struggle, did not know compromise. From the heights of our contemporary day, with its conception of 'the worth of all human beings', we can easily charge the past with lawlessness. But do we have the right to make such a judgement? It was said long ago that the task of the historian is not to laugh or cry, but to understand.'

Most of all, the editors hid their scoop within the layout of the magazine. The title of Ryabov's article was neither on the cover, nor in the table of contents. It was the last item in the issue for April 1989, save for the crossword puzzle. The article was divided into two parts, with Ryabov's dramatic announcement that he had found the Romanov remains consigned to the very last pages. Clearly, if trouble loomed, the serial would quickly be spiked. By the following month the editors of *Fatherland* realized that they had a sensation on their hands and gave the final part more publicity. Their caution had already cost them the element of surprise.

Ryabov was not shy about announcing his discovery even before *Fatherland* began the serialization of his article. Once it began to appear, it was material for other newspapers. *Moscow News* was one of the flagship publications of glasnost and perestroika, breaking major stories – something Soviet editors were specifically trained not to do – and pushing against the limits of the permissible. This was a story they were eager to cover. On 16 April 1989, *Moscow News* carried an exclusive interview with Ryabov by Aleksandr Kabakov, entitled 'The Earth Has Given Up its Secrets'. It was nothing if not sensational.

Ryabov supplied the paper with one of the pictures taken during the 1979 dig, showing a skull, described as that of Nicholas II himself, resting on a shovel. Ryabov described his visit to the Ipatiev House, his sense of an obligation to history and his determination to undertake this difficult, dangerous, 'secret mission'. He praised the 'brilliant professionalism' of Sokolov, even while lecturing him, 'as a veteran of our law enforcement organs', on where he had gone wrong. He revealed why he had published so little over the last decade: all his time had been devoted to this difficult task. Coincidentally, he had also completed a screenplay devoted to the Ekaterinburg events, which he hoped would soon be filmed so that people would know the truth. Such credit as Ryabov gave was to 'volunteer helpers'. One name was conspicuously missing from this account – Aleksandr Avdonin.

If Avdonin had benefitted from his ability to hide behind the protection of Ryabov, there was now little he could do to claim his share of the glory. Even more troublesome was the fate of the grave itself, over which Ryabov had apparently taken proprietary control. In another interview Ryabov announced that he would identify the location to the authorities only when he had been satisfied that the Romanovs would be given a proper, Christian burial.

If Ryabov was the master manipulator of Soviet glasnost, or publicity, Avdonin was forced to rely on perestroika, the reorganization of Soviet society. One of the distinctive features of the Gorbachev era was the rise of independent social and welfare organizations, free of Communist Party or state control. Activists scrambled to create and secure official recognition for political, cultural, religious and social groups. Avdonin and Gennady Vasiliev, another of the First-Finders, set up a charitable fund named Recovery (*Obretenie*), as a vehicle to carry on their activities. At first the stated object of Recovery was the continued hunt for Romanov artifacts, especially the two missing bodies, and the collection of materials devoted to the murders. As a natural offshoot, it became involved in a controversy over the proper burial place for the remains. A later project called for the creation of a memorial park and museum in the vicinity of the Four Brothers. Finally, Recovery pledged itself to the 'moral reconciliation of society'.

Throughout 1990 these grandiose plans lay in the future since Avdonin was not even able to move Recovery through the difficult process of certification. As an added distraction, both he and Ryabov had to fight off criticism in their own bailiwicks.

To put things in proper Communist terminology, if Aleksandr Avdonin is 'thesis', then his local rival Vadim Viner is 'antithesis'. The middle-aged Avdonin always sits warily, weighing his words carefully, a man warned by inclination and experience to give nothing away. The younger Viner – who announces himself as the eastern Siberian representative for Smirnov vodka – rushes into a room like the wind across the steppe. He is hyperactive, unable to sit still. Tall, thin, gap-toothed and balding, he dances about a room, examining every object in it. He has no doubt about the importance of the discovery in the Koptiaki Woods: 'This is our Kennedy assassination,' he proclaims. His comparison is not meant to be mere hyperbole. As every good conspiracy theorist knows, the death of John F. Kennedy on an autumn day in Dallas, Texas, was not only a murder but also a cover-up of momentous proportions. Viner is convinced that something similar has taken place in Ekaterinburg.

In the days before Smirnov vodka came to Siberia, Viner was a humble researcher on the staff of the Sverdlovsk Museum of the

History of the Youth Movement in the Urals. Whatever the merits of the museum, it was clearly not a springboard to fame. As the world began to descend on Sverdlovsk in the flurry of interest engendered by Avdonin's and Ryabov's find, Viner and some friends formed their own investigative team, the Group for the Investigation into the Circumstances of the Death of the Members of the Family of the Imperial House of Romanov. In April 1991 the Group was able to announce a significant find. One of its members had secured from his widow the diary of Stepan Vaganov, identified by Sokolov as one of the Tsar's assassins. The diary made an extraordinary claim: the family of a rich local manufacturer was executed at about the same time as the Romanovs. They were remarkably similar in number, age and sex to the Romanovs. The implication of this diary is that this family was burned and interred instead of the Romanovs.

This speculation failed to impress Avdonin. When the two shared a platform on one occasion, Avdonin spoke after Viner. He prefaced his remarks with the declaration that his audience should 'reject everything you've heard before me. It's rubbish.' Avdonin soon discovered that he was ill-advised to make an enemy of someone as determined and active as Viner.

Viner transformed his group of investigators into a Centre, complete with its own newsletter, *The Truth?*, and the approbation and support of a few visiting Romanovs. The declared task of the Centre is to gather information and materials connected to the Romanov murder – not incoincidentally the same task as Avdonin's Recovery association had set for itself. If Avdonin had created Recovery largely to pursue his version of events, then Viner's Centre seems determined to advance any scenario except Avdonin's.

Viner's cause was strengthened when he attracted to it a professional historian, Dr D. V. Gavrilov of the Urals Section of the Russian Academy of Sciences. Gavrilov frequently appeared in print with sceptical assessments of Avdonin's whole line of investigation. At an international scholarly conference held in Ekaterinburg in 1992 to legitimize Avdonin's claims, Gavrilov acted as the skeleton at the feast. He attacked the proceedings as badly organized and 'dilettantish'. He was especially scornful of the organizer's love of foreign expertise. 'The onslaught of the enthusiasts grows. Their representatives fly from one country to another, storming different research centres abroad, trying out new genetic expertise.'

Unpleasant as was this repudiation by his neighbours, Avdonin was lucky to escape with nothing more than being branded an incompetent. Ryabov, in Moscow, attracted much more vicious criticism from an unofficial monarchist and Russian Orthodox publication, *The Tsar-Bell*. An article entitled simply 'The Forgery' noted Ryabov's background, with its connection to the security forces, and asked how anything he touched could be considered reliable. Ryabov spread darkness, rather than light, wherever he went. Was it not suspicious that the Ipatiev House was torn down shortly after he visited it?

It was clear to all, the magazine argued, that Ryabov's 'tsarist burial' was a Cheka forgery, designed to mislead Sokolov's investigation. It was significant that Ryabov had found skulls, for the Sokolov-Diterikhs report demonstrated that the bodies were decapitated before cremation, and the grisly remains dispatched to Moscow. There was even a receipt for the heads, dated 27 July 1918 and allegedly signed by Lenin.

Why so much deception? Because the murder of the Royal Family was carried out by Jews. It was so brutal and inhumane precisely because it was a Jewish ritual murder. Ryabov was serving as the modern exponent of this deception. 'The most immediate goal of this forgery and the sensation artificially created around it – is to hide the ritual character of the murder and conceal the role of world Jewry in its organization and execution.'

At the beginning of 1991, under the barrage of criticism and fears that the Koptiaki site was no longer secure, Avdonin turned to the powerful head of the Sverdlovsk regional government, E. E. Rossel, with a formal report on his 1979 discovery. The news was an open secret, of course, but this formal declaration meant that Rossel had to take action. The situation was complicated by the fact that the Soviet Union was entering its last year of existence, with the consequent confusion over the lines of power. Boris Yeltsin, who had emerged as the principal critic of the slow pace of Gorbachev's perestroika, had been elected to head the Supreme Soviet of the Russia Federation, the largest component of the USSR. In June 1991 Yeltsin would consolidate his power when he was elected the first president of the Russian Federation. Because of his growing power, and because Yeltsin was his predecessor as head of the Sverdlovsk region, Rossel sought the approval of Moscow to take the matter forward. Yeltsin gave his blessing.

Matters moved quickly forward. Recovery was officially chartered. On 5 July the regional government voted to finance the investigation of the tsarist remains, and in the disintegrating USSR funding had become as important as official permission. To give the whole affair the appearance of legality and due process, Avdonin made a formal report to the Ekaterinburg authorities that he had found human remains in the forest of Koptiaki and was ready to show them to the police. The officer in charge of the investigation, V. I. Pichugin, assembled a team of experts, who were mostly police and forensic specialists and who were gathered in almost conspiratorial silence. The archaeologist L. Koriakova, about to depart for a summer dig, was lured to Pichugin's apartment – rather than his office – with the promise of 'something related to your work'. Pichugin confided that his task was to explore a secret burial, about which he could say nothing more. 'Oh, Nicholas II?' Koriakova replied to the disconcerted policeman.

The following morning, 11 July 1991, a small group of vehicles set out for the Koptiaki Woods, just as a truck from the central garage in Ekaterinburg had done almost 73 years earlier to the day. Their departure point was not the Ipatiev House, but the Ekaterinburg Central Stadium, located, ironically, on Ermakov Street, named in honour of the most murderous of the Tsar's assassins. Koriakova, as a professional archaeologist, was struck by the amateurishness of it all. There was a brief search as Avdonin tried to locate the exact spot, and then the remains were located and removed. A continuous rain turned the area into a swamp, but this had the advantage of keeping down the notorious Koptiaki mosquitoes. In all, portions of nine skeletons were recovered – Koriakova sketched them as they lay in the pit – along with bullets and pottery shards. The search team filled 12 empty Red Army ammunition cases.

The remains were taken to the laboratory of the Sverdlovsk

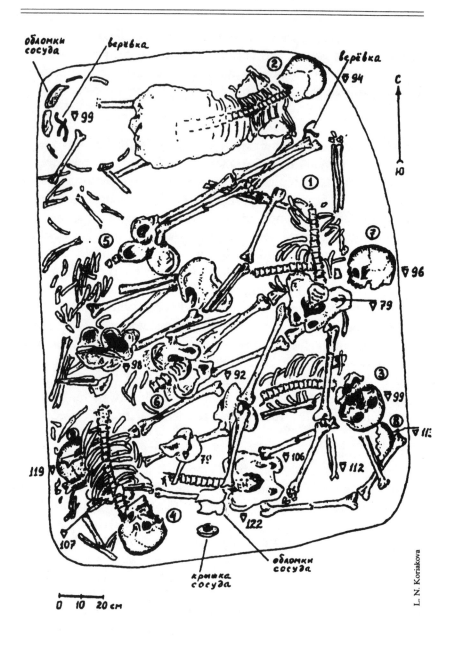

SKETCH OF THE COMMON GRAVE IN EKATERINBURG
[Showing Position of Bodies, Rope and Ceramic Fragments]

Bureau of Judicial Medical Expertise. At the beginning of August a series of committees was appointed to study the remains from the twin perspectives of a criminal and medical investigation. The Russian State Prosecutor's Office was notified in Moscow, and the inquiry took on a national coloration. Avdonin was now able to repay Ryabov with a surprise of his own: on 14 August the authorities in Moscow brought in Ryabov to record a statement of his involvement in the affair.

Throughout July and August, as Communist hard-liners plotted their coup against Gorbachev, and Yeltsin stood on a tank outside the Moscow White House, teams of experts from all over the dying USSR worked on the remains in Sverdlovsk, led by S. S. Abramov, Head of the Section for New Technology of the Bureau of Judicial Medical Expertise in Moscow. The researchers confirmed that there were parts of nine skeletons but, with a total of only 500 bones, they were far from complete. A team returned to the site in October and passed 20 tons of earth from the site through a small sieve. This yielded an additional 300 small bones, 11 bullets, 150 conglomerates of fatty tissue, 13 teeth – two of which were to prove of decisive importance – pottery shards and fragments of rope.

This operation virtually destroyed the integrity of the immediate site by damaging the strata levels. Other discoveries might nonetheless be possible, since more than half the bones of the skeletons have yet to be found. It is not inconceivable that some of the souvenir hunters and amateur archaeologists who flooded into the Kotiapki Woods have a genuine imperial relic tucked away in their collection of Romanov memorabilia.

Once the remains were removed to the laboratory, too many investigative cooks began to spoil the broth. Specialists led by Abramov, who tried to reconstruct the shattered skulls, hindered the rival Moscow team of V. N. Kriukov, which was investigating the injuries done to the bones. Other researchers complained that the bones had been cleaned, thus exposing them to the atmosphere.

The Ekaterinburg investigators were criticized for attempting preliminary reconstructions of the skeletons, thus reducing them to a gigantic jigsaw puzzle, but without the advantage of a complete picture on the cover of the box. In his review of their work, Dr William Maples, the American forensic scientist, predicts that the skeleton of Nicholas II will go to his final grave attached to the arm bones of his valet Trupp. Only the Russian team, which tried to match the skulls with photographs of the Royal Family, disturbed nobody else – nor did they produce findings that convinced anybody else. The investigation began to resemble an earlier chronicler's description of the Russian land itself: 'great and rich, but there is no order in it.'

The number of consultants working on the remains, and the sensational nature of the case meant that it could not possibly be kept secret. Fantastic stories began to circulate in the press, such as the claim that Boris Yeltsin had offered to buy the remains from Ekaterinburg. In the new Russia that followed the collapse of the USSR, everything was for sale, including information. *Izvestiia*'s correspondent in Ekaterinburg (as Sverdlovsk had again been renamed) complained that news stories on the research were appearing first in the foreign press, presumably because they were willing to pay. The whole investigation was degenerating into a 'cheap show'. Meanwhile, monarchist groups in the West, whom the new Russian regime was ready to court, complained that the inquiry was proceeding entirely without the participation of foreign experts. For them, nothing could be trusted if it bore the fingerprints of former Communists.

The Ekaterinburg authorities, still led by Rossel, had no objection to the participation of foreign experts, but they were not able to pay for them. Help soon arrived, along with the foreign politicians who were hurrying East in order to demonstrate their support for the new democratic Russia. In 1992 the American Secretary of State James Baker visited Ekaterinburg as part of a goodwill mission to Russia. The Ipatiev House was no longer available to show visitors, but Rossel had something better: the presumed bones of the last Tsar. In the course of Baker's tour of the remains, he was advised that the Russians would be delighted to have American assistance in their forensic work.

The Russians could not have made a better suggestion. In the aftermath of the Cold War, there was a vigorous debate in America about the extent of assistance that the USA should give her old enemy. American State Department officials were on the look-out for high-visibility aid projects – and so much the better if they were inexpensive. To help the Russians identify Nicholas II and his family – the romanticized Nicholas and Alexandra, the first victims of Communism – was almost too good to be true. Nor was there any shortage of volunteers. Dr William Maples, the director of the Pound Human Identification Laboratory at the Florida Museum of Natural History in Gainesville, identifies himself as the man for whom every day is Halloween, given the grim nature of his employment. He has built a high-profile career with his forensic investigations of notorious murder cases. When he heard of the Russian request, he assembled a research team and campaigned for the job.

It was a marriage made in heaven for both sides. Maples entered a case that was exotic even by his standards. The Russians received an internationally known expert, whose authority could be used to confound the complaints of critics. Maples and his team were able to provide tentative identification of all nine bodies in three days, where it had taken Russian teams half a year. They needed to work quickly because the Russians were slow to submit all the remains to their inspection. Dr Lowell Levine, the dental expert on Maples's team, was disconcerted to be handed a bag of loose teeth that had been found at the site, only a few hours before a news conference called to report on their findings. This was doubly irritating, because two of the teeth, as will be seen, had special significance. Despite these obstacles, Maples's team reached almost the same conclusions as the Russians.

Maples was also an active participant in an international conference organized by the Ekaterinburg authorities, with the active help of Avdonin's Recovery. It was designed to produce preliminary reports, which could be used to feed the world's media, as well as to still criticism at home by producing foreign experts. Specialists from all over the former USSR gathered in Ekaterinburg on 27–28 July 1992 to share their findings. Virtually every report strengthened the case that these were the remains of the Imperial Family. There was evidence of violent death. Dental work pointed to the turn of the century and to a wealthy patient – the Empress's fillings were made of platinum! The recovered bullets were compatible with those fired by a Nagan or a Mauser. The number of bodies matched the Yurovsky account. There was the proper differentiation by gender, height and age. Some of the bones and virtually all the skulls revealed the effects of sulphuric acid. All of the faces had been smashed in.

A scholarly consensus emerged: the nine bodies were those of the Tsar, the Tsarina, Olga, Maria, Tatiana and Dr Botkin and the servants Demidova, Kharitonov and Trupp. A Russian specialist, Professor Viacheslav Popov of the St Petersburg Military Medical Academy, expressed doubts as to whether body no. 5 was Maria or Tatiana, the two middle daughters who were two years apart in age. Maples had no doubts that the missing Grand Duchess was Anastasia. He pointed out that all the skeletonal remains in question are fully developed, while Anastasia at 17 years old, would not have fully matured. Subsequent comparative research in Maples's Florida laboratory strengthens his contention that, were these bones those of Anastasia, they would indicate unusual and unlikely physical development. The evidence strongly indicates that Anastasia's body has not been found.

These results were announced at a boisterous news conference at the conclusion of the scholarly debates. The world media instantly fixed on the absence of Anastasia from the common grave. The supporters of various pretenders both at home and abroad could breathe a sigh of relief, if they had ever entertained any doubts at all.

The language of the conference reports – as well as subsequent analysis – was drily scientific. The experts spoke of 'body no. 1' and 'body no. 2', about the calcination of bones and 'mechanical bone trauma', of the low quality of some turn-of-the-century dentures and of ballistic trajectory paths. The whole story could not be told because almost all soft tissue and the internal organs had rotted away. Even worse, none of the skeletons had as many as 50 per cent of its bones remaining.

Beneath the technical descriptions, however, the full implications of what happened in the Ipatiev basement becomes clear, even keeping in mind that the absence of so many bones and of all the soft flesh diminishes the full effect of the execution. A number of bones were shattered by bullets, and five skulls had bullet holes in them. Six of the bodies showed signs of damage by sharp objects, probably bayonets.

The work of Drs V. Popov and A. Kovalev on bullet trajectories is particularly terrifying. Yurovsky himself wrote in one of his accounts that 'it is not so easy to shoot people.' The forensic results reveal the outcome of his order to shoot at the heart to make death quick and reduce the amount of blood. The only wounds on the remains of Nicholas, standing in the centre of the first row, are gunshots to the chest. He was the principal target, and, as all commentators report, he died instantly. The corresponding bones of the Empress are missing, but she undoubtedly shared the same fate. The tall and burly Dr Botkin also took several bullets slightly below chest level. As he toppled forward, another bullet entered his head. The victims who were shot in the chest were fortunate: they probably died instantly.

Not so lucky were those who survived the initial fusillade. The guards began to fire wildly, wounding several of the victims in the thigh region. Tatiana turned her head away from the firing and was hit in the back of the head. She must have realized by then what was happening. Olga also died with a shot to the head, but from the front. Kharitonov and Trupp were shot in the head, but from different directions, probably as they moved around the room. Most melancholy of all are the remains of Demidova. Unlike the Romanov women, who stood stunned, like sacrificial lambs, she fought to live. Wounded, she still tried to ward off bullets. Her reward was 32 thrusts with a bayonet. Had the body of Anastasia had survived, it too would have shown the effects of Ermakov's Winchester bayonet, and the skull would have been staved in. All the existing remains show evidence of terrible trauma. For the Romanovs, 'death was never beautiful.'

Two bodies are missing and the scholarly consensus is that they are those of Alexei and Anastasia, whose corpses Yurovsky's detachment attempted to burn. These remains must be accounted for, since under the conditions of disposal described by Yurovsky, something must have been left behind. Human teeth will char, but they are particularly resistant to combustion. Parts of the larger bones of the bodies, such as the hip bone, invariably survive fires. Even modern crematoria are unable to reduce a corpse to pure ash. Two cremations would have left a considerable amount of ash. Yet nothing has been found.

There are several possible answers to this mystery. Yurovsky's account may simply be incorrect, but this seems unlikely, since it checks out in so many other respects. It is possible that the

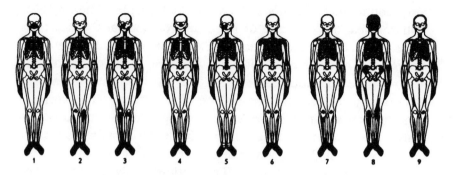

ATTRIBUTION OF SKELETONAL REMAINS
DISCOVERED IN EKATERINBURG
[Missing Bones Are in Black]

1. Anna Demidova
2. Evgeny Botkin
3. Olga Nikolaevna
4. Nicholas II
5. Maria or Anastasia
   Nikolaevna

6. Tatiana Nikolaevna
7. Alexandra Fedorovna
8. Ivan Kharitonov
9. Aleksei Trupp

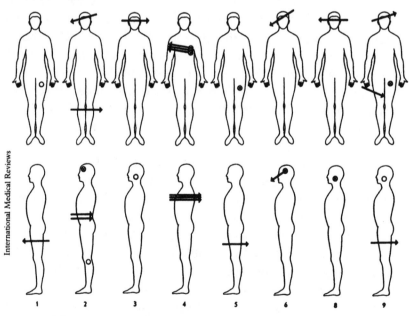

NUMBER AND DIRECTION OF GUNSHOT WOUNDS
[Based on Damage to Surviving Skeletonal Remains]

wholesale excavations that disturbed the integrity of much of the site, also destroyed the evidence of a strata of ash. But, whatever their shortcomings, the searchers were looking specifically for an ash layer, and they might have been expected to find some charred remains in the 20 tons of earth that they sifted through. Finally, Yurovsky's team might have done an exceptionally effective job of scattering the remains of the fire. But, given the haste and sloppiness that marked so much of their efforts, this also seems unlikely.

The answer may be found in a re-examination of Yurovsky's account of the operation. On the morning of 19 July the truck carrying the bodies from the Four Brothers to the deep pits in the forest got stuck in a marshy area in the road. Yurovsky decided to burn the corpses right there. It is probable that while one group was set to work extricating the truck from the mire, another would have been ordered to burn the bodies. Clearly they would have gone away from where their comrades were digging in the mud. They would not have appreciated smoke in their faces, or the stench of burning flesh in their nostrils. Since the immediate area was swampy, the burial unit would have had to move to higher or drier ground. They would have moved off the roadway, since they were planning to go back the way they had come. Only later did Yurovsky have his brainstorm of disposing of the corpses in the middle of the right-of-way.

There were remains from the cremations, since Yurovsky reported that 'they buried the remains under the fire and then scattered the fires in order to cover up completely any trace of digging.' At this point, Yurovsky hit on his alternative plan for disposing of the nine remaining bodies, exactly at the spot where the truck had just been dug out. Thus, the ashes and charred teeth and bones of Alexei and Anastasia should be in the general region of the main burial – but not too far away, since the burial detail would not have wanted to carry rotting corpses very far away. The remains could therefore be in any direction from the main burial, perhaps depending on the wind direction on the morning of 19 July. The site may well have reverted to swamp over the last 70 years, for the path of the original road has altered somewhat over time. No systematic mapping of the area has been done, so it seems logical to assume that somewhere in the near vicinity of the

Tsar's grave are the charred remains of his two youngest children.

One last mystery divides the specialists, and it is of special significance because it may provide physical evidence linking Alexei to the burial site. Dr Popov of St Petersburg has taken a special interest in the loose teeth recovered from the Koptiaki burial, which are useful for identifying characteristics of their owners. All the teeth attributed to the Grand Duchesses have dental fillings, an indication of their love of sweets, which were readily available in the royal household. The Tsar's teeth were a testimony to neglect, showing the effects of serious gum disease. Demidova boasted inexpensive dental work of indifferent quality. The Empress had magnificent teeth, with fillings of gold and platinum. Their splendour had initially convinced Ryabov that this was the skull of the Tsar himself.

Specialists have attempted to attribute all the teeth to one or another of the surviving skulls, a task hindered by the absence of half of an upper jaw for two of the three presumed Grand Duchesses. Two of the loose teeth in particular have aroused Popov's interest. They are two upper molars with incomplete root tips. On the basis of their size and structure alone, Popov has ascribed them to a young male of between 13 and 16 years of age. Since Tsarevich Alexei was 14 Popov believes that these are his last mortal remains.

Dr Lowell Levine, the dental expert on Maples's team, has been less than enthusiastic about Popov's conjecture. He argues that the gender of the teeth can only be resolved through genetic tests rather than simple observation. It is more plausible, he believes, that they are upper third, rather than second, molars, which would place them securely in the mouth of one of the Grand Duchesses. Levine concedes that the teeth are rather small for adult third molars, but argues that his attribution would not require the 'leap of faith' necessary to accept Popov's hypothesis.

Without further testing to determine the sex of the teeth's owner, this dispute cannot be resolved. What can be said is that the teeth display no trace of burning, so they cannot be remains from Yurovsky's pyre. If they could be shown to come from Alexei, they would be a further demonstration – should such proof still be required – that the Tsarevich did not escape the Ipatiev basement alive. One more scrap of Yurovsky's testimony would be confirmed.

Ever since Stalin decided that Mendelian genetics were anti-Soviet and liquidated some of the Soviet Union's leading geneticists, this particular field of biology has been underdeveloped in the USSR. But, as Dr P. Ivanov remarked in his short paper to the Ekaterinburg conference, so it was in many countries in the western world. That is why he was happy to announce that one of the most advanced human genetics laboratories in the world had agreed to participate in the hunt for the Romanovs. The previous year Ivanov, a researcher for the Moscow Bureau of Judicial Medical Expertise, had been in Britain to participate in a genetics conference hosted by the University of London. He had made the acquaintance of staff at Britain's Forensic Science Service. They foresaw many ways in which their work could assist the identification of the Ekaterinburg remains. All that was necessary was to find someone to pay for the expensive tests. Great Britain, like the United States, was eager for publicity-generating projects to demonstrate its support for the new Russia.

Exactly the same considerations as had appealed to James Baker now popped into the collective mind of Her Majesty's Government. A joint research project to establish, through DNA testing, the identity of the remains would be a glittering advertisement for British science and a wonderful goodwill gesture. And, as a final irony, the Romanovs would at last be admitted into Britain, 76 years too late. Their mode of transport would also be different: instead of a naval cruiser, they would come in an Aeroflot flight bag, carried through the Nothing to Declare channel at Heathrow Airport in London.

The science of DNA testing has revolutionized the identification of long-dead victims, whose remains have been reduced to a pile of bones. The first great success of this technique was, ironically, the identification of the remains of Joseph Mengele, the notorious SS doctor who carried out his own genetic experiments on his victims in the Auschwitz extermination camp. Mengele fled Germany at the end of the Second World War, after which journalists and the general public were titillated by many reported sightings in South America, where he lived until his death in 1979. Bones discovered in the late 1980s were said to be his. His son Rolf gave a blood sample. The DNA extracted from Rolf's blood was compared with the DNA recovered from the bones, showing that the Nazi geneticist had indeed escaped justice and, unlike his victims, lived a good long life. Scientists concluded with a 99 per cent certainty that the remains belonged to Joseph Mengele.

DNA analysis can also be used to establish family relationships where there are missing generations. In Argentina thousands of people disappeared during the military rule in the 1970s and 1980s, and in many cases their children were kidnapped by the military authorities. Since the establishment of civilian rule, grandparents have been searching for their lost grandchildren, and through DNA comparison over 50 children have been restored to their biological families.

Increasingly the science of DNA is being used in court cases, both in Britain and the United States, despite occasional misgivings as to its accuracy. The claims made initially on behalf of DNA were phenomenal. In one American court the prosecution described the chance of being wrong as one in 738 billion. It seemed that a spot of blood, saliva, sperm or hair would identify the criminal without doubt. After five years of practical experience, the picture is not so untroubled.

First, there is the obvious danger that even if the science is as infallible as was originally assumed, the scientists doing the tests can make mistakes or the material can become contaminated. There are also other arguments about matching DNA 'fingerprinting', which has led some courts to throw out DNA evidence. There is an estimated 2 per cent possibility that two unrelated DNA 'fingerprints' will match by chance. Nonetheless, the prosecution team in the O. J. Simpson murder trial made use of DNA evidence. In its opening statement the prosecution mentioned the DNA testing of Anna Anderson as an example of a successful identification by this method. The utility of DNA testing for criminal investigations means that the number of DNA laboratories is proliferating, and DNA databases are being set up. The British Forensic Science Service, an executive agency under the auspices of the Home Office, now has six centres in Britain equipped to carry out DNA testing, which are primarily used by the police for evidence in their investigations.

The DNA molecule is found in each living cell and is made

up of a pair of strands, the famous double helix, which wind up together like opposing spiral staircases. The 'rungs' of these stair-cases are composed of chemical units called nucleotides that are bonded together. DNA or deoxyribonucleic acid is the molecule that contains the genetic code. Contained in each cell are two types of DNA. Nuclear DNA is the first type, found, not surprisingly, in the nucleus. It is inherited from both the mother and father and can be used for establishing parentage.

The second type, known as mitochondrial DNA, is inherited from the female line only and lies not in the nucleus but in the cell itself. There are thousands of tiny structures within cells, known as mitochondria, meaning that scientists are more likely to find mitochondrial DNA even in badly degraded biological samples. The mitochondrial DNA from the mother is passed on to her children and remains constant from one generation to the next. Thus every person has the mitochondrial DNA present from his or her mother, who inherited it from her mother and so on. Changes in mitochondrial DNA are extremely rare, and scientists estimate they happen only once every 3000 or 4000 years.

'It is like a time machine, going from generation to generation unchanging,' says Dr Peter Gill of the Forensic Science Service. 'The same genetic code would be shared by mother, grandmother, great-grandmother, great-great-grandmother and so on.'

Only about 10 per cent of DNA governs such things as eye colour and brain development. The rest is known as 'junk' DNA. The pattern of sequences seems to have no special function, but they do provide an individual's precise fingerprint. Only identical twins have exactly the same code, but family links can be detected by matching sequences of the code. The nearest relatives will have the closest match. Gill emphasizes that if two people have the same mitochondrial DNA, then there is only the possibility that they are related. In other words, mitochondrial DNA testing can rule out people who are not related. But there is always a percentage of doubt in its positive identification.

There are four nucleotides that make up all mitochondrial DNA, consisting of 16,569 base pairs of nucleotides, arranged in a ring. A computer print-out of a DNA sequence produces the sequence of these nucleotides, whose sheer number would render them virtually unusable, except that scientists are able to concentrate on certain 'hyper-variable regions', made up of just 608 base pairs. When the sequences in the 'hyper-variable regions' match up, then it is assumed that the two are related. The last stage is to convert the molecular evidence of the skeletal DNA into a 'fingerprint', which looks remarkably like a bar code in a supermarket. These 'fingerprints' provide the precise evidence needed for identification.

The utility of DNA science has also recently developed following the invention of a new technique, known as polymerase chain reaction or PCR for short. This process enables scientists to grow the DNA in the test tube and thus amplify fragments of DNA to usable quantities. Nuclear DNA deteriorates with decomposition of the body very quickly, and it becomes more difficult to segregate nuclear DNA from decomposed bodies for testing. Mitochondrial DNA is generally easier to extract.

In September 1992 Dr Ivanov brought some of the Ekaterinburg bones to the Forensic Science Service, which was then headquartered in Aldermaston, and there Dr Peter Gill and his team set to work to extract DNA. The surface of the bones was ground down to remove any contamination, and then small sections were removed in sterile conditions using a hacksaw. The bone was pulverized and then dissolved to release the genetic material, DNA. Once purified and amplified to larger quantities using the PCR technique, the DNA was ready for examination. Conventional analysis was difficult because of the age and condition of the bones, said Dr Gill, but, nonetheless, Gill and his team succeeded in being the first to come out with the DNA sequence of the Tsar and Tsarina.

Peter Gill's team had to analyse DNA not only from the five skeletons thought to belong to the Russian Imperial Family but also those from the physician Dr Botkin and the three servants, Alexei Trupp the valet, Ivan Kharitonov the cook and Anna Demidova the Tsarina's maid. The scientists first determined the sex of the bones and confirmed the findings in Ekaterinburg, identifying four male and five female bodies.

Samples of both types of DNA were then studied to establish a family relationship between the five skeletons thought to belong to the Romanov family. Testing, known as short tandem repeat analysis, to analyse the nuclear DNA present, showed that the two skeletons assumed to be the Tsar and Tsarina were the parents of the three female skeletons, putatively thought to be the Grand Duchesses Olga, Tatiana and Maria. The three female skeletons had inherited nuclear DNA from the Tsar and Tsarina, establishing them as a family group. Tests on the four other skeletons, presumed to be the servants, revealed they were not related to this family group.

The forensic scientists then had to establish that this family was indeed the Russian Imperial Family. In order to prove this, mitochondrial DNA was compared with the mitochondria taken from surviving relatives, including Prince Philip.

In order to establish the mitochondrial DNA of the Tsarina and the children in the Romanov grave, Prince Philip, Duke of Edinburgh, was asked, and agreed, to give a blood sample. The Duke of Edinburgh is the nearest relative in the matrilineal line to the Tsarina. Tsarina Alexandra was one of Queen Victoria's grandchildren, the youngest daughter of Princess Alice, who married Ludwig, the Grand Duke of Hesse. Thus Alexandra would have inherited mitochondrial DNA from her mother Princess Alice and would in turn have transmitted the same DNA sequence to her five children. Prince Philip is likewise a direct descendant from Queen Victoria through the female line. His great-grandmother was the same Princess Alice, and his grandmother was Victoria of Hesse, the older sister of the Tsarina. Victoria in her turn passed the same mitochondrial DNA down to her daughter, confusingly also named Alice, who married Andrew of Greece. They had five children, one of whom is Prince Philip.

Dr Peter Gill was able to analyse the mitochondrial DNA from the blood sample released by Prince Philip. The DNA sample taken from the bones of the four female Romanov skeletons found in Ekaterinburg matched up with Prince Philip's DNA sequence. To carry out the analysis, the scientists focused on a stretch of the genetic code 800 'letters' long. A complete match was obtained between the samples taken from the Tsarina, the three children and Prince Philip.

The Tsar's DNA was checked against samples from two members of his family, descendants of Louise of Hesse-Cassel, Nicholas's grandmother. Both the donors had identical mitochondrial DNA, but the scientists found that the Tsar's DNA had a single 'spelling mistake' in the 800-letter stretch of code that was not present in the donor relatives.

The research team at Aldermaston was not satisfied. They therefore amplified the Tsar's DNA. A closer look at the results revealed that two types of DNA were present in the Tsar, probably as a result of a rare condition known as heteroplasmy. The research team was able to confirm this by mass-producing the Tsar's DNA by cloning it in bacteria, the PCR technique. One type of this mass-produced DNA matched the maternal relatives exactly; the other contained the single 'spelling mistake'. The mutation possibly occurred during his lifetime.

'We found what we suspected, that there were two different types of molecule in the clone,' commented Peter Gill. 'One was exactly the same as the descendants, and the other was the same as the apparent anomaly. Type two was the result of a rare mutation. The results we obtained were consistent with both paternity and maternity, indicating to us that this was indeed a complete family.'

The scientists say they are 98.5 per cent certain that their conclusions are correct, based on a neutral interpretation of the previous anthropological evidence and on the lowest interpretation of their own DNA evidence. Gill added that a conservative reading of the DNA tests would put the likelihood as high as 99 per cent.

As in all DNA analysis, there is a chance of getting a positive match as a result of chance alone. This led the scientists to conservatively estimate that they are 98.5 per cent sure of the correct match. In the words of Gill: 'This proves virtually beyond doubt that five of the nine skeletons found in the woods near Ekaterinburg were those of the Tsar, Tsarina and three of their daughters.'

He went on to explain that DNA analysis could not identify which daughter was missing. None of the bones showed any sign of being the remains of the Tsarevich Alexei. Peter Gill also made other attempts to gather material that could shed light on the discoveries. For instance, he took bandages for analysis that had been used by the Tsarevich and brought back to England by the tutor Sydney Gibbes. These have light brown stains on them, which could have been blood, but unfortunately they were unable to extract any material for use in analysis. The bandages are now on display at the Luton Hoo Foundation in Bedfordshire, as part of the Gibbes collection.

The Russian team also attempted to track down relatives of the servants for similar DNA analysis. They were unable to identify any, but Peter Gill was able to make some analysis on the putative bones of Dr Botkin. His granddaughter Marina Schweitzer sent some blood to the Aldermaston laboratory simply by pricking her finger and swabbing it with a tissue. Her half-sister, who was not descended from the Botkins, did the same, and Gill's team were thus able to isolate the Botkin-type of DNA from that of their mother. Gill was only able to identify Botkin's bones by a ratio of 3:1, because Marina Schweitzer was descended through the male line. Dr Botkin did have a sister, whose descendants would be able to provide the mitochondrial DNA for comparison, but they have not been able to locate her family.

Russian scientists have since put a further spoke in the wheel by developing their earlier assertion that the missing daughter was not Anastasia but the third daughter, Maria. A ruling on Maria was included in the report of an official commission, headed by Yury Yarov, a deputy prime minister, on 6 September 1994. Encouraged by Gill's assertion that the DNA sampling could not definitively assert which daughter was missing, the Russian scientists say the missing daughter is Maria. Russian forensic scientists spent four months piecing together skull fragments at a laboratory in Ekaterinburg and rebuilding their faces, using techniques sometimes employed in criminal inquiries. This was not an easy task. Some skulls had been badly damaged by rifle butts during the execution, and the executioners had attempted to destroy all traces of the bodies with grenades and sulphuric acid.

The researchers used computers to overlay images on the skulls. Then using plaster casts of the skulls, artificial 'flesh' was put on the bones. The depth of the flesh was calculated on physiological principles to enable the final masks to be made. Russian State Prosecutor Vladimir Soloviev said the resulting faces, along with DNA tests and dental records, positively identify Nicholas II, his wife Alexandra and their daughters, Olga, Tatiana and Anastasia. 'Now there is a clear answer,' he said. 'Anastasia is in the grave. There is no sign of Alexei or Maria.' Not everyone would agree with this confident diagnosis.

CHAPTER TEN

'How Shall I Tell You Who I Am?'

THE IDENTIFICATION OF the Romanov bones in Ekaterinburg at first sent shivers down the spines of the remaining Anastasians. Then their pious dedication seemed to have been rewarded when the Russian scientists announced finding only nine bodies. There was no trace of the other two – the Tsarevich and one of the Tsar's daughters. Dr Maples's assertion that the lost daughter was the youngest of Nicholas and Alexandra's girls, Anastasia, made perfect sense to Anna's supporters. The mystery of the missing bodies also fuelled the imagination of the general public. Was Anna Anderson's saga true? The absence of the Tsarevich's remains in the grave-pit was also a puzzle, but few gave credence to the possibility of long-term survival because of his haemophilia. It seemed absolutely incredible that the poor boy could have lived through a fusillade of bullets and blows from rifle butts, when his death had been close so many times from purely accidental causes.

When Peter Gill published the DNA sequences of the Tsar and Tsarina and of the three daughters, scientists were able to predict with some certainty Anastasia's likely DNA pattern. The problem for Anna's supporters was that she had left behind no bones for analysis. With her remains cremated, it seemed that proof of her identity lay lost in her ashes. There is no way that DNA or any other form of medical evidence can be extracted from dust.

Serendipitously it turned out that Anna had left behind more than dust. In 1979, when she had been admitted to the Martha Jefferson Hospital in Charlottesville for the operation to remove a gangrenous bowel obstruction and part of her small bowel, samples of her tissue were retained and sent to the hospital laboratory. In common with other US institutions, the hospital routinely keeps pathology samples from patients to use for comparative study and in case of future lawsuits over medical malpractice. Five one-inch biopsies of Anna's tissue were preserved by the pathologist and stored for their hospital records and research. It did not take long for those with medical knowledge to explore the possibility that they were still there.

The first person on the track of Anna's remains was a New Yorker named Sydney Mandelbaum, at work on a book promoting the use of DNA as a routine tool in legal cases. He was amused that the prosecution in the infamous O. J. Simpson case referred to the DNA investigation into Anna's identity as proof of the value of this new science. Mandelbaum plans to use Anna's story as the basis for a chapter in his book, for as a well-known mystery identity, she is certain to capture the imagination of readers, law-enforcement officials and courts throughout the USA.

Frustratingly for Mandelbaum, his first request to the hospital in connection with the tissue samples held there did not succeed. He had written in early 1993 to ask for information on samples of a former patient – Anna Anderson or Mrs Jack Manahan. At the time the hospital was in a chaotic administrative state due to a major refurbishment, and although officials conducted a cursory search of their files, they did not find any records under either of those names. Hospital officials claim they did not intentionally mislead Mandelbaum. Indeed there was no tissue sample stored in the hospital under either name proposed by Mandelbaum.

About one month later a postgraduate student from Texas, Mary DeWitt, wrote to the hospital asking that details of various files and tissue samples be made available for her academic thesis, which was to cover the DNA analysis and scientific research used in identifying Anna. Her seemingly straightforward demand was followed, within 48 hours, by telephone calls of a similar nature from a Dr Willi Korte, who said he was working with the Forensic Pathology Institute in Munich and phoning on their behalf. It does not appear that DeWitte's appeal was connected to that of Korte, but the proximity of their requests raised a few eyebrows at the hospital.

Korte's charming and insistent phone calls galvanized the hospital's acting director of medical records, Penny Jenkins, to take a more detailed look at the hospital's patient database. She made a thorough search of the files and the pathology department's vaults and found that, indeed, a tissue sample from Anderson was held there, albeit under the name of Anastasia Manahan.

Mary DeWitt, who said she purely wanted access to the sample to fulfil her thesis requirement, was advised by Penny Jenkins to contact Anna's biographer, James Blair Lovell. Penny Jenkins at that time was not fully appraised of the judicial regulations governing the release of forensic samples and patient records by the hospital. She suggested that Lovell could help obtain permission from Jack Manahan's cousins, apparently Anna's nearest relatives, who would have to sign a release form. Lovell quickly gained permission from the Manahan cousins, but then abruptly came to a full stop. He became anxious that Mary DeWitt would seize control through some legal means. He also realized he needed legal help to obtain release of the sample. This was when Dick Schweitzer, Gleb Botkin's son-in-law, came into the picture: 'He [Lovell] rang me up asking me to help him prevent Mary running off to Texas with the sample,' he recalled. A retired international attorney, Schweitzer quickly got to work on the legal ramifications.

Under Virginia law a hospital is restricted in its ability to hand out information on patients, which is strictly confidential. To release a patient's details the hospital has to have the permission of their so-called personal representative or executor; surviving spouse or children; and, lastly, next-of-kin by blood. By this time Jack had died, and Anastasia appeared to have died intestate and to have no blood ties – at least legally. She, of course, claimed various Romanov relations, but only the DNA testing would prove whether or not they were blood relatives.

The Schweitzers have held a life-long belief in the authenticity of Anna's Romanov claims. As Dick's wife, Marina, Gleb

Botkin's daughter, says: 'Father knew she was Anastasia and that was all there was to it.' The Schweitzers did not meet Anna very often, since Marina preferred to assume the role of a 'friend in the background', someone who could help Anna in a crisis, but who would not get involved in her day-to-day life. They were very sympathetic to Anna's plight, and Dick had sent money to her in Germany after the war, because his father-in-law was worried about her. As Dick put it, 'There was an intense family friendship' between them, emanating from Gleb's devotion to Anna.

Dick Schweitzer, a canny and persistent lawyer, applied to the Charlottesville court for a portion of the tissue sample to be removed from the hospital for the sole purpose of having it tested in a world-recognized laboratory that specialized in the scientific analysis of DNA. His reputation as a 'find a way' lawyer was severely tried over the next nine months. His original petition on 1 October 1993 was brought on behalf of Marina. As the grand-daughter of Dr Evgeny Botkin, who had died with the Imperial Family at Ekaterinburg, and whose presumed bones were found there with those of the Tsar's family, she could be considered an interested party to the case. She said the DNA examination would help in identifying her grandfather's remains.

Schweitzer drew up papers naming the Martha Jefferson Hospital requesting that a sufficient volume of the tissue sample be released for DNA testing; that no party should be able to sue the hospital for liability; and that the hospital was not to suffer from other lawsuits that might ensue, following the likely publicity the case would generate. Like his father-in-law, Gleb Botkin, Dick acted as a disinterested advocate for Anna, and he himself paid for all his legal costs as well as the expensive DNA analysis. At all times he has behaved in a patently honest manner, unlike some of his court opponents, who at best worked behind a secret agenda. Marina has said that she thought her father's directness could have been responsible for many of his problems – he did not flinch from saying what he believed to be the truth. Dick, with his lack of guile, has also suffered from attack.

Dick Schweitzer hoped to keep the lawsuit relatively low-key and to reach agreement in close cooperation with Martha Jefferson Hospital. He thought he had succeeded in getting a judge to hear the case privately in chamber, but his cover was blown when James

Lovell gave an interview to both the *Washington Times* and the *News of the World* in August 1993, just three months before he died. In the interviews Lovell publicized the prospect that Anna's identity could be established through DNA testing and told the newspapers that the Forensic Science Service would carry it out, although no full agreement had then been made. Dr Gill had been in touch with Lovell, simply expressing his willingness to do the work, if the legal problems could be resolved.

The ensuing publicity was 'dead wrong' in Dick's words, and it broke his allegiance to Lovell as well as unnecessarily complicating the procedure. It forced the Virginia lawyer to make his request to the hospital public, thus protracting the process and making it much more expensive for all concerned. It also invited the intervention of less disinterested parties.

The mysterious figure of Willi Korte continued to charm Penny Jenkins on the telephone, trying to find a way to gain access to the pathology sample. Out of the blue, or so it seemed to the participants in the courtroom drama, the little-known Russian Nobility Association intervened in Dick's petition, which he had by then filed at Charlottesville City Court. The Association said it had an interest in the results of any test on Anna because its purpose is to authenticate the identity of members of the Russian nobility who had come to live in America and Europe since the 1917 revolution. Strictly speaking, this was a moot point. Grand Duchess Anastasia was not a member of the mere 'nobility' but of the much more elevated Imperial Family. In its depositions to the court, the Association claimed to want independent scientific testing of the sample to establish Anna's DNA sequence and consequently her claim to be a Romanov. In practice, as the court case dragged on, it only appeared interested in obfuscating the issue, presumably to delay or prevent DNA testing of the tissue.

Penny Jenkins, who fielded the requests of the various parties to the case on behalf of the hospital, had no illusions about the various demands.

> We all had an agenda. I saw the film in the [19]50s and since then I believed. It was an enchantment from my childhood. I guess I wanted to see her [Anna] come out to be the princess because of the romance of it all. Others were sure she was

while others [the Russian Nobility Society] certainly didn't think so. It was a feel good story. That made us all [at the hospital] very much want to make this work. But we also have a responsibility to our patients and to our whole community. We had to stick absolutely by the letter of the law.

By this time two film-makers, unbeknownst to each other, were both on the track of this dramatic story, vying to win a world exclusive in finally revealing the identity of Anna Anderson. Julian Nott, an Englishman, had been commissioned by British television's Channel 4 to make a documentary feature on solving the mystery of Anna Anderson. His 60-minute film concentrated on the scientific aspects of the story, going through the evidence that had held the attention of German judges for more than 30 years. Discussions of her handwriting, her knowledge of languages, the shape of her ears, all built up to the climax of the film, a report on the latest scientific identification technique – DNA. A story that lumped together dead Nazis, O. J. Simpson and the Grand Duchess Anastasia was a film producer's dream come true.

In his search for exclusive access to the results, Nott decided 'to hitch my wagon to Schweitzer'. Dick's philosophy remained constant throughout the struggle – he was willing to cooperate with anyone who might conceivably help achieve the outcome he wanted – bona fide DNA testing on Anna's sample. Dick subsequently allowed Nott exclusive access to filming the key stages in the scientific operation, and Nott also gained Gill's permission to film at the Forensic Science Service.

The second film-maker on the trail of the story was Maurice Philip Remy, the German television producer who is well known in his own country for hosting their version of *Candid Camera*. Remy has also made a documentary on the Russian treasure lost during the Second World War and was in Ekaterinburg with the Maples team, after which he hoped to tie up the major loose end – the fate of the Grand Duchess Anastasia. Remy had hired Willi Korte, who lived in the United States, to do all he could to gain access to Anna's last remains. Remy's first thought was to commission the Forensic Pathology Institute in Munich to carry out the DNA analysis. Remy's plans were unknown to Schweitzer, Lovell, Nott and the hospital itself. Willi Korte, in his turn, played a behind-the-scenes role through his client, the Russian Nobility Association, with the support and backing of Remy.

One month after Schweitzer's original petition was lodged, the Russian Nobility Association filed its own petition to intervene, complete with Washington lawyers, Andrews & Kurth, and the local Charlottesville firm of Feil, Deinlein, Pettit & Williams. For three months the Schweitzers were, not surprisingly, at a loss to understand the underlying motivation of the Association. Most of the petitions began with the monotonous introduction from the Association's Washington attorney, Lindsey Crawford:

> The association is an historic and philanthropic organisation whose purpose is to protect the authenticity of the line of the Imperial Family of Russia and the events prior to 1917 in Russia. The association is a not-for-profit corporation and was incorporated in 1938 under the laws of the state of New York.
>
> The association was formed by former members of the Russian nobility in the United States to work together with former Russian nobility in France and the rest of Europe and Latin America. The general purpose of the organisation is to preserve and promote the history and culture of the Russian nobility. Such an organisation was needed after the Russian Revolution, since nobility was then outlawed in Russia.

As Marina Schweitzer put it: 'I thought I would go mad if I had to hear Lindsey Crawford say that again in court.'

Dick Schweitzer well understood that nothing in Anna's life had been simple, and, in his view, the intervention by the Russian Nobility Association was only one more instance of a string of unnecessary complications. Despite its declared concern for Russia's noble culture, the Association appeared to have one purpose only – to block proceedings or delay the process of discovery, while taking over the responsibility for the testing and announcement of the results. Dick Schweitzer knew exactly how much Washington lawyers cost and doubted that the Association by itself had access to that level of funding. He also recognized the name of the Washington lawyers – they had been in touch with James Lovell seven months earlier on behalf of Korte asking that the laboratories in Munich should carry out the analysis of Anna's sample. Naturally Schweitzer began to conjecture that Korte could be backing the Association, but who was behind Korte?

The advocates of freedom of information also made an appearance. The Richmond Newspaper Group filed a petition to intervene to prevent the case from being heard privately. The Group's proprietors no doubt recognized a scoop of the century and demanded that they be allowed full access and coverage of all proceedings, which, of course, Dick Schweitzer had tried initially to circumvent by trying to get the case heard in the judge's chambers.

The court case, with all its litigants, had just got under way in October 1993 when Penny Jenkins arrived at work early one morning to find a woman sitting in her office and demanding access to the Anderson sample. She introduced herself as Anastasia Romanov and declared it had taken her three days to arrive in Charlottesville from Mullan, Idaho, because she only travelled by train. To the consternation of all concerned, the trial judge accepted her brief. She became the fourth party officially represented in the court case, the most bizarre and in some ways the most poignant. She claimed to be Anna Anderson's daughter. This Idaho Anastasia had changed her name by deed poll, when she realized her true antecedents.

Anastasia Romanov said that her original name was Ellen Margarete Therese Adam Kailing and claimed that she was born in Germany on 27 October 1937. She was later rescued from a concentration camp, and her adoptive mother was paid to raise her. Her story thereafter confirmed the dangers of convent girls reading romantic novels. The key evidence of her 'true' identity came from a Princess Ileana, who was then Mother Alexandra, Abbess of the Orthodox Monastery of the Transfiguration at Ellwood City, Pennsylvania. She told Ellen Kailing in June 1990 that she was the daughter of Grand Duchess Anastasia. Later, after reading James Lovell's book on Anastasia, where he conjectures that Anna had a love affair with Prince Heinrich von Reuss zu Schleiz, she drew the logical inference that the Prince was her father. The raw material for her new identity was drawn from three authors who have written about Anastasia and the Romanovs: Peter Kurth, James Lovell, and most recently Edvard Radzinsky. In her affidavit she stated:

> When I did see the pictures in Peter Kurth's book, *Anastasia the Riddle*, I knew this was my story.
>
> Actually Lovell in his book, *Anastasia the Lost Princess*, gave me the right information. Nadejda Mamysheva from Russia pointed this information out to me. Now the picture was complete and fitting.
>
> The last information came from Edvard Radzinsky and it is now clear that my mother protected her brother, she tried to protect her husband and she certainly protected me, her daughter . . . It is also clear that my mother's brother was living in Russia and was married. Did he have children, it is not clear.

She claimed the right as Anna's nearest relative to sole access to the tissue sample. Her testimony was melancholy and incoherent, especially as she recounted her unhappy life, which included a divorce, where her former husband was given custody of their children. Her dream of being a lost princess, based on nothing more than reading three books, is sad testimony to the potency of the Anastasia story.

Anastasia Romanov was admitted as a party to the court hearing, since Judge Jay Swett and hospital attorney Matthew Murray agreed that this case should only 'happen one time'. The judge allowed all interested parties to put forward their claims at once so as not to take up future court time nor add to the hospital costs by reapplying for access. In the event Anastasia Romanov, having declared her identity and demanded good notice of future court hearings so that she would have time to take the train from Idaho, faded away, appropriately enough, to St Petersburg, Florida. Before she left she donated blood samples so that she could later prove her relationship to her famous mother. They were never used.

• • •

The significant feature of the existing lawsuit was that the protagonists ostensibly had no quarrel. Anastasia Romanov, the Russian Nobility Association and the Schweitzers all claimed to want the same outcome – the DNA testing of the Anna Anderson tissue sample by qualified scientists. Dick Schweitzer had approached the Forensic Science Service in England, where the Peter Gill team had established the DNA sequences of the Tsar and Tsarina from the bones removed from the pit near Ekaterinburg. Schweitzer was prepared to pay for the testing himself. He appointed an old college friend, Edward Deets, who lives in Charlottesville, to act as local counsel.

Dick Schweitzer's first petition in October asked that the DNA testing be carried out by the Forensic Science Service, then based at Aldermaston, as it was the 'acknowledged leader in developing and conducting forensic procedures through polymerase chain reaction in DNA genetic testing'. He also invited the Armed Forces Institute of Pathology in Washington, DC, to carry out a parallel DNA investigation to confirm the integrity of the English laboratory's results. He requested the Charlottesville court to order Martha Jefferson Hospital to release the material and required that all further demands for access to the sample be denied until the Aldermaston scientists had concluded their research. Schweitzer's appeal included an affidavit from Nancy Leeds Wynkoop, whom Anastasia considered her 'closest relative on American soil'. As the daughter of Princess Xenia of Russia and granddaughter of Grand Duke George of Russia and Princess Marie of Greece and Denmark, who was a first cousin of Nicholas II, she was the same Nancy who, as a little four-year-old girl, had made Anna sob when she stayed at the Leeds mansion at Oyster Bay in 1928. Nancy was wearing the sailor's cap that Anastasia said reminded her of her lost brother Alexei. Attached to the Wynkoop papers was her mother's affidavit, submitted in 1958 in support of Anastasia's claims before the German courts.

The first petition from the Russian Nobility Association was lodged on 4 November 1993. It noted there were at least four Romanovs living in the United States who were not informed of the court proceedings, although if their petition were consistent with their apparent belief that Anna was an impostor, they did not have to be informed as they were not 'blood relatives'. Ignoring this nicety they then denied Marina Schweitzer's right to petition the court as she was not a blood relative. Perhaps more reasonably they asked how Anastasia's tissue would help establish the identity of Dr Botkin's bones in Ekaterinburg. On the very same day Anastasia Romanov, hot off the train from Idaho, had filed her affidavit, supporting her claim to being Anna Anderson's 'closest relative'. Thus the main players had staked their claims to Anna's bowel, and the battle lines were drawn.

In its memorandum, filed in support of the petition to intervene on 12 November 1993, the Russian Nobility Association rejected the choice of the Forensic Science Service, implying that a laboratory paid for by the Schweitzers would not be impartial. The Association contested Marina Schweitzer's application because 'Schweitzer admits that she premises her petition on her life-long belief that Mrs Manahan was Anastasia Romanov.' The Association said it wanted the sample to go to laboratories at the University of California, Berkeley, and filed an affidavit from Dr William Maples in support of the Berkeley claim.

William Maples's statement on oath was an astonishing piece of judicial evidence since it cast doubt on Peter Gill's work with the Romanov bones. Maples had led the team from the University of Florida that provided anthropological assistance to the Russian scientists at the Romanov grave. Philip Remy had met Maples and his team in Ekaterinburg, when the results of the studies on the Romanov bones were announced. Maples had then sent samples of teeth and bone from Ekaterinburg to Dr Mary-Claire King, a DNA specialist at Berkeley, but in contrast to Dr Gill, who quickly published his findings in *Nature Genetics*, she has yet to make her work public.

This did not stop Maples from recommending that Dr King work on Anna's tissue-sample analysis. Maples pointed to Peter Gill's report, which showed that the Tsar had a single mutation, and said that Dr King had found no such anomaly in the bone and teeth samples she had received from Ekaterinburg. Maples wrote in his affidavit that: 'In particular, she [Dr King] has had no difficulty identifying the Tsar's remains.' As Dr King had not published whether or not she had encountered any difficulty, Schweitzer, in his response to the court, affirmed that her scientific findings had not been subjected to a peer review. In fact Gill was able to locate the single mutation because he had more advanced equipment than King, which permitted him to do more detailed work.

Maples also criticized the 98.5 per cent certainty of a familial match that Gill had found between the carriers of mitochondrial DNA in Ekaterinburg, which he said was not 'scientifically significant because several of the mitochondrial DNA sequences found in Prince Philip and his sisters and Tsarina Alexandra and her daughters are very common in Europe, particularly Germany'. This was not the view Maples put forward in his recently published book, *Dead Men Do Tell Tales*. In his chapter discussing his work on the Romanov bones, he wrote that Gill reported the DNA match was 'almost 99 per cent' and that he believes 'the British DNA work to be the final word in resolving this old mystery'.

Prince Alexis Scherbatow, the elderly president of the Russian Nobility Association, did not hesitate to pick up on this expert opinion in his affidavit. He said that science would not be served by biased participants and that the British laboratory represented 'second best scientific testing'. Peter Gill is an acknowledged world-leader in his field, the laboratory has the largest DNA database in the world, and Gill had already published the DNA sequences of the Romanovs, work done at the request of the Russians. But it got worse. Scherbatow cast aspersions on Gill's integrity by intoning that the 'samples may be contaminated to "prove" their conclusions.'

One problem for the Russian Nobility Association was that Dr King at Berkeley had not shown a burning desire to work on the Romanov case. She failed to respond to telephone calls or other messages. She did, however, send a notarized affidavit dated 7 December 1993, in which she stated that she had worked for seven months on various samples of bones and teeth taken from all nine bodies found in Ekaterinburg.

Far from supporting Dr Maples's allegations that there were problems in connection with the DNA identification work at the Forensic Science Service in England, Dr King offered to work collaboratively with Dr Gill if there were sufficient DNA material in Anna's sample. 'It would be ideal to have two qualified laboratories carry out the mitochondrial DNA testing in parallel and compare their results,' she testified. King told Dick Schweitzer she had the utmost respect for Gill's work and was horrified to hear that aspersions were being cast on his scientific integrity. She also called Gill and distanced herself from Maples's assessment of Gill's work. Dick Schweitzer added that he would have been happy for her, as a qualified DNA expert, to work on the case, but she was apparently not interested in the assignment.

By this time Dick Schweitzer was becoming more and more frustrated by the spoiler action of the Russian Nobility Association in the lawsuit, which he attributed to their apparent fear that the DNA testing would prove that Anna was indeed Grand Duchess Anastasia. He still did not know who was backing the Association, why it was so concerned to delay the testing nor why the Association had become involved in the first place. Penny Jenkins had perhaps the simplest answer: 'They just didn't want her at their cocktail party, I guess.'

Actually, she was right. Remy, through Willi Korte, was able to interest the Russian Nobility Association in the case precisely because Anna's presence had divided the Russian *émigré* community for so many years. They wanted the matter cleared up. In fact Remy did try to attract support for his suit one rung higher – from the Romanovs themselves. Prince Nicholas was nearly persuaded to appear in court but was dissuaded at the eleventh hour by his relative, Prince Rostislav. He was advised that as the Romanovs had managed to avoid going to court over the case for 70 years, it was hardly appropriate for them to become involved a full 10 years after Anna's death.

Paranoia, rumours and accusations were heightened by Korte's approach to the whole affair as a cloak-and-dagger mystery story. In direct contrast was Dick Schweitzer. Although a declared partisan of Anna, he consistently acted in a clearly straightforward manner. He did not confirm that Korte was behind the Russian Nobility Association until January 1994, and he did not discover that a German television company was behind Korte until much later. Remy and Korte had together been able to build up the paranoia among the Romanovs and others by referring to Schweitzer's father-in-law, Gleb Botkin, and his embarrassing public letter condemning the Romanov family back in 1928. Remy said that Korte indulged in the secret-behind-the-scenes manoeuvres before Remy knew Dick Schweitzer. In retrospect Remy says it would have been better to attempt a clear-cut arrangement with Schweitzer as Nott had done. Such an agreement, however, would have cost him his scoop.

The frustration felt by the Schweitzers was admirably summed up by Judge Swett, who concluded in court that however many testing sites were designated, it still would not be sufficient to satisfy the Russian Nobility Association. In common with the Schweitzers, the Association wanted at least two separate tests done, but they could not come to an agreement as to which laboratories should be commissioned. Dr King did not appear willing to carry out the DNA analyses. Dr Gill who did not contribute directly to the court case was ready and willing to do the work, while the laboratories in Munich, originally cited by Willi Korte, fell out of the picture as proceedings continued. The Armed Forces Institute of Pathology in Washington, DC, was the other contender for the testing, and they appeared willing to cooperate.

Meanwhile Dick Schweitzer sought ways to move the court case forward. He discovered that Anna had made a will in Germany in 1953 and appointed four executors. Only one was still alive, Baron Ulrich von Gienanth, and it was possible that he could qualify as Anna's personal representative under Virginia law. Von Gienanth was interested in the case, but by now was an old man, and due to difficulties over travel and translation of documents, he was never qualified to act in Charlottesville. He is also deaf, which did not help in transatlantic telephone calls.

Schweitzer was set to announce his discovery of von Gienanth at a meeting scheduled for 10 January 1994, in obedience to an order from the judge that the parties to the case sit down and try to hammer out a mutually agreed programme for the testing. This attempt at reconciliation degenerated into a Keystone Kops farce. Willi Korte, as he explained in a letter to the judge, tried to contact Lindsey Crawford, the Washington lawyer for the Association, before the start of the meeting. He arrived at her office to see her driving off and presumed she was heading out for the two-hour drive to Charlottesville. In fact she was only going off to re-park her car.

Korte then hired a car, as his own would not start, and arrived in Charlottesville late for the meeting, clutching a paper stating that he was a representative for the Russian Nobility Association. Schweitzer was not allowed to put any questions to him there, but at least he now had proof that Korte was behind the Association. He was becoming suspicious that Remy was Korte's true employer and demanded that Korte confirm it. Korte said nothing. Crawford did not turn up at all as she had discussed the developments with hospital attorney Matthew Murray, who wanted to delay negotiations until the legal standing of von Gienanth could be established. This meeting and the failure of Dick Schweitzer and Lindsey Crawford to reach agreement on the testing caused Schweitzer to press for a nonsuit, which was granted on 1 March 1994.

It was then that sweet reason seemed to shine, finally, on the proceedings. One of Matthew Murray's colleagues accidentally stumbled on the answer. An old Virginia statute enables a judge to appoint an administrator if the executor of a will has died or is unable to carry out the appointment. Schweitzer then asked his local attorney, Edward Deets, to petition the court to act as administrator, which the judge allowed on 16 March.

Naturally this did not satisfy the Russian Nobility Association. They brought a second lawsuit contesting the appointment on the grounds that Deets could not act impartially, as he had been the local lawyer for Schweitzer. They also repeated their demand that Dr King carry out the primary tests, with another laboratory appointed to conduct parallel testing. Finally on 19 May the judge dismissed all claimants to the second lawsuit, saying the court lacked jurisdiction to entertain the petitioner's claims and that the petitioner lacked sufficient standing to assert claims to the tissue sample. After that it was plain sailing.

The eight-month affair cost the Martha Jefferson Hospital at least $15,000, and estimates for Remy and his teams of lawyers have been put at between $40,000 and $100,000. Schweitzer always refuses to talk about how much he spent, but just travelling and attending the court hearings in Charlottesville must have taxed his pocket, although he himself represented his wife.

Dr Peter Gill arrived in Charlottesville just one month later, on 19 June, to take the samples back to England. The event was scheduled for a Sunday afternoon, because hospital officials were nervous that the heightened interest in the case could lead to a dangerous mishap – or something worse. Julian Nott was quite worried that if the Russian Nobility Association got wind of the transfer they might serve an injunction on Gill in person or try to prevent the removal of the sample through other means.

Although the weekend appointment was designed to reduce outside interest in the event, it was scarcely conducted in secrecy. The removal of the biopsy sample was watched by hospital administrators and the attorneys connected with the case together with the Schweitzers, while a British film crew captured every moment of the transaction. The crew was there to provide material for Nott's television documentary as well as film footage for the United States public television science programme, NOVA.

Betty Eppard, a registered histology technician, who coincidentally had conducted the routine blood tests required by American law on Jack and Anna before their marriage, performed the actual cutting of the tissue. Eppard operated the slicing device, known as a microtome, which was wiped with absolute ethanol after each use and its blade changed with each tissue block. Each segment was also washed in the sterile solution prior to being mounted on the microtome. The same procedure was repeated five times: Dr Hunt MacMillan of the Martha Jefferson Hospital gave Dr Gill a tissue block and identified it; Peter Gill sterilized it before handing it on to Betty Eppard. Eppard sliced three to six pieces off each block, the slices each equal in thickness to two hairs. The tissue slivers were so thin they immediately curled up before Gill, using a special tweezer, gently picked them up and placed them in sterilized vials. The samples had been fixed in formaldehyde and preserved in paraffin wax. Dr MacMillan then put the vials into tamperproof plastic bags and sealed and labelled each one. To test for possible contamination a piece of wax containing no tissue was cut from each block for use as a control, to check that it wasn't randomly contaminated by DNA from human handling.

Gill, ever the cautious scientist, told the press at that weekend: 'I can't be sure at the moment how likely it is we'll get DNA from the samples. One problem is that they have been subject to harsh chemical treatment which destroys DNA. We also have to bear in mind the age of the samples.' This was probably not what the Schweitzers wanted to hear.

After nearly a year of legal wrangling and up to $100,000 later, Gill, on that hot Sunday afternoon, put the plastic bags containing the samples of Anna's tissue loosely in a backpack, which he slung over his shoulder as he set off for the two-hour drive back to Washington, DC. That backpack seemed a prosaic end for something that had taken up so much time and proved of such value to so many people. And if indeed Anna Anderson had been a Romanov, that anti-climactic treatment was almost in keeping with the many accidents that had beset her life. A second sample was sent to the United States Armed Forces Institute of Pathology for parallel testing. Only one-third of the tissue kept by the hospital was removed, the remainder is to be retained for further scientific work, if not for future dynastic claimants.

Despite Gill's words of caution, scientifically speaking, it was not a difficult task to ascertain whether the last mortal remains of Anna Anderson contained Romanov blood. He tested the specimens of tissue for both nuclear and mitochondrial DNA. When he announced the results at a press conference in October 1994, he was able to make a forthright statement: 'The results show that the sample could not have originated with the Tsar and Tsarina.'

Gill told the media there was no connection between the tissue sample's DNA and the established DNA patterns of either the Tsar or Tsarina. Five strands of nuclear DNA, which establishes parentage, were extracted from the sample, despite the fact that the DNA was highly degraded. Gill's team found that four of the five different strands were inconsistent with those of the Tsar and Tsarina. In addition the mitochondrial DNA did not match that in the blood given by Prince Philip, thus ruling out any maternal relationship. Gill was extremely careful to relate all his statements to 'the sample' he examined, rather than naming Anna outright. He did say he had checked the serial numbers on the tissue biopsy, which corresponded to the hospital records at the pathology laboratory, before removing it, thus implying that the tissue he had analysed did originate from Anna Anderson.

The courageous manner in which the Schweitzers faced the press at that conference, in the light of Gill's findings, impressed all concerned with the case. Prince Alexis Scherbatow even wrote a letter to *Royalty* magazine in response to an article about Anna's DNA results. Among other things he writes: 'The RNA, of which I am president, was never a party to these deliberations.' This letter seems to be almost an apology for the obfuscation perpetrated in the Association's name, given the uncomplicated way the Schweitzers handled the announcement of the results.

Gill's findings were corroborated by the work of Dr Mark Stoneking at Pennsylvania State University, who extracted DNA from six strands of hair said to emanate from Anna. This is where Sydney Mandelbaum, the first sleuth to approach the hospital at Charlottesville to ask for the release of Anna's tissue biopsy, re-enters the story. Well might Mandelbaum joke that Gill thanks him every day for the corroboration that came from Pennsylvania.

The hair sample used by Dr Stoneking and his researchers does not have an impeccable provenance. Susan Burkhart, a lover of the Romanov legend, one day dropped into a bookshop in Chapel Hill, North Carolina, to browse through the latest selection of Anastasia and Romanov memorabilia made available to the shop from the sale of part of Jack Manahan's estate. As Susan was looking through one of the books she found an envelope, with the legend 'Hair of Princess Anastasia' written on the envelope. The hair was in a clump, as though it came from a hair brush, and it was dyed. Jack washed and tinted his wife's hair throughout their marriage. Of most importance, perhaps, from the scientific point of view, the hair had roots. While mitochondrial DNA is easier to obtain from a piece of tissue, it can also be recoverable from a small amount of material, such as a hair follicle. It is very difficult to extract DNA from a cut lock of hair.

Susan Burkhart contacted one of Anna's biographers, Peter Kurth. In partnership with Mandelbaum, they chose Dr Stoneking to assist them in their search, offering 'to make him famous'. Dr Stoneking is a member of the Department of Anthropology at Pennsylvania State University and has conducted wide-ranging research on population genetics, from which he has developed an extensive database. Six strands of hair were placed in an envelope and sent by Federal Express to Stoneking's centre, where he arranged for graduate student Terry Melton to do the actual scientific analysis.

Like many others, Terry Melton had come under Anna's spell sufficiently to recall with excitement the time she had run into her in a casual way, while living in Charlottesville where she worked at the University of Virginia. She and her husband saw the Manahans eating at a cafeteria one evening, with the station wagon parked outside. As usual there were several dogs in the car. One of them had escaped, and Melton recalled how she 'grabbed it' while her husband went into the restaurant to tell the Manahans. Anna came out and silently retrieved the dog.

'She was a very eccentric woman, she did not talk to me at all,' says Melton. 'She was very well known in Charlottesville and actually had an exalted status in the community although she ran into trouble at the end of her life.'

Melton received the six hairs and used five of them to extract the available mitochondrial DNA. Using the polymerase chain reaction (PCR) technique to tag the mitochondrial DNA available from the hair, she was able to sequence it and compare it with the patterns from the Tsar and Tsarina published by Gill in *Nature Genetics*. She said there were six differences across the region examined, which indicated no possibility that the hair came from a person related to the Imperial Family.

She informed Peter Kurth and Sydney Mandelbaum two days before Gill's press conference, and they released a press statement through the international news agency Reuters, on the Monday before the Wednesday press conference. Gill immediately got in touch with Stoneking, entered an agreement and compared DNA results. The two separate research laboratories had come up with exactly the same DNA sequence. Melton only tested the hair strands for mitochondrial DNA. In corroboration, the Armed Forces Institute also produced a matching mitochondrial DNA sequence from their section of tissue. There is about a 2 per cent likelihood of two people having identical DNA by chance.

'It was extremely gratifying to us,' comments Mandelbaum, as this parallel testing appeared to add to the proof that Anna was not Anastasia. Perhaps, more importantly, it corroborated the provenance of both samples, lessening the possibility that the tissue biopsy held by the hospital had been tampered with.

Melton, like many others working on the case, was disappointed that her own scientific investigations could not come up with proof that Anderson was indeed who she claimed to be. Peter Kurth, on the other hand, was devastated by the results, she said. He had publicly proclaimed his belief that Anna was the Grand Duchess, not only during the testing process but even concluding his biography with the words: 'I believed her, yes. I believed her, I liked her, and I am proud to have stood on her side of the struggle.'

Having established who she was not, the question for the scientists and journalists involved in Anna's search for an identity had to be: 'If she was not Grand Duchess Anastasia, who was she?' At the same time as conducting the scientific testing commissioned by the Schweitzers, Peter Gill also carried out a DNA test on a blood sample supplied via film-maker Julian Nott. This sample came from the great-nephew of Franziska Schanzkowska, a man named Carl Maucher, who was the grandson of one of Franziska's sisters. His mitochondrial DNA matched the pattern established at the Forensic Science Service.

Peter Gill, in his characteristically dry and scientific manner sums it up thus: 'This finding supports the hypothesis that Anna Anderson and Franziska Schanzkowska were the same person.'

The Forensic Science Service has a database of more than 300 Caucasian samples. The British scientists searched through the examples and found no matching sequence, meaning that the Maucher sequence and that taken from the Charlottesville sample is rare. This led Gill to say 'the chance of matching the profiles is less than one in 300.'

Anna had been confronted by members of the Schanzkowski family twice – first by Franziska's brother Felix in 1927 and secondly by four of her siblings in 1938. On both occasions, they did not identify her as their sister. Franziska Schanzkowska was born on 16 December 1896, in Bororwihlas, a small town in Kashubia, one of the Polish provinces at that time forming part of the German Empire. She was five years older than the Grand Duchess Anastasia, which coincides with the many descriptions of her 'premature ageing' noted by doctors and visitors alike. Her father married twice, and she was a child of the second marriage and close to her brother Felix. The first family were very religious and straitlaced, while Franziska and Felix were more open-minded. Franziska was noted for reading books, which led to comments that she had airs above her station.

'My auntie Franziska was the cleverest of the four children,' said Waltraut Schanzkowski, who now lives in Hamburg. 'She did not want to be buried in a little one-horse town in the depths of Kashubia, she wanted to come out into the world, wanted to become an actress – something special.'

Shortly before the outbreak of the First World War, Franziska left Bororwihlas for Berlin, fell in love and got engaged. Her future husband was called to the army, and Franziska got a job at a munitions factory owned by the electrical company AEG in Berlin. In 1916 her fiancé was killed on the western front. Shortly after this tragedy, Franziska let a grenade slip out of her hands as she was working on the assembly line, and it exploded. She was injured slightly in her head, but a foreman was blown to pieces in the accident before her very eyes. She was deeply shocked, left the factory and worked on a farm, becoming apathetic and spending long periods in bed. The last the Schanzkowskis heard of their sister was a birthday card she sent to her brother Felix in February 1920. On 17 February 1920, Fraulein Unbekannt was rescued by a police officer from the Landwehr Canal.

The remaining Schanzkowskis are quite suspicious of investigators into the Anna Anderson case. Felix's daughter has told reporters that her father talked about his sister Franziska with pride, saying she got away and made a new and successful life for herself as Anna Anderson. However, she does like to be paid for her reminiscences. Margarete Ellerik, the daughter of Gertrude who tried to make Anna admit to being a Schanzkowska, generally refuses to have anything to do with investigators and is apparently afraid that the family will be prosecuted for Anna's activities.

Among Anna's foremost true believers, the Schweitzers were most upset by the DNA test conclusions. While accepting the findings as presented by Peter Gill, they are convinced that 'something went wrong' with the sample that was tested. The results from the Forensic Science Service and the US Armed Forces Institute do corroborate each other, although the US institution only took mitochondrial DNA from its sample. The parallel testing fulfilled its purpose as it proved that the specimens were not tampered with or damaged after their removal from Charlottesville. The outcome of the hair test, despite its questionable provenance, also corroborates what Gill and his colleagues discovered. The Schweitzers suggest that switching or tampering with the samples is possible, but if that had happened, both the hospital sample and the clump of hair would not only have had to be planted but would also have had to come from the Schanzkowski family through the female line to produce the same mitochondrial DNA sequence.

Dick Schweitzer is now looking at possible reasons for what he considers to be the negative answer found by Gill and his team, since he accepts the integrity of the DNA testing. He is contemplating renewed scientific investigations, including possible analysis of materials held in Germany as well as further comparison with the Schanzkowski family. The experience of the court trial has made Dick Schweitzer more tight-lipped about his future plans, but additional tests are planned for the hospital tissue sample. These would determine whether the gangrene found in the sample was the same type as found in the surgery, as recorded in the hospital notes by the doctor who had performed the operation; that the sample came from someone who was 78 years old; and include a study of the techniques used for storage. He is also searching for other clues in Germany, where Anna spent time in such a large number of medical institutions, and indicates he may have found new material that could cast further light on Anna's identity. He is working constantly to exclude possibilities and is considering further tests on members of the Schanzkowski family to see if any loose ends can be tied up. 'I guess I have a few more years yet,' he says.

Was tampering possible? The Martha Jefferson Hospital in Charlottesville has been storing specimens from patients since 1978, when it opened a pathology department. The basement department was relatively easy to enter, according to visitors. When the Manahan biopsy became the subject of such intense interest, the hospital authorities moved it to a safer place for storage, suggesting some concern by the hospital management that the existing site was not secure.

Penny Jenkins acknowledged that something could have gone wrong in the storage – where human beings work there is always the possibility of a mix-up. An outside hand could possibly have perpetrated a switch. But, she thinks Schweitzer will have little success with his quest. The medical-records room is always staffed or locked, she says, and any person wanting to tamper with the specimen would have to search for the patient records number and then the specimen file number, which is stored in a different place. In addition to the tissue blocks kept in the pathology department, the hospital keeps a surgical slide from all operations. A technician at the hospital cross-checked the surgical slide with the specimen taken by Gill, and it showed no visible differences. Jenkins said she did not know of the existence of surgical slides until this case, and they are kept in a different place from the biopsies.

The weekend before Schweitzer's press conference and Julian Nott's film, which was premièred on 5 October 1994, Philip Remy had planted a spoiler story in *Der Spiegel*, which was picked up by the *Sunday Times*. It reported parallel testing that had been ordered by Remy and was able to debunk Anna's claims before Gill's announcement. After losing control of the Charlottesville sample, Remy had set about to discover alternative scientific proof of Anna's identity, which would be exclusive. Although Nott was the first to proclaim the findings on film, the exclusivity of the news was damaged by Remy's early revelation that Anna was not a Romanov. There had been other behind-the-scenes negotiations with the *Sunday Times*, who were interested in the story and wanted to splash it in their weekend edition, but the newspaper could not find enough corroboration of Gill's results and so went with the Remy story. In the end Gill's verdict stayed a well-guarded secret until the press conference.

Remy's discoveries centred on a glass slide containing a drop of blood allegedly given by Anna in 1951 in Germany. Professor Stefan Sandkuhler, a former blood expert at Heidelberg University, had examined Anna, taken a blood sample and smeared a drop on a glass plate. Scratched into the glass and clearly legible is the name of the patient: Anastasia. The sample was divided in July 1994 and sent to two independent scientists, Professor Bernd Herrmann at the Anthropological Institute of Gottingen University and Dr Charles Ginther at the University of California. Two months later Herrmann announced that he had obtained four DNA particles from the sample, none of which tallied with the DNA found in the Romanov bones. Remy also took a sample from Margarete Ellerik, daughter of Gertrude, but so far there has been no report on that comparison.

The problem with Remy's scientific investigation was that Gill did not agree with it. In his most categorical statement at the press conference, he affirmed: 'I have compared the results, and they were different. I therefore concluded that the samples he analysed and those I analysed had different origins. One of these samples has to be false.'

Remy argued at the press conference that his German scientists affirm there are ten possibilities why the samples came out with different DNA sequences. Only one of these possibilities is that the samples originate with different people, leaving nine scientific reasons for the discrepancy. While Remy blustered, Gill grew more grimly impassive, refusing to countenance a scientific explanation for the obvious differences in their DNA sequences. Remy is still awaiting the results from Dr Ginther in California and plans to complete his film about Anna Anderson in the autumn of 1995.

The fact that Schweitzer invited Philip Remy to the press conference at all indicates his character. Despite Remy's backing of the Russian Nobility Association, which cost Schweitzer time, effort and money, he was only concerned that all interested parties should lay out their wares and contribute any information they might have to solving the mystery. Remy appreciated Schweitzer's generosity. Nonetheless Remy found himself in a lion's den as he was verbally attacked by another interested party, the writer Michael Thornton, who accused him of attempting to scoop Nott's film by publicizing results obtained from a blood sample of spurious authenticity. There was also a more serious side to the conflict, as it is possible that Remy broke a Virginia statute by paying a third party to appear in court. This is illegal as it allows someone to attempt to ruin his opponent by tying him up in court on spurious charges, without revealing their true nature. But all this is the past. Schweitzer and Remy are now on good terms and compare notes on the Anna story.

Dick Schweitzer's outgoing and guileless nature has been all the more battered by some of the comment surrounding the announcement of the results. Dr Gill had telephoned him with the results one full month before their public announcement, so the Schweitzers had had time to prepare themselves. They were, of course, dreadfully disappointed, but at all times they have been extremely careful to praise the work of the scientists. As Dick

Schweitzer says:

> I still believe Anna Anderson is Anastasia. Dr Gill's method-
> ology and science showed that Anna was not a member of the
> Imperial Family, that was excluded first by the nuclear DNA.
> But when you go further and say the mitochondrial DNA
> indicates it has some relationship to a Polish factory worker,
> that fits none of the rational experiences of people who knew
> her. It's just too pat.

Marina Schweitzer is a little more direct. She describes the
assumption that Anna Anderson was actually Franziska
Schanzkowska as 'for the birds. I'm disappointed but they don't
change my opinion.' Neither of them can accept that the regally
imposing Anna could fool princes and princesses of Europe if she
had been born into a poor family. All her supporters described her
manner, particularly the way she lifted her hand to be kissed, as
being unmistakably royal. She also appeared genteel in her conversation, her style of speech and her interests, so they feel sure that,
whoever she was, she was not a semi-educated Polish factory
worker. Witnesses are also clear that she was not acting a part.
Despite her travails she was never exposed, a feat that could not
have been achieved if she had been acting. She believed herself to
be the Grand Duchess, taking on her persona. It is perhaps
enough that those surrounding her believed she was from the
Imperial Family, making 'proof' of her identity almost irrelevant.
If they knew she was Anastasia, then that was who she was.

In addition to the Schweitzers, there is a small band of
Anastasians who continue to cling to their beliefs, despite the
obvious set-back of the DNA results. They tend to view this latest
'evidence' as another in the long line of controversial tests that
Anna was subjected to during her life. 'Life became almost
unbearable for her,' comments a Charlottesville friend, Mildred
Ewing. 'I'm sorry that it turned out like this but I still believe she
was she.' Other supporters rely less on faith and continue to point
to the many 'proofs' that were substantiated during the German
court trials. For Ian Lilburn, his judgement is more succinct: 'I
think there's something we don't know about DNA.'

As well as bearing the disappointing results, Dick Schweitzer has been personally attacked on the editorial pages of *Nature Genetics*, the leading scientific journal devoted to genetic biology and DNA. The editorial, which contains some errors, bemoans the fact that he does not accept the outcome of the DNA results.

> Why is it then that Schweitzer and his supporters refuse to accept the results and are even now exploring other ways of proving themselves and the late Anna Anderson right? What, given such reluctance, does the scientific community have to do to convince the public that it knows what it is talking about and is accurate in its assessments?

It is true that Dick Schweitzer does not concur with the DNA findings, but the editorial writer has missed the point. From his knowledge of Anna, Schweitzer feels that the test conclusions are so improbable that the tissue biopsy tested had to be switched or contaminated. He has never challenged the outcome of DNA analysis, the accuracy of DNA science in general nor the particular work done by the scientists involved. He has always been very careful to state that the results came out wrongly not because of the science or the scientists but because of the material used.

It may never be proved entirely to everyone's satisfaction whether Anna emanated from the Polish/German provinces or from Tsarskoe Selo. The weight of opinion has now moved to the astonishing conclusion that she was the most successful impostor of the twentieth century, but, for most people, their opinion is formed by the media, without first-hand knowledge.

Michael Thornton, who held power of attorney from Anna in England, was one of her friends. Thirty-five years ago as a student, he trekked out to Unterlengenhardt with the sole purpose of meeting Anna. He had seen the film, *Anastasia*, starring Ingrid Bergman, and its romance had captured his imagination, as it had that of so many other people. He had to wait three weeks before being admitted by Anna, but in the meantime he went to dine with Gunther Berenberg-Gossler in Basle, an occasion arranged by Lord Mountbatten. Gossler was the lawyer acting for Barbara of Mecklenburg against Anna in the German law courts. Thornton says he has always remembered Gossler's words:

'She will win you over because she has astonishing suggestive power, and you will find she is Franziska Schanzkowska.' Thornton said he never took a position on her identity because he had not known her in childhood. His sympathy had been piqued by the film, and his attention then held because she was a remarkable woman.

> I don't think I was particularly deceived by her. I did like her as a person, she was a charming and often impressive figure. She caught the imagination of the world and she achieved the fame largely by herself. Somewhere along the way she lost and rejected Schanzkowska. She lost that person totally and accepted completely she was this new person. I think it happened by accident and she was swept along on a wave of euphoria. Then she was incredibly lucky in that forensic scientists find such a close similarity with her ears, her eyes, her height. To me she was utterly fascinating. I'm pleased to have known her. She was probably a much more interesting person than the Grand Duchess Anastasia would have been.

For Dick Schweitzer, the case is not so simple. The DNA results have challenged a certainty that his wife Marina has known all her life and that Dick himself accepted as indisputable knowledge when he married into the Botkin family. Despite the scientific rationality of the DNA investigations, Dick feels the 'rational experience' of those who knew her outweighs scientific evidence. 'It's like saying she was a man,' said Dick. He is right in that DNA is not absolutely foolproof, but, equally, if the results had come out the other way, there is no question that he would have leapt on them as the last scientific word, while Anna's opponents would have had their doubts.

As Anna Anderson is now a figure of legend, perhaps it is unimportant who she was. As she once told an interviewer on the American ABC television network: 'How shall I tell you who I am? You believe it or you don't believe it. It doesn't matter. In no anyway [sic] whatsoever.'

CHAPTER ELEVEN

Criminal Case No. 18/123666–93

'IT'S NOT EASY to kill someone,' says Vladimir Soloviev with a smile, echoing Yurovsky's contemporary account. He should know, for he is a long-serving member of the Russian State Prosecutor's Office. He has served on a number of notorious murder inquiries, including that of Father Aleksandr Men, a popular Moscow priest who was killed by muggers. He is now working on the most high-level investigation of his career: the murder of Tsar Nicholas II and his family. Did he get the case because of his successful record in chasing the criminals of Russia's capital? 'I got the job because the Chief State Prosecutor didn't want it!'

When nine bodies are found in a pit, it warrants a criminal investigation, even in Russia, where there are more than enough mass graves waiting to be discovered. When the bodies are clearly not evidence of a recent crime, there is a tendency to file the case away. But when the corpses may well be those of the last Imperial Family of Russia, they warrant a second look. This was even more so since every aspect of the 'Romanov business' has become a political hot potato, touching on more than one special interest.

In October 1993 Russian President Boris Yeltsin appointed

Deputy Prime Minister Yury Yarov to head a high-level commission, comprised of clergymen, politicians, scientists and historians, to make recommendations to him about the future disposition of the murdered Romanovs. Until Yarov submits his report to Yeltsin, newspaper speculation about a royal burial in St Petersburg, Ekaterinburg or anywhere else is premature. The Yarov commission faces one great obstacle: it must satisfy itself that the remains are those of the Romanovs before it makes final recommendations. With talk of a possible canonization of the Tsar and his family by the Russian Orthodox Church, there is real determination to ensure that the relics are genuine.

It has been left to the lawyers such as Soloviev to still the doubts of politicians, clergymen and the general public. Soloviev took up his burden and set to work on the case numbered 18/123666–93. Seldom can an investigator have had so many people looking over his shoulder, offering so much criticism and advice. The first of these volunteers were self-proclaimed Romanovs, who emerged from every quarter once his investigation was publicized. Each week brings him a pile of letters from assorted Olgas, Tatianas or their children. He tosses a file across the table. 'This is a typical one. Adult male, Donets region. Claims to be the Tsarevich Alexei. Age in passport – 28.' He rolls his eyes heavenwards.

As Anna Anderson discovered, the real Romanovs are even more contentious. The White Russian *émigrés* have neither forgotten nor forgiven the 70 years of Communism and continue to distrust all agents, past or present, of the Soviet state. When Gelli Ryabov announced the discovery of the Sverdlovsk grave site in 1989, monarchist groups in Europe and the United States announced in chorus that no investigation could be credible unless it included foreign specialists. The Russian Nobility Association formed a Russian Expert Commission Abroad and offered assistance to the Yarov commission. Mistrust poisoned all efforts at cooperation, however, particularly when the State Procurator's office sought 'Romanov DNA' to test against the burial remains. The obvious candidate was Tikhon Kulikovsky-Romanov, offspring of the morganatic marriage of Grand Duchess Olga Aleksandrovna, the Tsar's sister, who was then a resident of Toronto, Canada.

When Tikhon refused to cooperate with 'Communists', Soloviev found a candidate who could not refuse: Nicholas's brother, the Grand Duke Georgy Aleksandrovich, who had died of tuberculosis in 1899 and was buried in the Peter and Paul Fortress in St Petersburg. He proposed to exhume the body and secure a sample for genetic testing. When Kulikovsky-Romanov heard of these efforts, which he saw as a desecration of a forebear's remains, he contacted the Russian Orthodox Church Metropolitan of St Petersburg and Ladoga, Ioann, to protest. It took Soloviev a year of quiet diplomacy, and the intervention of Orthodox Patriarch Aleksei II himself, before permission was given in May 1993. The blackened remains of Georgy again saw the light of day, however briefly.

Tikhon's wife, Olga, was of fighting Cossack stock, and after his death she took up the struggle with a vengeance. In a letter published in *Izvestiia*, she branded Soloviev a 'political timeserver ... ready to sacrifice his reputation and to offer the court of history findings and conclusions which only benefit the present political masters of Russia'. In Olga's opinion, he was letting himself be taken in by a crude fabrication of the KGB.

Equally hostile to Soloviev's investigation were those on the extreme right wing of the Orthodox Church, organized as the Union of Russian Orthodox Brotherhoods. They had deduced what Soloviev was up to. It was only necessary to look at the number he had assigned to the case: was not '666' the mark of the Beast of the Apocalypse, the Antichrist himself? If Olga Kulikovskaia-Romanova was content to attribute a cover-up to Communist agents, the Brotherhoods found enemies who were more sinister still. The bodies found by Aleksandr Avdonin and Gelli Ryabov in Ekaterinburg could not possibly be those of the Imperial Family because, as General Diterikhs had shown in his report, the corpses had been decapitated and taken to Moscow. The present burial was designed to obscure that fact. Why? Any reader of Diterikhs could provide the answer to that question: it was to disguise the ritual murder of the Tsar carried out by the Jews! That hoary legend still has its supporters in the Orthodox Church. During one meeting with the Patriarch, Soloviev was stunned when Patriarch Aleksei asked him if he was investigating the possibility of a ritual killing.

Soloviev pronounced himself sceptical about the reality of ritual murder, but he was willing to follow any good lead, even those that touched on foreign pretenders. The KGB had always known that all the Romanovs were dead – they were told so at agents' training school when the first news of Anna Anderson's claims came in from the West. Soviet foreign agents maintained surveillance over all significant émigré figures. Aleksandr Kerensky, for example, was still being observed in Palo Alto, California, 50 years after his overthrow. Did the security organs keep tabs on the young pretender – or perhaps even more? Aleksandr Avdonin is one of many concerned with the case to remark on the striking knowledge Anna Anderson appears to have had of the royal court. Could she perhaps have been 'prepared' by the Soviet secret service, ever eager to sow confusion and discord in émigré circles? Soloviev's appeal to the relevant archives produced not a single scrap of information. This in itself is suspicious, given the Organs' avaricious appetite for information. Soloviev remains undecided whether it is old-fashioned inefficiency, or something more sinister.

What Soloviev can predict is that a recommendation from the State Prosecutor's Office is nowhere near ready. The Yarov commission will just have to wait. 'I'd like to get all the scientists in one room and knock their heads together. Get them to furnish a majority report, and as many minority reports as they want. The government has even offered to pay for another international conference, so they must be taking it seriously.' The phone rings again for the prosecutor. 'It's my boss. He says to pack my bags and be ready to go to Chechnia tomorrow.' The 'Romanov business' will just have to wait while Vladimir Nikolaevich explores other cellars filled with the corpses of slaughtered families.

In December 1994 the authors were in the German capital of Bonn to do research for this book. Our hotel was located across the street from the Bonn City Opera, whose posters announced the evening's entertainment as Tchaikovsky's *Sleeping Beauty or, The Last Daughter of the Tsar*. It was too great a coincidence to ignore. We purchased tickets.

The Sleeping Beauty worked surprisingly well as a metaphor

for the story of the real Anastasia, whose birthday celebrations, during which her sisters dance for her, forms the romantic centre-piece. Another Anastasia is also featured, a young woman dressed in black coat and heavy boots, who throws herself from a bridge into a Berlin canal.

The Grand Duchess Anastasia Nikolaevna is dead, murdered by bullets, bayonets and rifle butts in a dark cellar in Ekaterinburg, Russia, at 2:30 in the morning of 17 July 1918. The young woman who rose out of that Berlin canal lived on in the person of Fraulein Unbekannt, Anna Tchaikovsky, Anna Anderson, Anastasia Manahan. The second undoubtedly believed she was the first. And, truly, she kept alive the memory of that other Anastasia. Without her there would have been no films, no books, no romantic legend.

The two Anastasias represent the two faces of the twentieth century. One is a century that really existed, full of war and the slaughter of the innocents. The second is the century we longed to have, of peace and family pleasures, and the dreams of any little girl who would close her eyes and become a princess.

Select
Bibliography

Newspapers and Journals

Istina? (Ekaterinburg)
Izvestiia (Moscow)
Moskovskie Novosti (Moscow)
Nature (London)
Nature Genetics (Washington)
The New York Times (New York)
New Scientist (London)
Pravda (Moscow)
Royalty (London)
Tsar-Kolokol (Moscow)
The Times (London)

Articles and Monographs
Russian Titles Are Given in Translation
and Marked with an [R]

Alekseev, Veniamin. *The Death of the Tsarist Family: Myths and Reality.* Ekaterinburg, 1993. [R]
Alexander, Grand Duke. *Once a Grand Duke.* London, 1932.
Alexandrov, Victor. *The End of the Romanovs.* London, 1966.
Aucleres, Dominique. *Anastasia, qui êtes-vous?* Paris, 1962.
Avdonin, A. N., 'In Search of the Place of Burial of the Remains of the Czar's Family,' *Historical Genealogy*, 1 (1993): 96–8
Avdonin, A. N., 'Investigation of Sources on the Death of the Romanovs and the Search for their Remains,' *Historical Genealogy*, 2 (1993): 83–6.
Avdonin, A. N., 'The Secret of the Old Koptiaki Road: A History of the Search for the Remains of the Imperial Family,' *Istochnik*, 5 (1994): 60–76. [R]
Bolotin, Leonid, 'Where Does the Path of the 'Grand' Prince Lead?', *Tsar-Kolokol*, 1 (1990): 11–42. [R]
Botkin, Gleb. *The Real Romanovs.* New York, 1931.

Botkin, Gleb. *The Woman who Rose Again*. New York, 1937.

Botkine, Tatiana. *Anastasia retrouvée*. Paris, 1985.

Buranov, Iu., Khrustalev, V. *The Death of the Imperial House*. Moscow, 1992. [R]

Bykov, P. M. *The Last Days of the Romanovs*. Sverdlovsk, 1926. [R]

Chavchavadze, David. *Crowns and Trenchcoats: A Russian Prince in the CIA*. New York, 1990.

Chupriakov, M. E., ed. *The Secret of the Tsarist Remains*. Ekaterinburg, 1994. [R]

Clarke, William. *The Lost Fortune of the Tsars*. London, 1994.

Diterikhs, M. K. *The Murder of the Tsarist Family and Members of the House of Romanov in the Urals*. Vladivostok, 1922.

Enel (Skariatin, M. V.). *Sacrifice*. 2nd edn. Brussels, n.d.

Ferro, Marc. *Nicholas II: The Last of the Tsars*. Tr. by Brian Pearce. London, 1991.

Gavrilov, Dmitry, 'The World will Never Know What We Did with Them,' *Ural*, 12 (1993): 206–223. [R]

Gill, Peter et al. 'Identification of the remains of the Romanov family by DNA analysis,' *Nature Genetics*, vol. 6, February 1994.

Gill, Peter et. al.. 'Establishing the Identity of Anna Anderson Manahan,' *Nature Genetics*, vol. 9, January 1995.

Gilliard (Zhil'iar), P. *The Emperor Nicholas II and his Family*. Vienna, 1921. [R]

Gilliard, Pierre, and Savitch,

Constantin. *La Fausse Anastasie. Histoire d'une pretendue grande-duchesse de Russie*. Paris, 1929.

Iakovlev, Vasilii, 'Years and Fates. The Last Journey of the Romanovs,' *Ural*, 7 (July 1988): 147–67 [R]

Ioffe, Genrikh, 'The House of Special Purpose,' *Rodina*, 4 (1989): 84–95; 5 (1989): 79–92 [R]

Jones, Steve. *The Language of the Genes*. London, 1993.

Kadish, Sharman. *Bolsheviks and British Jews: The Anglo-Jewish Community, Britain and the Russian Revolution*. London, 1992.

Kasvinov, M. K. *Twenty-three Steps Down*. Moscow, 1982. [R]

Kerensky, Aleksandr. *The Crucifixion of Liberty*. London, 1934.

Kheifets, M. *Tsar-Murder in 1918*. Moscow, 1992. [R]

Knightley, Phillip. *The First Casualty*. London, 1975.

Krug von Nidda, Roland. *I Am Anastasia*. Tr. Oliver Coburn. New York, 1958.

Kurth, Peter. *Anastasia. The Riddle of Anna Anderson*. Boston, 1983.

Lovell, James Blair. *Anastasia. The Lost Princess*. Washington, 1991.

Maiakovskii, V. V. *Collected Works in Eight Volumes*. Vol. 6, Moscow, 1968. [R]

Maples, William R., with Browning, Michael. *Dead Men Do Tell Tales*. New York, 1994.

Marie, Grand Duchess of Russia.

A Princess in Exile. New York, 1932.

Massie, Robert K. *Nicholas and Alexandra*. New York, 1967.

Meier, I. P. *How the Tsarist Family Perished*. Moscow, 1990. [R]

Moiseev, Aleksandr, 'The Ballad of a Lost Name,' *Ural'skii sledopit*, 1 (1991): 4–13. [R]

Nepein, I., ed. *Before the Shooting. Last Letters of the Tsarist Family*. Omsk, 1992. [R]

Nicholas II. *The Diary of Emperor Nicholas II*. Moscow, 1991. [R]

Occleshaw, Michael. *The Romanov Conspiracies. The Romanovs and the House of Windsor*. London, 1993.

Paganutstsi, P. *The Truth about the Murder of the Tsarist Family*. Moscow, 1992. [R]

'Forgery,' *Tsar-Kolokol*, 2 (1990): 10–28. [R]

Popov, V. L. 'The Identification of the Remains of the Tsarist Family of the Romanovs,' special supplement to *International Medical Reviews*. St Petersburg, 1994. [R]

Radzinsky, Edvard. *The Last Tsar: The Life and Death of Nicholas II*. Tr. by Marian Schwartz. London, 1993.

Rathlef-Keilman, Harriet von. *Anastasia*. Tr. F. S. Flint. New York, 1929.

Richards, Guy. *The Hunt for the Czar*. New York, 1970.

Ross, Nikolai. *The Death of the Tsarist Family*. Frankfurt am Main, 1987. [R]

Ryabov, Gelli, '"We have to shoot you" . . .' *Rodina*, 4 (1989): 84–95; 5 (1989): 79–92. [R]

Sokolov, N. 'Report of Mr. N. A. Sokoloff, Examining Magistrate, into the Circumstances of the Murder of the Russian Imperial Family.' Typescript, Paris, 1920. British Library, CUP 24 aa 19.

—— *The Murder of the Tsarist Family*. Buenos Aires, 1969. [R]

Summers, Anthony, and Mangold, Tom. *The File on the Tsar*. London 1976.

Trewin, J. C. *Tutor to the Tsarevich. An Intimate Portrait of the Russian Imperial Family Compiled from the Papers of Charles Sydney Gibbes*. London, 1975.

Wheeler-Bennett, John W. *Brest-Litovsk: The Forgotten Peace, March 1918*. New York, 1971.

Wilton, Robert. *The Last Days of the Romanovs from 15th March, 1917*. London, 1920.

Yeltsin, Boris. *Against the Grain*. London, 1990.

Zaitsev, Georgy, 'Seventy-eight Days,' *Ural*, 6 (June 1993): 73–173. [R]

Index

Abramov, S. S., 189
Alapaevsk, 38, 80
Aleksandr Mikhailovich (Russian
 Grand Duke), 12, 13, 118
Aleksandra (Abbess of the Monastery
 of the Transfiguration), 211
Alekseev, General M. V., 10, 15
Aleksei (Patriarch of Moscow), 233
Alexander III (Emperor of Russia),
 117
Alexandra Fedorovna (Empress of
 Russia), 16, 26, 35, 41, 57, 62, 70,
 75, 92, 153, 165–6, 191, 213;
 attitude to Brest-Litovsk Treaty,
 21–2, 25; character of, 5–6; DNA
 testing on remains of, 200–201,
 220, 222; execution of, 48–51;
 identification of remains of, 192–3,
 196; political role of, 7–13
Alexei (Aleksei) Nikolaevich (Russian
 Tsarevich), 5, 15, 25–6, 33, 35, 38,
 41, 47, 77, 83, 90, 172, 200–201,
 202, 204; destruction of corpse of,
 62; execution of, 49–52, 166–7;
 missing body of, 192–3; search for
 remains of, 180, 196
Alexis, Prince d'Angou, 93
Alice (Grand Duchess of Hesse), 5,
 200
Alice, Princess of Greece, 133
Anarchists, 36–7

Anastasia (American film), 132, 137
Anastasia Nikolaevna (Russian Grand
 Duchess), 33, 87, 90, 95, 143, 161,
 200–201, 208–9; description of,
 88–9, 156–7; destruction of corpse
 of, 62, 195–6; 'escape' to Perm of,
 70; execution of, 49–51, 73, 86,
 235; search for remains of, 180,
 192–3, 203–4
Anderson, Anna (Anna Tschaikovsky;
 Anastasia Manahan), 77; American
 tour of, 109–13; character of,
 87–91; courts cases involving,
 132–40, 142; DNA testing of,
 204–30; and Franziska
 Schanzkowska, 105, 128–9, 135,
 223–5; knowledge of languages,
 135–8; last years of, 162–4; life in
 America, 142–5; life in Germany,
 93–108; marriage to Jack Manahan,
 145; mental health of, 151–7;
 physical characteristics of, 157–8; in
 Unterlengenhardt, 130–41
Andrei Vladimirovich (Russian Grand
 Duke), 90, 103–4, 109, 147
Anglo-International Bank, 122–3
Argentina, 198
Armed Forces Institute of Pathology
 (Washington, DC), 213, 217, 220,
 224
Aucleres, Dominique, 135, 139

Dobrynin, Konstantin, 52
Dolgoruky, Prince Aleksandr, 25, 32,
  37
Duma (Russian Parliament), 7–8, 16;
  Progressive Bloc in, 10
Dzerzhinsky, Felix, 37

Eickstedt, Professor Baron von,
  159–60
Ekaterinburg (Sverdlovsk), 23–4, 26,
  28–31, 42, 58, 65, 75, 81, 165, 167,
  187, 191
Elizaveta Fedorovna (Russian Grand
  Duchess), 38
Ellerik (Schanzkowska), Margarete,
  224, 226
Enel (Mikhail Skariatin), 84–5
Eppard, Betty, 219
Ermakov, Petr, 37, 45–6, 49, 51, 53,
  56–7, 63, 73–4, 165–6, 173–5, 178,
  193
Ernst Ludwig (Grand Duke of
  Hesse–Darmstadt), 97, 100–101,
  103, 105, 117, 128, 150
Ewing, Mildred, 228
Extraordinary Commission for
  Struggle with Counterrevolution
  and Sabotage (Cheka), 37, 45–6,
  60, 70, 82, 186

Fallows, Edward, 110, 112–13, 121–4,
  127–9
Fedorov, Dr (court physician), 16
Fesenko, Ivan, 45, 74
Figaro, Le, 135, 139
First-Finders, 180, 184
Ford, Henry, 81
Forensic Pathology Institute
  (Munich), 206, 209
Forensic Science Service (Britain), 1,
  198, 209, 213–15, 223–4
Four Brothers, 45–6, 53, 57, 60, 65–6,
  68, 73–4, 167, 174, 180, 184, 195
Frederick, Prince of Saxe-Altenburg,
  91, 114–15, 126, 130, 132–3,
  138–41, 143, 153, 161, 163–4
Furtmayr, Dr Moritz, 133–4, 160–61

Gallop, Arthur, 121
Gavrilov, Dr D. V., 185–6
George, Duke of Leuchtenberg,
  105–6, 109, 152, 157–8, 164
Georgy Aleksandrovich (Russian
  Grand Duke), 233
Georgy (Prince of Russia), 146
Germany, 21–3, 36, 39, 42–3, 46, 70,
  78, 81
Gibbes, Charles Sydney, 33, 88–9,
  135–6, 156, 202–3
Gienanth, Baron Ulrich von, 137, 217
Gill, Dr Peter, 1, 2, 199, 202–4, 209,
  213–28
Gilliard, Pierre, 21, 33, 76–7, 80, 84,
  98–104, 109, 126, 132, 134–5, 136,
  148–51, 156, 158–9, 170
Gilliard, Shura (Aleksandra Tegleva),
  99, 136, 150, 157
Ginther, Dr Charles, 226–7
Girsh, Captain, V. A., 65–6
Golitsyn, Major-General Vladimir, 69
Goloshchekin, Filipp, 32–3, 38, 41–2,
  44–6, 48–50, 79, 165, 168
Gorbachev, Mikhail, 181, 186, 189
Grandanor Corporation, 110, 112–13,
  121, 124
Great Britain, 75
Grunberg, Franz, 97–8
Guchkov, Aleksandr, 15

Hannoverscher Anzeiger, 126, 157
Hardenberg, Count Kuno, 100
Heine, Heinrich, 85
Hermine, Empress of Germany, 126
Herrmann, Professor Bernd, 226
Heyden-Rynsch family, 127
Hitler, Adolf, 143
Holtzmann, Fanny, 121
Houghton Library (Harvard
  University), 125

Ioann, Metropolitan of St Petersburg
  and Ladoga, 233
Ioann Konstantinovich (Russian
  Grand Duke), 38
Ioffe, Professor Genrik, 182
Ipatiev House (House of Special